Nailed

The failures of government education policy from 2010 onwards, and how to fix them for free.

Andrew Chubb

"Nailed" charts the 30-year journey of a teacher who, having almost given up after his first year, went on to become the principal of an academy in one of the UK's poorest areas, and then CEO of a Multi Academy Trust. A lifelong curriculum innovator, Chubb charts how the freedoms enjoyed by schools up until around 2012 were gradually eroded, and how this process, coupled with an ever-tighter accountability regime, resulted in the needs of our most Vulnerable Young People (VYPs) being increasingly less well met. In making his case for the need for radical change, Chubb discusses how ministers' desires to promote 'equality of opportunity' has actually reduced the ability of schools to develop curricula that promote the 'equity' that our VYPs so desperately need. He goes on to demonstrate that current secondary school performance metrics take little account of 'value-added' in spite of government claims to the contrary, and that consequently, schools now have 'perverse incentives' to offer our VYPs programmes of study to which they are all too often not well suited. On the back of this analysis, he offers suggestions as to how changes need to be made at national level to reverse this trend, arguing that in basing policy around the needs of VYPs, all pupils would benefit.

Acknowledgements:

This book would not have been possible without the help and support of many people. Firstly, I would like to thank the pupils, staff and governors of both Archbishop Sentamu Academy and the Sentamu Academy Learning Trust, whose support for me during our most difficult times as an academy were inspirational. I would also like to thank Archbishop Sentamu himself for his own unwavering support during that period, and for my wonderful PA, Laura Fillingham, whose unending humour and efficiency made my job so much more enjoyable.

If the book is readable, it is thanks to Colin Campbell, Emeritus Professor of Sociology at the University of York. He was kind enough to read the initial script and point out whole areas for improvement, as well as helping with the book's title and also the title for one of the chapters.

I am also very grateful to Ryan Norman, who gave me invaluable advice on how to approach agents and publishers, and to Wayne Ross, who helped me greatly with the stylistic presentation of the text.

Lastly, and of course by no means least, I want to thank my amazing wife Maxine, whose support and belief that I had 'something to say' encouraged me enormously as I slaved over the laptop.

Table of Contents:

Introduction:

The plight of vulnerable young people in our schools is rarely far from the headlines. Often unwanted, excluded or simply choosing not to turn up for school at all, many will continue to experience significant levels of disadvantage and deprivation throughout their lives.

Re-engaging them in their learning during their teenage years is a major challenge, and one for which schools are, quite reasonably, highly accountable. And yet despite this being a real priority, leaders often struggle to help them. Pressures from government to demonstrate success often lead to these pupils being caught in the crossfire of a statistical struggle between schools and ministers. Adding to the overall seriousness of the situation is the constant concern that Ofsted will deem a school to be employing 'perverse incentives' or, worse, to be 'off-rolling' vulnerable pupils to manipulate their statistics. Tragically, ministers and school leaders all want the same thing – to improve the life-chances of our young people. This being so, how have we arrived at a point of such conflict? And are there any solutions?

In Nailed!, I analyse changes in government policy with respect to curriculum, school performance metrics and Ofsted over the past 14 years. Drawing on my extensive experience as an Academy Principal and CEO of a Multi Academy Trust during that period, I argue that the reforms introduced by successive ministers have made it far harder for schools to provide an appropriate education for vulnerable young people – or 'VYP's.

Taking in turn the policy areas of curriculum, school performance metrics and the accountability regime of Ofsted, Parts One to Three draw attention to how a piecemeal approach to educational reform in these three areas has impacted with disproportional negativity on our most vulnerable pupils. Arguing that these problems demonstrate the need for a 'system re-set', in Part Four I offer proposals for how a series of straightforward and cost-neutral changes to policy could vastly improve outcomes for VYPs.

Acknowledging that bringing about such change is not without its problems, in spite of the opportunities offered by the new government, Part Five explores how this might be achieved. I argue that a major requirement in this respect is for the main teaching unions to formulate and agree upon a key set of proposals. Importantly, I argue that by avoiding all discussions around the traditional and contentious areas of pay and / or conditions of service, and instead focussing a campaign on meeting the needs of our VYPs, the chances of success are far greater.

'Nailed!' champions the cause of our vulnerable young people and the schools that work so hard to serve them. It celebrates the skills of the teaching profession and calls for government to give our leaders in education far greater agency over the policies by which they operate than is currently the case. It calls for the devolution of decisions on curriculum, allowing headteachers to decide locally those areas of study which will best promote equity for their pupils. Finally, it argues that if government policy treated our VYPs as VIPs, then all pupils would benefit.

Andrew Chubb

December 2024.

Prologue

'I Fought the Law'

I loved my job. But walking in to the academy on a bright morning in May, nothing could have prepared me for the storm that was about to unleash itself upon us. Having made my final preparations for Collective Worship, I was just grabbing a quick coffee when I received a call from our front desk:

'Andrew – Ofsted are here'.

Unannounced. That was bad – awful – in fact. The education inspectorate was supposed to give 2 days' notice before landing, so that could only mean one thing...

'You'd better show them up then...'

There are no words to describe, adequately, the truly awful experience of being 'doorstepped' like that. Grounds opening up, bottoms falling out of worlds, pits in stomachs ...

....' We've received a complaint....'

...were the first words to come out of the Lead Inspector's mouth, standing in front of me in my office, whilst simultaneously thrusting out of her hand a copy of a letter she had received. Apparently, this anonymous person had sent it to Ofsted, the press, the BBC, the headteachers of all the other academies in our trust, the local press, our patron – Archbishop Sentamu – but not to me.

'How could anyone do this? Does someone really hate me and our academy that much? Is this how anonymous complaints are investigated? Why didn't somebody phone me and ask what was going in? Why are they sending in a whole team?...'

Just a few of the thoughts that flashed through my mind as I struggled to contemplate the implications of this *blitzkrieg*. I read through the letter – it was a combination of *'lies, damn lies and insinuations'*. I told our inquisitor that it was rubbish – but the damage had been done. An hour later, my PA researched her profile - the little 'bio' on the official Ofsted website proudly stated that she specialised in 'schools causing concern'. And so it was to be as, two days later, my senior team and I sat, stony-faced, around the long white table in our conference room.

I had never liked either the table or the room, and the words of the lead inspector did nothing to improve my mood:

'Overall outcomes at KS4 in English and Maths are significantly lower than the national average'…

Well, on Ofsted's criteria, they would be. Six months earlier, we had taken the decision to continue 'early-entering' our pupils for their key exams, in the full knowledge that these results, whilst giving our pupils a second chance to achieve the grades they needed, would count against our school.

'Staff are working hard…' – *a glimmer of hope* - 'but progress is not rapid' – *glimmer extinguished.*

'If outcomes in any key subject are inadequate, then outcomes overall are inadequate…'

Nail One banged in firmly.

'SLT make accurate judgements about the quality of Teaching and Learning…'

Better. As a team, we had spent most of our days going into classrooms, supporting colleagues, coaching, training, encouraging,

'But there are weaknesses in Science…'

Well, yes there were. In the past 12 months, we had been forced by a change of government policy to change from delivering BTEC Science – assessed primarily through coursework – to GCSE Science – assessed mainly through exams – and we were struggling. Surely the team would understand?

'As a consequence, their progress lags behind that of their peers nationally…'

So, no reprieve there then.

'Homework across the school is variable..'

I could feel the hammer being raised, as the Lead Inspector droned on

'Overall, Teaching and Learning is inadequate'

Nail Two firmly banged in.

'Child Protection Policy meets requirements..'

Good – it should do, given the army of people we have employed to ensure our young people feel safe.

'Vulnerable pupils feel safe, and there is a strong Christian ethos...'

That sounded better.

'Spirituality is a strength of the school...'

Things are looking up.

'This is a very nurturing school...'

Great!

'There is an excellent house system in place with strong links to pupils in other countries..'

At last, they're beginning to see some of the opportunities our pupils would otherwise not have..

'However, we saw children cycling to school without helmets...'

Where on earth is that in the Ofsted schedule?

'We saw some off-task behaviour when children were bored..'

In my experience, most adults display far more of this when bored than do our pupils.

'We saw a piece of paper being thrown in one lesson...'

Seriously? 1400 pupils in one of the most deprived areas of the country and you bring that up?

'...and pupils dawdle between lessons.

I don't ever remember personally rushing as a child to conjugate verbs or tackle Pythagoras when I was at my selective grammar school.

'Attendance also needs to improve…'

For the third time in 15 minutes, I sensed a hammer being raised..

'Overall, Behaviour Personal Development and Well-being require improvement..'

Well, only a 3 inch as opposed to a 9 inch nail, but a nail, nonetheless.

'In considering our judgement on Leadership and Management, we note that governors are aware of the context of the school and the challenges it faces in recruitment..'

That was certainly true.

'However, middle leaders need to improve their monitoring in English, Maths and Science…'

Weigh the pig even more? I begged to differ.

'…and the progress of pupils supported by the pupil premium is still too slow'.

Along with many, if not most, schools in the country

'Taking all our findings into consideration, we find the Leadership and Management of the school to be inadequate..'

Another 9 inch nail hammered in

'..and as a result, we are of the opinion that the school requires Special Measures

There it was, the coffin banged tightly shut.

'…And the Law Won'.

Utter humiliation for our academy, our staff, for me personally. Over the coming weeks and months there would be a detailed appeal and an almost filmic set of events that threatened to completely annihilate our Trust of schools. We would experience a roller-coaster ride, and, ultimately, incredibly, remain in control of our destiny. But at that moment, all that I could see, and feel, was a sense of abject failure. Selfishly, I wondered how I would go into school the next day, what I would say to our wonderful, hard-working and committed staff, and what I would say to our amazing pupils. The de-brief ended. I escorted the inspectors out of the school, shook their hands, wished them a safe journey, drove home. In the words of The Clash, we would spend the coming years forever 'Breaking Rocks in the Hot Sun'.....

Part One

The impact of Government Curriculum Policy on Vulnerable Young People

Chapter 1 – 'A tale of two inspections'

Abstract:

This chapter describes the very different outcomes of two Ofsted inspections – the first being in 2014 when the academy I was leading was judged to be almost 'outstanding', and the one two years later when the same academy was judged to be 'inadequate'. The chapter explores some initial thoughts on the reasons for this, and sets out how these will be examined in more detail in the rest of the book. Included at this point are my main contentions and thoughts on the changes in educational policy that I believe are needed if the needs of our most vulnerable young people are to be better served:

1. *That curriculum policy over the past decade has been influenced more by misguided notions of equality than by principles of equity, and that this has negatively impacted our most vulnerable young people;*
2. *That government metrics around pupil performance continue to force schools to act in the interests of the performance tables themselves rather than pupils, in spite of ministers having tried to abolish these so-called 'perverse incentives';*
3. *That curriculum, examination and accountability systems have been neither viewed nor developed as a whole, and that this piecemeal approach to educational reform has impacted with disproportional negativity on our most vulnerable pupils. Put another way, a succession of education ministers, starting with Michael Gove, have*

acted like insouciant doctors, dishing out an ever-increasing number of pills to be taken without considering how they interact with previous prescriptions;

4. *That we have a long-term moral duty to ensure our 'VYPs' become 'VIPs', and that the solutions proposed in this book will not only help achieve this, but also raise aspirations for all pupils; and*

5. *That many (though not all) of these problems can be solved through a 'system reset' without either the state or individual schools incurring any further costs.*

'Ch ch ch ch changes'

(Bowie, 1971)

And yet just two years earlier in February 2014, in the very same room, sitting around the very same table, a different Ofsted team had judged our academy to be 'Good' – indeed, almost 'Outstanding'. At that time, the East Hull February gloom had been totally dispersed by our lead inspector's comments, which had been full of praise for our efforts at transforming the fortunes of our pupils:

'The proportion of students attaining five or more good GCSE and equivalent qualifications, including English and mathematics at the end of Year 11, is now just above average. This represents good progress over time; achievement across the school is improving strongly, particularly in English where students now make outstanding progress.' (Swallow, 2014)

'Great – all of our hard work in developing the curriculum, in matching course to pupils' skills, in allowing them a number of opportunities to sit key exams, has paid off..'

'The sixth form is good. Student numbers and courses are rising, and provision is good. Most students make at least expected, and some good, progress, particularly in vocational subjects'.

'Delighted for my sixth form team, who have worked so hard to encourage our young people to stay on with courses they enjoy...'

'Teaching is typically good, with examples of outstanding practice. Teachers are committed fully to creating a positive climate where students can do their best. As a result, students achieve well.'

'So very pleased that 6 years of hard work from our staff have finally been recognised officially'.

'Arrangements to keep students safe are outstanding. Parents and carers say how much this is a top priority of the school's leaders. Behaviour is equally outstanding. Students' spiritual, moral, social and cultural development is promoted extremely well. It is promoted very effectively through the excellent relationships in school, and a wide range of exciting experiences.'

'I haven't been deluding myself – this really is a happy school where our pupils feel safe, valued, and inspired'.

'The principal, governors, and key leaders and managers are hugely ambitious on the part of all young people. They constantly communicate high expectations, and are relentless in their drive for improvement. As a consequence, teaching is improving strongly, standards are rising, and students are keen to learn, and eager for success.'

'I am so lucky to have such a great team around me – this really is the best job in the world'.

As the inspection team left, we were on cloud nine.

And for the next two years, Archbishop Sentamu Academy continued to ride high. Serving one of the most deprived communities in the country, we continued to enjoy leading a happy, thriving school community. Pupil achievement was indeed impressive – our students were gaining good exams results given their starting points, and our flourishing sixth form was the launch pad for many of our students to reach university – most of them being the first in their family ever to do so. In sum, we had found a way of making school a highly positive experience for our students, and we had done so whilst maintaining an extremely low exclusion rate. On the back of that success, we bid successfully to open a second facility - one of the largest Alternative Provision academies in the country, educating over 150 young people at serious risk of long-term exclusion – and by 2016, we had become one of the government's new 'academy trusts', comprising our own two academies and three local primary schools.

So, what on earth had changed in those two years? How could we have gone from being an academy which achieved good results against all the odds, to one which had been slated by Ofsted as inadequate? The answers I would offer are both complex and concerning. Complex, because they involve a deconstruction of a swathe of government policy over the past two decades, and concerning because they show just how hard this increasingly inchoate spread of legislation has made it for schools to serve our most vulnerable and disadvantaged pupils.

All of which has led to this book. The main answers as to how Archbishop Sentamu Academy went from 'hero to zero' in little over two years lie, I believe, in an analysis of government education policy development. This is not to absolve myself of blame for the outcome of our 2016 inspection – indeed, almost every day for the past 8 years I have castigated myself for it, as will become apparent. But I do believe that this analysis should be brought into the open and discussed. In short, I believe that our 'tale of two inspections' can be used as a lens through which we can examine the shortcomings of current policy, their impact on our most vulnerable young people, and a view to offering solutions for improvement. With this in mind, I want to take a journey into the inner workings of our secondary schools. I want to 'lift the lid' on some key changes of government educational policy over the last 20 years or so and assess their impact on our most vulnerable young people. In particular, I want to examine three key issues - the links between national curriculum policy, the metrics used to judge pupil progress, and the Ofsted system which is tasked with evaluating a school's success with pupils based on these criteria. Examining the interplay between these three factors is important if we are to understand policy successes and failures and crucially, suggest ways in which 'the system' should change in order to serve better those most at risk of long-term exclusion.

As I hope will become clear through this book, my life-long passion has always been to do all I can to improve the life-chances of the most vulnerable through education. Being given the opportunity to lead Archbishop Sentamu Academy was therefore a dream come true, as our pupils were in top 1% of the most deprived communities in the land. This commitment to serving the disadvantaged continued when we became a 'Multi Academy Trust' (MAT) and in 2020, our group of 5 academies included three in the top 10 most deprived in the country, of which one - an Alternative Provision academy – was actually the top-most deprived, bar none.

'Getting it right' for this cohort of young people really matters. Good schools are important for all pupils. But there is a well-worn axiom that 80% of a child's success is down to the family into which they are born. Well-functioning, aspirational families can often make up for the limitations of provision which will exist in almost any school, whether these limitations are the result of government policy (as I will indeed argue is the case), or the shortcomings of a particular aspect of the school itself. To give two simple examples, socially advantaged families will often be able to pay for additional tutor support if a child is struggling in a particular subject, or pay for additional music or drama classes if the school doesn't provide sufficient of these. Schools serving areas of high deprivation however generally find themselves having to make up for the educational bonuses provided by the better-off. In stating this, I am in no way complaining about the level of challenge involved in serving pupils in deprived communities. What I will be proposing in this book however is that some relatively straightforward changes in government policy could make a huge difference to schools faced with this challenge, and thus, to our most vulnerable young people, or 'VYP's, themselves.

A more 'traditional' approach to writing a book such as this might have been to research as much as possible anything written about these themes over the past decade, and then to add my thoughts to this body of expertise. I was concerned however that in working this way, I might be unduly influenced by the writings of people I respect greatly, and in so doing, not think hard enough about the issues for myself. With this in mind, I took a different approach, deciding to rely on my own thinking as far as possible about the problems posed by 'the system' for our VYPs, and then to check my thinking ruthlessly against what has already been written. This process has led me to make five key contentions:

1: That curriculum policy over the past decade has been influenced more by misguided notions of equality than by principles of equity, and that this has negatively impacted our most vulnerable young people, or 'VYP's;

2: That government metrics around pupil performance continue to force schools to act in the interests of the performance tables themselves rather than pupils, in spite of ministers having tried to abolish these so-called 'perverse incentives';

3: That curriculum, examination and accountability systems have been neither viewed nor developed as a whole, and that this piecemeal approach to educational reform has impacted with disproportional negativity on our most vulnerable pupils. Put another way, a succession of education ministers, starting with Michael Gove, have acted like insouciant doctors, dishing out an ever-increasing number of pills to be taken without considering how they interact with previous prescriptions;

4: That we have a long-term moral duty to ensure our 'VYPs' become 'VIPs', and that the solutions proposed in this book will not only help achieve this, but also raise aspirations for all pupils; and

5:That many (though not all) of these problems can be solved through a 'system reset' without either the state or individual schools incurring any further costs.

Whilst the first three contentions are highly negative in nature, the last two give us hope. I strongly believe that with sufficient will and political courage, we can, fairly rapidly, develop educational policy in ways that will make it vastly easier for schools to improve the life-chances of our most vulnerable young people. For decades, a key educational challenge in the UK has been how best to achieve this. By the time this cohort reach secondary age, many of them, already typically highly socially disadvantaged, have become disengaged. Often lacking the structure and support of a stable family, they begin to drift, putting themselves at risk of further educational and long-term social exclusion. The impact of the pandemic has only exacerbated these problems, adding to the challenges already experienced by schools and academies who serve these young people.

Unlike so many of our society's problems however, I believe that there are some relatively straightforward solutions to improving significantly the life-chances of our 'VYPs', and that this will, moreover, benefit all pupils. Between 2004 and 2018, I had the privilege of leading two schools – one 'Local Authority Maintained', and one academy. During that time, I worked variously under the constraints of a local authority, the freedoms of the original academy movement, and latterly, the constraints of the ideologically driven reforms introduced by Michael Gove and carried on for 14 years, first by the Conservative/Liberal Coalition and since 2015, by the Conservative party alone.

However, the recent change of government in 2024 has opened up the chance for a reset in education policy. In line with the five contentions above, I argue that a 'system reset' is needed, to ensure the following:

1: It becomes in schools' interests to have the most disadvantaged pupils on roll. Currently, the opposite is the case;

2: Linked to this, that there are incentives for schools and academy trusts to collaborate at a local level to ensure the most vulnerable have quick access to school places. Currently, there are many disincentives for this;

3: The curriculum promotes equity, as well as equality. The dogma of the so-called 'English Baccalaureate' works against this, especially for our most vulnerable pupils who often achieve the lowest outcomes;

4: Pupils are enabled to be tested on a mix of exams and continuous assessment. At the moment, almost all assessment is exam-based;

5: In light of the above, the current measurement of a school's success known as 'Progress 8' is radically overhauled; and

6: The inspection framework evolves to take these changes into account.

Ironically, between the mid-1990s and the introduction of Gove's reforms, much of the above was possible. The good news however is that many of the changes advocated here could be, broadly, cost neutral.

This book is written in light of my own 31 years in education (14 of which were in headship and 5 as CEO of our MAT), the particular strategies we employed during this to meet the needs of our most vulnerable pupils, and the impact of changing government strategy on that work. Understanding this requires a detailed deconstruction of policies around pupil admissions, curriculum, assessment and inspection policy. Wherever possible, I illustrate the issues highlighted in Part One with vignettes drawn from my own personal experiences, in an attempt to spare the reader having to wade through a series of potentially arcane, dreary and indeed turgid definitions.

In Part Two, drawing on this analysis and experience, we will look at a number of broadly cost-neutral strategies that would, in my view, bring much greater hope to pupils, and in particular to those who are currently highly vulnerable, as well as to their teachers, who work so hard to support and encourage them. In 1997, one of New Labour's mantras was 'Education, Education, Education'. Drawing on this rallying cry, I would suggest that 2024's incoming government needs to give schools a renewed framework in which they can 'Innovate, Innovate, Innovate'. To achieve this, there will need to be a shift in the current relative balance between 'top-down control' and 'bottom-up development' not only in terms of the curriculum and the ways in which schools are actively encouraged to work collaboratively, but also in the development of the metrics by which pupil achievement is measured and school effectiveness judged.

I am fully aware that these issues are regularly discussed in the press, are the subject of national and international research conducted by highly respected scholars, and of lobbying from our own teaching unions. Indeed, a criticism of this book could be that it is very heavy on 'what is wrong', and too light on 'what to do about it'. I have taken this approach however quite deliberately, for two reasons. First, so much high quality material has already been written on this subject. For example, a series of excellent proposals for policy change in these areas has been produced by my own former union - ASCL – in their 'Blueprint for a self-improving system' (ASCL, 2015) and 'Blueprint for a fairer system' (ASCL, 2021). This being the case, it is clear to me that the profession already has well thought-out ideas as to 'what to do about it'. Second however, I wanted to drive home the impact of what I see as successive failures of government policy on school leaders, and therefore by definition, on our VYPs. Where I hope this book *can* add value therefore is in spelling out very clearly and in significant detail through a 'case study' approach the issues which underpin the urgent need for this change, if our VYPs are to be given the opportunity to flourish. As such, the main aim of the book is a 'call to arms' for leaders in the profession – particularly those who lead the teaching unions, to work out new ways of collaborating effectively both amongst themselves and with school leaders to present this 'case for change' to government ministers and to impress upon them the urgency to act.

Following on from this, I have also taken the deliberate decision not to discuss the issue of resourcing, or lack thereof. There are two main reasons for this too. First, detailed analyses and accounts of this issue abound elsewhere, and lobbying on this issue is already taking place. As such, I don't feel I have anything to add to this area of justifiable concern. Second, and perhaps more controversially, I do not actually believe that this is the main issue behind so much of the malaise and unhappiness in the profession, as evidenced for example by the recruitment crisis. It is certainly true that a lack of funding present huge challenges – indeed I remember all too well the weekly meetings over many years with my Finance Director, combing the budget line by line in an attempt to find areas in which we could save money. However, I believe it is the corrosive lack of trust in school leaders displayed by central government which is the root cause of so much unhappiness in the profession – it was certainly the case for me. Michael Gove, Secretary of State for Education between 2010 and 2014 embodied this scathing distrust, referring to educational experts as 'The Blob'.

This cynical, indeed contemptuous view, was clearly deeply held, as leading up to the Brexit referendum, he famously declared as Lord Chancellor : 'I think the people of this country have had enough of experts with organisations with acronyms saying that they know what is best and getting it consistently wrong'. This sweeping level of arrogance is as staggering as it is dangerous – the experts of the educational world in this country leading the two main Headteacher unions ASCL and NAHT for example actually, in my view, 'get it pretty much absolutely right'. Indeed, without wishing to stray too far from the central point of this book, recent history would indicate that it is actually our elected leaders and many of their ministers with whom 'the people of this country' have more than had enough. Returning to my point however, I believe that reforms designed to address the profession's concerns around curriculum, assessment and inspection would do much to improve morale, and would probably mitigate at least to some extent frustrations around levels of resourcing.

But why the focus on Vulnerable Young People? There are three main reasons for this. Having worked in a number of schools during my career serving both highly affluent (in the case of Arden School) highly deprived communities (Archbishop Sentamu Academy) and those in between these two extremes, I want to make the case that changes in government policy in the three areas of curriculum, assessment and inspection have impacted most negatively on pupils who already suffer the worst deprivation – our Vulnerable Young People or VYPs. Second, if these pupils' needs are not adequately met in school, it is they who go on to have the most impoverished lives, with all the costs both to their own well-being and to society in general that this entails. Third, the families of these pupils often have little voice or influence to bring about the changes that would improve the life-chances of their children, and so I believe that we have a moral imperative to speak up for them. To these three main reasons however, I would add a fourth – a focus on improving policies for our VYPs would actually improve opportunities for all pupils. I hope therefore that by digging deep into the issues of curriculum, assessment and inspection through the lens of their impact on VYPs, we can paint a detailed picture of what it's like to serve a deprived community under the current body of educational legislation – in other words, without the kinds of changes for which organisations such as ASCL are calling. In short, improving the quality of educational policy in terms of its impact on VYPs should improve the quality of policy for all pupils, much as 'a rising tide floats all boats.'

In stating this, I am of course aware that it would be very easy to point to any number of headteachers, principals and CEOs who could, quite justifiably, point to making 'the system' work more successfully for their pupils as they tackle the issues discussed in this book. At the very least however, I hope that this book can contribute to a discussion for changes that are, I believe, urgently needed as, sadly, there is little evidence to suggest that central government has acted on the recommendations of experts in the field such as ASCL, or indeed any of the teaching unions. This leads me to a seventh contention which we will look at in the second part of this book – that education's professional associations need to work together to present a united front on these issues. When researching this book, I specifically looked for occasions where all the main unions had managed to issue joint statements on any issues. I found two such examples, both linked to the management of the COVID crisis, but could find no examples of agreement on the issues of curriculum reform, performance data or the functioning of Ofsted.

If the main trigger for this book is my reflection on the negative impact of government education policy on vulnerable young people, then our analysis must start with the obvious question – who are our VYPs? As I attempt to answer this, the reader will notice immediately that this book has a secondary school bias, and in particular, that it deals in the main with the challenges of compulsory 11-16 education. It would be completely correct to point out that the challenges in serving our VYPs begin in primary school, and that addressing system-level problems at that stage would help enormously to reduce the challenges on which this book focusses. However, as almost all my experience has been at secondary level, I simply don't feel qualified to comment in detail on how these issues work themselves out at primary level. This was brought home to me in no uncertain terms by one of the best heads with whom I have every had the privilege of working - Jane Daniels, a very good friend and head of the excellent St. James' primary school in Hull. St. James' joined our academy trust in 2016. When another headteacher joining the trust expressed concern that I would suddenly start asking successful primary schools to 'change things', she remarked quite candidly in front of me – 'Oh, don't worry about Andrew – he doesn't make any difference!' In honour of Jane's comments therefore, the focus of this book will be on secondary education.

In his best-selling book 'But what can I do?' (Campbell, 2024), Alastair Campbell urges those who want to see things change not to stand on the side-lines, but to get involved. Rather than become another grumpy, superannuated armchair critic of government education policy, this is therefore my own small attempt to take up Campbell's challenge and present a 'case for change' to the current and future generations of policy makers in this field. Whilst this may seem a significant challenge, I give two examples in chapter 21 from my own experience of how it is indeed possible to bring together large numbers of professionals to solve a common set of problems.

This book is also, however, written with a second audience in mind. Set against my determination to rise to Campbell's challenge was a long list of reasons for not writing it. Top of that list was a sense of shame. I felt, and still feel to this day, the awful responsibility for a cataclysmic failure that brutally yanked away the fruits of many years of work of so many of my committed colleagues, dissolving our dreams and leaving us in a ditch of despair as a series of 'educational thuggernauts' repeatedly rolled over us.

It is often said that failure need not define you. I would argue however that failure does inevitably do just that – the only question is – how? The answer, I believe, depends on how you respond to it. In all honesty, I wish that there was a way in which I could have all the memories of my own failure erased. Given that such a solution as seen in the film 'Men in Black' is not possible however, there are essentially two alternatives. On the one hand, you can allow failure to become your own personal accuser, suffocating your self-esteem and robbing your life of the oxygen of optimism. In this scenario, failure defines you as, well, a failure. However, it is equally possible to embrace failure as 'fertiliser' that can nourish you. During my time at Archbishop Sentamu Academy, I used to play a game I invented called 'Spot the Silver Lining' with my senior team. The aim was to find something positive in each of the setbacks we experienced on a regular basis, with the aim of 'never wasting a good crisis' but using it as a stimulus for improvement. Viewed this way, failure can lead you to becoming even more fruitful.

With this in mind, I hope that these thoughts will bring implicit encouragement to any leader who is currently looking at the balance sheet of their career, and at the bottom line, writing the word 'failure', whether in the increasingly demanding and at times merciless arena of educational leadership, or some other area of life. My own experience is that it most certainly **is** possible to react to failure positively, and with work, to avoid the corrosive (if completely understandable) damage of self-pity, and the sheer waste of 'just giving up'.

Chapter Two – (Un)Fair Access

Abstract:

This chapter starts by defining the concept of a 'VYP', and looks at a number of reasons for which they may not have access to schools. Readers may be shocked by the tactics employed by schools to achieve this, but I try to balance this with explaining why schools often find themselves in such an invidious position when asked to accept VYP's. This is all illustrated with reference to practices in Hull, through meetings which I attended over a number of years, and can therefore verify.

'Left Outside Alone'

Anastacia, 2004

So, who are our most vulnerable young people?

Education has long been the subject of ministerial intervention. Back in 1976, my wonderful Y9 form teacher Vince Cross was bemoaning to us all during a tutor period that 'education was a political football'. He was probably upset about the fact that our Grammar school was 'turning Comprehensive' at about that time, as Shirley Williams, Education Secretary, eagerly promoted the policy in her own attempts to improve standards for all. As I entered teaching and indeed headship, I never forgot his comments, often reflecting myself on how intense this 'political football match' had become. I don't doubt that successive Education Secretaries have been sincere in their desire to usher in policies that enable all children to achieve, including the most vulnerable. I do doubt however their ability to foresee the unintended consequences of their actions, consequences which in my view have, over the past decade, in fact made school a far worse place for many of those who 'don't really fit in', young people who find themselves at, or near, the bottom of the educational heap – excluded, unwanted and without any real hope for their lives. Since retiring in 2020, I have observed how education's football match has continued, as successive politicians and policymakers have grappled with the challenges of COVID and the post-COVID era. Central to these

28

efforts, just as was the case I believe for Shirley Williams, is the recognition that school 'just doesn't work' for too many of our young people, as evidenced by low attendance rates, high exclusion rates and poor outcomes for many. Reports of this abound, but one example is an article by Eva Wiseman, which appeared in the Guardian in December 2023. In it, she notes:

'The Chief Inspector of schools in England claims that parents and pupils now disregard rules they once took for granted, like attending daily, and headteachers say they agree. The DfE's advisor on behaviour policy said it was Covid that 'broke the spell'….. Rates of absence have increased dramatically since COVID – more than a quarter of all secondary pupils are now defined as persistent absentees, missing at least 10% of classes.' Eva rightly points out the impact on those who find themselves at the bottom of the pile: 'To see schools failing like this seems to reflect what's happening in the wider world – the most vulnerable pupils being failed or forgotten, the bonds within communities weakening, a kind of social crumbling. And when a person drops out – when they crash, or falter or get ill, or get it wrong…there is nowhere else for them to land.' (Wiseman, 2023)

Of course, it would be wrong to overlook the fact that many schools and academy trusts do enable their pupils to succeed against all the odds. But even here, there are exceptions. In another Guardian article from December 2023, Ana Fazackerley and Michael Savage draw attention to the fact that some of the most successful schools and trusts suspend vastly more pupils than the national average, and that doesn't include, according to former Ofsted inspector Julie Price Grimshaw, the probability that '…some academies would have much higher exclusion rates if they counted the parents who felt pressurised to leave because their children kept being suspended'. (Fazackerley, 2023). They quote Anne Longfield, chair of the Commission on Young Lives and the government's former children's commissioner for England, who warned that, depending on the school they attended, poorer children and those with special educational needs were more likely to be suspended or excluded, which in turn made them vulnerable to being exploited by criminal gangs.

And it is precisely this cohort of teenagers who are the most vulnerable. All headteachers recognise these pupils. They may be disaffected, disruptive, difficult to manage. They know they don't fit in, that school 'isn't for them' and that sadly, and often quite truthfully, they are simply not wanted. The luckiest of these (including those who have an official 'Educational and Health Care Plan', or EHCP, for 'Behaviour, Emotional and Social Difficulties', or BESD) may end up in an 'Alternative Provision' (or AP) academy. As already mentioned, I bid for, built and opened one of these up for our own vulnerable young people in 2014. The problem with this definition of 'vulnerability' however is that it is fairly narrow, and ignores the fact that there is a far larger cohort of pupils who also experience significant disadvantage. For this reason, I would choose to include in the category of 'VYP' any pupil who suffers socio-economic disadvantage. For the purposes of this book, I would define them as those who attract the 'pupil premium' – additional funding given to schools to support them. This widens the pool of VYPs to around a quarter of all pupils. Here therefore, the term 'VYP' is used to denote both those who are recognisably 'the most difficult' to manage' for the reasons outlined above, and also those who, even if they are not hard to manage, nonetheless face significant disadvantage through no fault of their own.

It is worth noting of course that in practice sadly, the 'most difficult' will invariably already be in the larger group of pupils who attract the pupil premium. As we progress though this book, it will hopefully be clear that the policy failures discussed have the potential to impact to a greater or lesser extent *all* pupils defined in this way as 'vulnerable'. However, I would like to begin our investigation by looking in more detail at some of the reasons for which those right at the bottom can, as noted by Anne Longfield above, simply 'drop out and disappear'. I would like to point out at the outset that almost every colleague with whom I have ever worked wants their school to be inclusive. With this in mind, the accounts that follow are not meant to be judgemental, but rather an indication of one of the many ways in which government policy has failed to link curriculum, performance metrics and accountability coherently, and an illustration of the consequences that this has had on our most vulnerable young people. The cost of inclusion for schools has, in all truth, has become incredibly high.

So how is it that an increasing number of young people fall out of school? There are a number of answers to this, but one of the first problems is that they may not appear in the first place. To understand this, we need to look closely at the principles of 'Fair Access', a system which enables young people move between schools. There are a number of main reasons for pupils needing to change school – for example moving house, experience of bullying, permanent exclusion or moving to avoid a permanent exclusion. Whatever the reason, moving to another school can often impact negatively on a pupil's academic success.

In his seminal book **'Visible Learning for Teachers',** John Hattie carries out a meta-analysis of the factors and strategies that impact pupil achievement, either positively or negatively. His analysis concluded that the single most negative factor is a pupil moving schools. Unless the pupil moves to a new school during the last year of the compulsory schooling (Year 11), the new school becomes accountable to the DfE for his or her exam results. According to Hattie's research, it should therefore be clear from a Headteacher's point of view that accepting any new pupil onto their school roll risks their overall 'pupil achievement' score being depressed, with common sense suggesting that the risk of this is greater if the reason for the pupil moving was linked to poor behaviour. (Hattie, 2012)

In an ideal world, headteachers would naturally take their fair share of these 'hard to place pupils. However, because the accountability stakes in this country are so high, there is a permanent disincentive to do so. We will spend some time looking at this issue in future chapters, but for now, agreeing to take in challenging pupils through 'Fair Access' can be akin to 'turkeys voting for Christmas', to use an overworn analogy. I can illustrate this best with my own experience.

In 2004, I took over as Headteacher of Campion School in Leamington Spa. Campion was at the time an 11-16 school with around 500 pupils. It was situated in the most deprived area of Leamington, and was characterised by very poor behaviour and correspondingly low pupil achievement, falling rolls (meaning that the incoming Y7 roll was smaller than the outgoing Y11 roll) and struggling finances. The previous headteacher had become ill, and one of the results of this was that the school had accepted over a period of time a disproportionately large number of pupils from other local schools who had either 'been encouraged to leave' or actually expelled. The situation was intolerable – the school was chaotic and meaningful learning was very difficult to achieve, no matter how skilled the teachers were. Local Authority advisors had placed it their own 'Special Measures' – the lowest category of overall effectiveness.

To turn the school around, we had to improve behaviour, and to do this, my team and I very quickly established some very clear boundaries. As a consequence of this, exclusions rocketed and over the next four years, I permanently excluded 40 pupils – an appallingly high number. However, half-way through my time there, in 2006 Ofsted judged the school to be securely 'Good', with Leadership and Management judged 'Outstanding'. We will unpick other aspects of this story in later chapters, but at this point, I simply want to draw the reader's attention to the negative impact that accepting difficult pupils from other schools can have on 'your' school. At this point however, it is worth looking at just one more strand of the issue surrounding permanent exclusions. Up until 2012, a permanent exclusion had not only to be upheld by the governors of the school or academy trust, but was also subject to an appeal process. If the parents or guardians of the permanently excluded child so desired, they could call for an independent review of the exclusion. This review panel had the power to re-instate the pupil in the school if they felt that the exclusion was unwarranted. From September 2012 however, the powers of such a review panel were significantly reduced from 'being able to reinstate' to 'recommending reinstatement' – a recommendation that the school or academy would not need to follow, and indeed would have almost zero interest in doing so.

With all this in mind, it should be clear that the process of 'Fair Access' needs very careful management, and during my time at Campion, this actually worked quite well. As local Headteachers, we would meet regularly with Local Authority officers to place pupils who needed to move schools. There appeared to be a tacit understanding that Campion had been very badly served in the past, and so colleague Heads never complained (at least to my face) about my own very high level of exclusions. The situation was perhaps helped by two factors – the accountability stakes were not as high then as they subsequently became, and we had an excellent Pupil Referral Unit whose Headteacher put in additional support to schools who accepted pupils that had been expelled from other institutions. Ultimately however, the Local Authority was able to direct a school to take a pupil against the wishes of the Headteacher. This only happened once to me. A young boy who had been engaging in 'sexually inappropriate behaviour' applied to join the school. I was tremendously worried by this, and refused point-blank to take him. In the end, I was directed to take him, albeit with a full programme of support from the local authority psychologist. In the event, I need not have worried – the boy was well-behaved, did not repeat his behaviour in the school, and worked quietly until he left at the end of Y11.

With the advent of academies however, implementing Fair Access at a local level became much trickier. To explain why this was the case, we need to spend a few moments looking at how the role of Local Authorities had been changing, and crucially, where they found themselves in 2010.

Up until the late 1980s, Local Authorities had a powerful role to play in the running of schools. They determined budgets, appointed headteachers and ran their own inspections. However, in 1988, the Education Reform Act (ERA) introduced (amongst other things) the concept of 'Local Management of Schools' (LMS). The next 30 years saw a gradual decrease of the Local Authority's role in running schools, a process which accelerated with the establishment of academies. Academies were established as independent, state-funded schools which importantly for this discussion, were free of Local Authority control. Amongst other things, this meant that they were able to set specific criteria for their own admission of pupils, and thereby control these much more closely than had previously been the case under 'local authority' rule. For example, whereas in the past a school would be more or less obliged to accept a pupil that moved into its 'catchment area', an academy could now state in its admission policy that it would adopt a system of 'fair banding', meaning (for example) that it would only admit a certain proportion of low-attaining pupils. A far higher than average percentage of 'difficult' pupils come from this band, so an admissions policy such as this could enable the academy to turn a certain number of these away.

By 2008, there were approximately 85 such secondary academies. The academy of which I was Principal, Archbishop Sentamu Academy was founded in 2008, and was academy number 84. At the time, there were around 3500 secondary schools, so proportionally at around 2.5% of all secondary schools, their impact on 'the system' (including the principles around Fair Access) was relatively low. However, with the Academies Act of 2010, Education Secretary Michael Gove gave the right for all local authority maintained schools to 'academise'. Up until that point, a school had needed a 'sponsor' to academise. Typically, the sponsor was required to put up a sum of around £1,000,000 in return for the privilege – perhaps the best example of this is the highly successful London-based Harris Academy group. However, from 2010, the only criterion was that a school should have an Ofsted rating of 'good' or better. This led to an explosion in the number of academies to the extent that today, 80% of England's 4190 secondary schools are now academies.

Because academies were established as independent schools, they were directly accountable to the Secretary of State, not (as was previously the case) to the Local Authority. Gove recognised that the expansion of academies would not only leave a vacuum in the 'middle-layer' of running schools – a role previously carried out by the Local Authority – but would also make the schools' minister's job unworkable! With this in mind, he put measures in place to replace the 'middle layer'. Nowadays, that function is mainly (but not exclusively) carried out be a system of Regional School Directors and their associated bureaucracy, but in 2010, an immediate problem to solve was that of ensuring Fair Access to pupils who needed to move schools. To recap for a moment: By 2010, almost all Local Authority areas now had a combination of on the one hand, traditionally run local authority maintained schools, and on the other, academies and so-called 'University Technical Colleges' (UTCs), essentially a specific type of academy which focussed on technical education. However, academies were able to set their own admission criteria, and could not be directed to accept pupils by the Local Authority. This resulted in an environment in which academies were, in theory, able to 'duck' notions of shared local responsibility for accepting challenging pupils onto their roll either by:

1. Not admitting them in the first place through a specific admissions policy designed to do this;
2. Expelling pupils with no possibility of the Local Authority preventing this (remember that from 2012, it was almost impossible for permanent exclusion to be overturned through and independent appeals process); or
3. Refusing to accept pupils from other schools with no possibility of the Local Authority directing them to do so. (Academies can in theory be directed to take pupils by the secretary of state, but in practice, this happens very rarely).

To resolve this whole problem of how to ensure that all schools and academies in a local area took their fair share of pupils moving schools for whatever reason, the government required every Local Authority to establish 'Fair Access Panels', along with clear guidelines as to how these should operate. Their aim was to ensure that all schools and academies in a given area both recognised, and acted upon, their shared responsibility to ensure that all pupils moving schools were enabled to do so in a timely fashion. These principles all appear perfectly reasonable. However, we need to remind ourselves of the freedom of academies to set their own admission policies (which, if used in certain ways could 'filter out' VYPs from the outset), and the increasing freedoms academies had to permanently exclude pupils (From 2012, they had the freedom to expel pupils without fear of having them returned to the school through an appeals process). These factors, coupled with the statistical disincentive for schools to accept pupils through Fair Access (particularly in the light of increasingly high accountability stakes), meant that in practice, it was perfectly possible for academies to duck their responsibilities if they were so inclined.

The Fair Access system is thus the first example in this book of how the piecemeal approach to developing central education policy has actively worked against the interests of our most vulnerable pupils. To illustrate this more clearly, we will now look at how the system used to work in Hull during my time as an academy Principal. What follows may be shocking to some. However, I put the root of the blame for these questionable practices firmly at the door of successive education secretaries, who either refused or were simply unable to see that the principles of Fair Access were incompatible with the accountability regime to which schools are all subject.

(Un)Fair Access

Hull was one of the first authorities in which all its secondary schools fairly quickly became academies, meaning that the Local Authority had in effect very little hope of directing any school to take a particular pupil. The ultimate success of the panel relied therefore on colleague headteachers working together for a common good. This potential 'Wild West' was made worse as the years went on by three additional factors – the establishment of both a UTC and an 11-16 'arm' of a local sixth-form college that were set up in Hull, and practices adopted by our neighbouring Local Authority – the East Riding of Yorkshire. Taking these in turn:

The UTC and Sixth form were able to contact all pupils in Year 9 across Hull, offering them the prospect respectively of either a technical or more vocationally based curriculum. However, if after a year or so the pupil proved disruptive, they could be expelled back into the academy from which they had originally come. This was, quite naturally, resented by the other schools in Hull, who would be made accountable for the results of pupils who were almost certainly problematic, and with whom we would have little time to work (typically a year or less) to enable them to succeed. A similar situation pertained with the East Riding – schools 'just over the border' would do their best to attract pupils from Hull whom they saw as potentially advantageous to their results, but if they turned out to be problematic, would expel them and expect Hull (not East Riding) schools to take them onto their rolls. This practice caused particular resentment, as it was felt that wherever possible, a whole local authority (the East Riding) was doing its best to shift its responsibilities for managing and supporting challenging pupils onto schools in another local authority which had more than enough challenges of their own.

With all these factors in play, the monthly meeting of the Fair Access panel was never going to be easy! The process would begin a few days before the meeting itself, when paperwork would be sent out from the Local Authority on each of the typically 80 or so young people we needed to place in our schools. On every form, the parent put a choice of school, so at that point, our first priority was to examine carefully the potted histories provided and try to work out the truth about the pupils. The forms themselves were often both deliberately misleading and very badly filled-in, so it was crucial for us to assess, for example, whether accepting any given pupil was likely to be a catalyst for further disruption. In this respect, two categories of children were particularly worrying – those 'wanting a fresh start' (generally a code for the fact that they were being encouraged by the school to 'jump before they were pushed'), and of course pupils with a long history of fixed-term exclusions.

Parental choice was a key reason for having to accept a child though Fair Access, and if the reason for that choice was that the pupil was in our catchment area – i.e. lived near to our school – the school would probably have to accept him or her even if the year group was 'full'. However, if the overall profile of the pupil gave cause for concern (for example a listed history of persistent disruption), it was common practice to delay their entry – for example if it was known that they would immediately hook up with equally nefarious friends they had at the school, or would bully others. These and other reasons meant that challenging pupils were not immediately admitted to a school they had chosen, in the hope that they would give up, or try another school.

However, if the child didn't live in the catchment area, schools had a much better chance of refusing them entry. Firstly, it could be claimed quite legitimately that the year group was full. All schools have a 'Pupil Admissions Number' (PAN) for each year group. However, this figure can fluctuate. On occasions a school can end up with more pupils in a year-group than was originally planned, if for example it suddenly becomes very popular and lots of local children apply to attend. On other occasions however the actual number of pupils in a year group may decline – if for example a number have opted to leave to attend a UTC from year 10 onwards, or if there is simply a drop in the birth rate. Where numbers decline, the school makes appropriate adjustments in the number of classes it puts on for the following year – for example having only 7 instead of 8 sets of English, Maths and Science. In this case, the year group is 'full' from a teaching provision point of view, even if there is still physical space in the building. In order to protect the size of teaching groups therefore, schools could legitimately alter their official PAN for any given year-group, making it harder for pupils to be admitted in-year. But in the final event, schools could simply stand their ground anyway, refuse a pupil entry, and say that they were not prepared to take 'another disruptive pupil', secure in the knowledge that only the Secretary of State could overrule this decision, a process which in itself was extremely lengthy. At that point, the child would remain out of school until the next Fair Access meeting.

A final problem was that, for many years, the meeting was attended mainly by Deputy Heads, who had been briefed in advance of the meeting by their headteachers as to which pupils to accept. If pressure was brought to bear on the luckless Deputies in the meeting to take a pupil that the school in advance of the meeting had decided against, they would invariably simply inform the panel that they had been instructed by their Head not to accept them. We will see in a later chapter how, as a group of headteachers, we improved the workings of the FAP, but for several years, the system was, to varying degrees, subverted.

At this point, the attentive reader will be asking 'So what happens if a child can't get into a school through Fair Access?' The simple answer is that at best, they spend more time out of school than is needed, and eventually do find a place in a school at a subsequent Fair Access Panel meeting. A lucky few may be given a place at an Alternative Provision academy (such as the one that I established). However, places are limited, and demand far exceeds supply. So, for many, the process of Fair Access is 'rinsed and repeated', meaning that in the worst cases, pupils can find themselves out of school for months, or even drop out entirely. At that point, we can remind ourselves of some of the words of Anne Longfield, chair of the Commission on Young Lives and the government's former children's commissioner for England who was quoted earlier on in this chapter: 'Young people who end up being excluded are vulnerable to being exploited by criminal gangs, and their life chances are diminished'. Indeed.

The inability to be admitted to a school in the first place is not however the only reason for which vulnerable young people find themselves out of school. The second biggest reason is pressure from the school itself to leave. Even though schools now have fairly strong powers to permanently exclude pupils with little chance of the decision being overturned, a high level of these exclusions is frowned upon by Ofsted. To avoid this official opprobrium, another tactic employed by schools is for pressure to be brought on a disruptive pupil to 'leave before they are officially expelled'. In these cases, one of the following scenarios generally applies:

1. The parent or guardian agrees to apply for a place for their child at another school;
2. The parent or guardian agrees to 'home educate' the child; or
3. The school simply 'loses contact' with the child, and after a while, drops them off their roll. This is one example of a practice called 'off-rolling', which we will look at in much more detail in a future chapter.

In the first scenario above, the application will be put through the Fair Access panel. As already discussed however, there is a good chance that this will not work unless two headteachers can agree a 'quid pro quo', in which they effectively 'swap' a pair of disruptive pupils. To be fair, this can work in the interests of all concerned and such agreements made by Headteachers whether through, or independently of, the Fair Access Panel can be effective in improving the life chances of vulnerable young people.

The second scenario may often arise when the first one has failed. In this case, the parent, desperate to avoid a permanent exclusion, removes their child from the school and agrees to take responsibility for educating their child themselves. I do not intend to debate the general pros and cons of home-schooling here. Suffice it to say, it was my experience that those parents who took this decision were woefully ill-equipped to home-school their children.

If the practices outlined in the first two examples are morally questionable (the exception arguably being the situation where two headteachers try to help two pupils and each other with a 'swap'), the third scenario is completely illegal – a school must not drop a pupil from their roll before they are either on the roll of another school, or being home-schooled. You would rightly think that no headteacher would ever contemplate off-rolling. The fact that between around 2017 and 2020 the practice became quite widespread, and the subject of numerous investigations, is indicative of the huge pressures under which schools had by that time been forced to operate. To use another overworked metaphor, it was an indication that the piecemeal approach to the development of educational legislation was 'squeezing the orange' to such an extent that the pips were beginning to pop out.

Concluding comments:

In this chapter, we have attempted to define the concept of a 'VYP', saying that for the purposes of our discussions, it will include any young person who attracts the 'pupil premium' – this being around a quarter of all pupils. We then went on to look at a number of reasons for which our most vulnerable pupils find themselves, in the words of Anastacia's 2004 hit, 'Left outside alone'. We have seen how parents can be put under pressure to withdraw their child if they become persistently disruptive, how they can be permanently excluded and once expelled, find it very difficult to find a place in another school. We have also begun to explore how a disconnect between various aspects of government policy (in this place Fair Access legislation and accountability systems) acts as a powerful disincentive for schools to 'do the right thing', the end result being that whilst some vulnerable people may ultimately gain a place in an Alternative Provision academy, too many find themselves outside of education, and highly vulnerable to gangs, crime and long-term exclusion. It is, I am aware, a profoundly depressing picture. I was always troubled by our own Fair Access system in Hull and on a personal level, resolved to try to find ways to fix it. I believe that in the end we were able to improve it considerably, but that is the subject of a later chapter where we begin to offer ways of improving 'The System' for our most vulnerable young people. For now, however, I would like to look at another key issue that causes our most vulnerable young people to drop out – the curriculum itself.

Chapter 3 – A brief history of curriculum policy

Abstract:

This chapter gives an overview of the development of curriculum policy from the 1950s, and the extent to which it has ensured our 'VYP's receive an education suited to their needs. Following this, and explaining how I almost gave up teaching very early on in my career, I go on to chart my own experience as a curriculum innovator, charting the ways in which I made use of increasing freedoms to devise programmes of study and assessment routes that suited many VYPs much better than the traditional routes followed in many schools at various points in time. In particular, it looks at how 'GCSE equivalencies' such as GNVQs and BTecs were allowed to develop. The chapter ends however with an early experience of how government dogma (in this case applied to the Specialist College programme in place at the time) almost derailed one of my initiatives, and forced me to adapt in a way which was to the detriment of many pupils – especially our VYPs.

'We don't need no... education...'

Pink Floyd, 1979

Pink Floyd's words have always challenged me to ensure that school is as enjoyable, creative and useful as possible. A key plank of that success has to be the design of the curriculum - what our pupils learn during their time at school both within and outside of formal lessons. In the last chapter, we noted that schools serving deprived communities need to make up for deficits in experience which more affluent families typically provide at or through home. To achieve this, a strong curriculum for these schools is therefore all the more crucial. Since the introduction of the National Curriculum under Kenneth Baker in 1988, curriculum design has been hugely influenced and steered through successive developments of government legislation. Along with the exam regime and the accountability system of Ofsted, it is one of the three key elements of what can be described as our 'educational system'. Indeed, if we break down schooling into its simplest terms, we could define it as follows:

1. Pupils come to school and learn (Curriculum)
2. At various ages they take exams (Metrics)
3. Schools are judged on how successful the pupils are (Accountability through Ofsted)

With this in mind, both this and the following chapters in Part One focus on how government policy has affected curriculum design and through this, how it has impacted the life-chances of our most vulnerable young people. But first, a little history on the development of school-based qualifications themselves.

Between 1951 and 1986 there was relatively little change in the exams that pupils were required to sit at age 16, the main options being 'O' levels (introduced in 1951) and CSEs (Certificates of Secondary Education) introduced in 1965 as alternatives to 'O' levels, following a report carried out by the Beloe committee between 1958 and 1960. In simple terms, 'O' levels were what would be understood as 'academic' exams, with CSEs being more 'practical' in nature. There was a loose currency whereby a top grade CSE was judged to be of equivalent value to a 'C' grade (minimum pass) at 'O' level.

In 1986 this all changed, with the introduction of GCSEs. GCSEs amalgamated and replaced both 'O' levels and CSEs, becoming the main exam sat by all pupils in a variety of subjects at 16 from 1988 onwards. But if the 30 years prior to the introduction of GCSEs was marked by a period of calm, the next 30 years saw an explosion of change and with it, the arrival of a huge variety of qualifications, all of which led to a great many options in the delivery of the school curriculum. 'Mode 3' GCSEs, GNVQs, BTECs and other so-called 'vocational' qualifications all appeared on the scene and with them, the potential to customise the learning for the individual pupil much more closely. My own time in education matched this period almost exactly – I started in 1989 – and for a teacher with an interest in curriculum design, the 25 years between 1990 and 2015 were genuinely exciting, especially in terms of how we were able to cater for the most vulnerable. A thorough analysis of this period, and how it came to a crashing halt around 2015, will serve us well as we look at one of the key contentions of this book – that government curriculum policy is currently having a highly negative impact on our most vulnerable young people.

I first became interested in curriculum design at the age of 12, when the grammar school I attended presented me with my first choice. From Year 8 (or '2nd year' as it was called back then) the school had quite rightly picked up that I had little interest in sciences and thus put me into an alternative 'languages stream', meaning that I studied French, German and Latin. I loved all three, and was therefore extremely disappointed to learn that I would have to give up one of these in order to study either Geography or History for GCSE. Both of these options bored me senseless at the time, so I was most unhappy at having to give up a language. In the end, I opted to carry on with French and German, and much to my displeasure, opted for Geography, a subject I just managed to pass at 'O' level two years later. To say that this choice forced upon me at the age of 12 was a formative experience is perhaps a bit of an overstatement, but looking back over my career in education, I see now that an interest in curriculum design was always a key driver in my teaching practice, as I sought to find ways to motivate as many different groups of pupils as possible. In spite of the enthusiasm that was to drive my career however, it was almost over before it even started, as 18 months after beginning teaching, I was on the point of giving up.

My last period at 'school' was in 1987, when I attended Birmingham University for my PGCE course. I didn't rate it at all. Although Birmingham itself is a fairly prestigious so-called 'Red-Brick' University, I found many of my lectures crushingly dull. Indeed, if I learned anything from them, it was how **not** to teach. To make matters worse, our course leader took the view that his trainees should complete their teaching practice in 'good' schools – by which he meant schools in which there were few challenging pupils. Instinctively I knew this would not prepare me well for the rigours of the average, let alone 'difficult' school, so whilst I was obliged to complete one of my placements in a grammar school, I managed to persuade him to let me carry out the other one in a normal comprehensive school.

Sadly, my suspicions about the relevance of my teaching practice were proven to be correct. My first real job teaching French was at an inner-city school, which at the time was ranked 100/106 in terms of exam results at the time when so-called 'league tables' (although successive governments insist on calling them' performance tables') were first introduced. In all honesty, in spite of all my efforts, I thought I was perhaps one level above 'catastrophically bad'. The term 'Education' is derived from two Latin words - educere – means 'to lead out', the other – educare – meaning to train or mould. Unfortunately, my first few terms as a teacher were a failure in both senses of the word. I led only a few to see any value in learning French, and was able mould even fewer of them to hand in any homework. I struggled, struggled and then struggled some more.

After 18 months of not making much progress with my classes, I decided to take stock. I could see that not only was my initial approach not working, but that worse, *any* approach I took failed to motivate the great majority of the pupils I taught. This most fundamental of failures almost led to my giving up teaching all together, or at least teaching in the UK. Somewhat discouraged by this, I decided to do an additional qualification for 'Teaching English as a Foreign Language' (TEFL). This had a notoriously difficult written exam, and a relatively straightforward practical exam. I loved the course, and flew through the written exam. For the practical exam, we all had to teach an aspect of English grammar to a class we had never previously met. I prepared my materials meticulously, rehearsed my delivery fastidiously, taught the lesson energetically...and was told that I had failed. To this day, I don't really understand what 'went wrong' – the learners certainly seemed to be engaged and making progress - but needless to say, I was pretty devastated. So, there I was. Aged 26 – failing in mainstream education, failing in TEFL teaching – what to do? I considered my options. I worked out that I could either apply for another job in teaching, hoping that I would receive a strong enough reference to be given a second chance, or apply for another job altogether. In the final event, I did both.

I remember very little about my interview with Scottish Widows insurance. I must however have convinced them enough about my enthusiasm for selling pensions and other financial products, because I was offered the job. I told them I would consider their offer. The following day, I had an interview with another school. I had actually summoned up the courage to apply for a job which entailed a slight promotion – which in hindsight was a bit overoptimistic – but the interview seemed to go well. After an hour or two of sitting around to find out if they wanted me or not, the Deputy Head, with whom I was later to become good friends – explained the situation: 'We have a bit of a problem here..' he began. 'We would like to take you on, but somebody else in the school has applied for the actual promotion, so would you be prepared to take the teaching job but without the promotion?' I considered his offer for perhaps three nanoseconds, made him wait a further four, then gratefully accepted. Having endured 20 months of relative failure and absolute misery, that job offer was to open up 25 years of joyful fulfilment.

Arden was, without doubt, a school situated in a 'leafy suburb'. However, like every school, it had its fair share of challenges, including its own rump of pupils who were 'actively disengaged' from their studies. In their own way, they too were 'VYPs' – most from broken families, some with mental health issues, but all of them having to learn French. It was clear to me very early on in my career that insisting on a 'Full-Fat 9 GCSEs' diet would not serve this group of pupils well. There are a number of reasons for this, and to understand them, we need first to grasp the role given by the government to a frightening array of acronyms:

- NCVQ – the National Council for Vocational Qualifications (established in 1986)
- SCAA – the School Curriculum and Assessment Authority (established in 1993)
- QCA - the Qualifications and Curriculum Authority (established in 1997 upon the merger of NCVQ and SCAA); and
- Ofqual – the Office of Qualifications and Examination Regulations (established in 2010).

The role of these bodies is to regulate the curriculum and associated assessment of exams taken by pupils at 14 (KS3 SATs), 16 and 18. KS3 SATs were abolished in 2008, and for the purpose of this section of the book, we will focus on the role played by the aforementioned QUANGOs in the assessment of exams taken at by pupils at age 16. The observant reader will notice that QCA and Ofqual were formed immediately after two significant changes of government – in the case of QCA when Labour came to power under Tony Blair in 1997, and in the case of Ofqual, under the Coalition government led by David Cameron in 2010. We will return to this specific point later on.

Following the establishment of the NCVQ in the late 1980s, pupils were able to study a variety of accredited exams up to the age of 16. These included GNVQs (General National Vocational Qualifications), as well as GCSEs. GNVQs, as the name suggests, gave a more 'practical' or 'applied' slant to study. They included areas such as Business Studies, ICT, Leisure and Tourism and Health and Social Care, with two-thirds of the course being assessed by coursework. Although it was possible to study 'Part One' GNVQs, full GNVQs (the type taken by the majority of pupils following these courses) were given the 'equivalency' of 4 GCSEs. The main difference between the two types of exams was that generally, GCSEs were (and today are even more so) assessed through so-called 'terminal examinations', whereas for GNVQs, two-thirds of the final grade were awarded through a process of 'continual assessment'. Arguments around the relative merits of these two approaches are commonplace. As is said to be the case with economists, put three educational specialists together in a room and you will end up with four different viewpoints on the subject! At the most basic level however, the assessment process of GNVQs had four advantages in comparison to GCSEs.

Firstly, they had a very practical focus. A common complaint of almost every pupil who has ever lived – i.e., all of us – is 'What's the point of doing this?', which on occasions, is a very fair complaint. With the vocational orientation of GNVQs however, pupils were able to study a subject in which they were in theory at least quite interested, and for which they could see a practical purpose. The most famous of these was perhaps the GNVQ in ICT studied by all pupils at Thomas Telford Academy, which in the late 1980s and early 1990s enabled pupils to prepare themselves for the use of computing in everyday life. Whilst we may take the development of these skills more for granted now, thirty years ago this was a very big deal.

Secondly, the ability to draft and re-draft (an almost inevitable by-product of the process of continual assessment) are very useful skills to develop in themselves, whether it is for the production of a specific text (such as this book), or more generally to develop resilience. The defeat of the English by the Scottish at Bannockburn in 1314 was perhaps down to the words of Robert the Bruce, who is famously said to have told his troops 'If at first you don't succeed, try, try, try again'. However, you don't need to be a soldier to realise the benefits of resilience, as in practice, we all have to persist at various points in our lives to meet our goals. Indeed, Education Secretary Michael Gove himself famously had to take his driving test seven times before he passed it.

Thirdly, in my experience, some pupils who are otherwise perfectly capable and hard-working perform far more poorly in exams than they deserve. There are many reasons for this, including the fact that in the main, GCSEs test memory skills, as well as conceptual understanding. For pupils such as these, the option of being able to demonstrate competence through a process of 'continual assessment' is clearly of great benefit.

Fourthly, and perhaps most crucially of all, GNVQs (and indeed other vocational qualifications) are criterion-referenced, rather than norm-referenced. We will look at this key difference in much more detail when we look at the whole issue of assessment in later chapters. For now, however, it is sufficient to note that with criterion referencing, any pupil who meets the required standard can pass. With norm-referencing (which applies to all GCSEs), only around 70% of pupils can achieve the current 'minimum pass' grade of a level 4 or above in any given exam sitting.

Just before entering the 'rabbit hole' of exam assessment policy, we were discussing the delivery of French to our VYPs at a school in a leafy suburb. The challenge I faced was this: At the time, most of the pupils were studying at least 8, if not 9, GCSEs, including French. I knew that for many of the VYPs, taking this number of exams at one time with such an emphasis on memory recall was going to be difficult. I also knew that for many, French would be fairly low on their list of priorities. I therefore set about finding a solution which would enable my VYPs to study French through a process of continuous assessment which, in my view, would prove more immediately engaging.

We noted a few moments ago that the continual assessment method of examination applied to vocational qualifications – not GCSEs. However, after researching the options available, I discovered that the Southern Examining Group – SEG - offered a 'Mode 3' style of GCSE, which did indeed allow the course to be examined differently. Under this arrangement, modules or 'chunks' of the course were examined over a period of time – typically the two years of Key Stage 4 (Years 10 and 11). To my great delight, I discovered that this approach worked really well with my groups – my pupils found it very motivating to learn a manageable amount of material over a number of weeks and then be tested on that section of work. In short, they enjoyed eating the 'exam elephant' one bite a time. Unlike almost all other GCSEs, this particular course was criterion referenced – if pupils were able to meet the standard, they passed. The result of my experiment was that GCSE success shot up for this particular group of pupils.

Following on from this success, we decided to pilot this approach with a wider group of pupils during Year 9, to see if it suited others. We discovered that not all pupils enjoyed it, with many preferring a more 'traditional approach' to examination. This should of course no surprise - it is perfectly reasonable to expect that different methods of course delivery and exam assessment will suit different people. Over the course of the next four years, during which time I took up a post as Head of Languages at another school, I continued to do my best to match the method we used to teaching languages to the individual pupils. By introducing the 'Mode 3' approach to all pupils in Year 9 as part of their normal, pre-GCSE studies, we were able to determine quite reliably which ones were best suited to this approach, and which ones preferred a more traditional approach.

The experience served to confirm my initial observations that the Mode 3 approach appealed in particular to our VYPs. In turn, this early 'longitudinal' study led me conclude that different types of assessment suit different types of people, that there was a strong correlation between VYPs enjoying and succeeding in a course with regular 'bite-sized testing', and that this being the case, we have a moral obligation to find the best ways for all pupils to achieve the standards we set them.

These conclusions may not appear that staggering. What I do find staggering however is that from 2010 onwards, successive Secretaries of State for Education have, in my opinion, wilfully ignored these considerations, to the detriment in particular of our VYPs. This is a theme to which will keep on returning throughout this book. In the 1990s however, we were still in a period of great 'curriculum opportunity', which brings us neatly to our next point – the development of the 'specialist schools' programme.

Introduced in 1993 by the education secretary Gillian Shephard, the programme gave schools the opportunity to 'specialise' in a particular area of the curriculum. The first such colleges were based on a Technology specialism, but the programme quickly expanded to include Sports, Languages, Arts and Business Studies. In order to qualify for a specific designation, schools had to raise £100,000 in sponsorship and write a very detailed three-year development plan, outlining how the specialism would be used to raise standards not just in the area of specialism, but across the school as a whole. In return for this, the school received an additional capital investment of £100,000 to develop the specialism, plus £100 per pupil per year additional on-going funding. Anecdotally, according to my then headteacher, the DfE saw this programme as a 'bargain', as for an average cost of £73 per teacher nationally, they would be ensuring that schools wrote detailed development plans - which apparently was not always the case at the time. I have no way of confirming the truth or otherwise of this view!

Be that as it may, the programme offered genuinely exciting opportunities for curriculum development. In 1996, having returned as Head of Languages to Arden School where I first introduced the

SEG French GCSE described above, I proposed that we should apply for Language College status. Whilst many schools employed specialist bid-writers to do this, I agreed with the Headteacher that I would undertake this myself as part of my day-job. After endless drafts and hundreds of pages of writing, the bid was written. However, raising the necessary sponsorship was more challenging. Email had only just been invented at that point and was not widely used, so the quickest form of communication at the time was the fax. Sadly, the only fax-machine was in the office of the school bursar, which led to my disturbing him several times a day as I chased the elusive £100,000. He became so sick of this that in his leaving speech, he said he would give me a ticket for a trip to the moon in NASA's space shuttle – one-way. However, my perseverance paid off, we raised the money, and our bid was finally able to be submitted. After waiting for 3 nail-biting months, we heard that we had indeed been granted Language-College status, and so began four incredibly enjoyable years.

For curriculum innovators, the specialist college programme as a whole was 'manna from heaven' at the start, giving schools the opportunity to put into practice the sort of observations I had made about how best to match various curriculum and assessment methodologies to different groups of pupils. Having had the privilege of travelling widely thanks to my degree in Modern Languages, I have always had a passion for languages and learning from other people's cultures – a passion I was keen to share with my pupils. The additional funding from the Specialist Colleges programme enabled us to do just this, and interest in languages blossomed as we organised a wealth of trips, visits and exchanges. This included China, to support our introduction of Mandarin Chinese into the Curriculum. After much haggling with suppliers, we were able to use the capital funding to install language laboratories and a full computer network in every languages' classroom, a network which was happily maintained by a group of tech-savvy pupils. We were in the very early days of the Internet but managed nonetheless to video-conference with a partner school in France, which we even managed to demonstrate to an Ofsted inspector during an inspection. Exam results continued to rise, and the programme overall was a great success for our pupils.

Until it wasn't, quite as much. If the start of the specialist college programme showcased the extent to which central policy could influence outcomes positively for all pupils, its development showed the extent to which government tinkering around, without consultation, had the opposite effect. A key requirement of the programme was that all pupils should take a subject linked to the specialism in some form or other. That was arguably a reasonable policy, as long as the requirement did not become too much of a straitjacket. When we look at what we now know as the 'English Baccalaureate' or 'Ebac' later in this book, I will argue that the level of curriculum prescription engendered by this policy is injurious to pupils, especially our VYPs. At the start of the specialist college era however, the requirement for all pupils to study the subject specialism in one form or other was not too much of a restriction, given the number of different courses and exams that were available at that time. We will look at more examples of these later on. In the case of our languages' specialism, the initial requirement was that all pupils should take a modern language. That worked well for us, as we had found an alternative qualification – the SEG 'Mode 3' GCSE – that enabled all our pupils to succeed.

However, a few years into the programme, new requirements were added in order to qualify for ongoing funding and 'specialist designation'. In our case, it was suddenly decided by central government that all pupils should have to study 2 languages to GCSE. I fundamentally disagreed with this, as did the school's senior leadership team, and so at that point, the school was on the horns of a dilemma – should we follow a policy which, in all honesty, we felt was not in pupils' best interests, or should we risk losing our specialist designation and associated funding? In the end, we found a rather messy fudge whereby pupils studied at least one full language GCSE, and one 'half-GCSE', which was possible at the time. I was never happy with the situation – for many pupils the additional half-GCSE was not the best use of their time. The solution did however enable us to continue with both our designation and our funding. This was one of the first examples I encountered of ideologically driven, ill-thought out initiatives being introduced without any consultation impacting negatively on pupils. In the simplest of terms, the government had 'moved the goalposts' without warning, making leaders' lives needlessly more difficult, and pupils' lives correspondingly worse. This behaviour was perhaps a small cloud on the horizon of the otherwise beautifully clear skies of curriculum development opportunity, which were a feature of that time. Little did I know at that point that this small cloud would become an immense storm that, in 2016, threatened the survival of both our academy and our Trust.

Chapter 4 – Developing new qualifications.

Abstract:

This chapter starts by outlining how I helped to develop one specific 'GCSE equivalent' - the 'Young Arts Leader Award' (YALA) during my time as a deputy-head at Langley School, and then continues with an account of the various curriculum innovations I introduced during my first headship at Campion School in Leamington Spa. A key observation here is the extent to which these so-called 'alternative' qualifications were able (to misquote a lager advert form the 1970s) 'to reach those pupils that other qualifications could not reach'. This was especially the case at Campion, where my curriculum initiatives were framed in the successful bid for the school to become a specialist 'Arts and Enterprise' college, a key strategy in turning around the fortunes of the school and its pupils.

'…..Fame!'

Irene Cara, 1980

The years I spent at Arden were amongst the most enjoyable of my career. Our department had great teachers, we had great resources from the additional language college programme, and we had the freedom to innovate with the curriculum, enabling us to find motivating courses for the vast majority of our pupils. However, after four years there, I felt that I was able to leave the department in very good hands, and so I moved to Langley School as Deputy Head in charge of the Curriculum. Langley too was a great school, blessed with an excellent, visionary Headteacher, and an incredible Performing Arts department. Prior to my arrival, thanks to a bid to the Arts Council, the school had constructed and was running a fully professional theatre, enjoyed by both pupils during school hours, and the general public in the evenings and weekends. This amazing resource opened my eyes to the power of the Arts to transform young people's lives – I saw that success in the Arts had the power to transfer to other areas of the curriculum too. With such an incredible resource already on-site, I therefore proposed that we should bid for 'Performing Arts College' status.

Whereas the decision to apply for Language College status at Arden had been relatively straightforward, convincing the Langley senior leadership took more work. Eventually, a change in the programme introduced by Education Secretary Estelle Morris in 2001 set out the vision that all schools would either become specialist colleges in their own right, or attached to one through a 'community outreach' programme. The choice was pretty stark – either become a specialist college, or become a (probably very) poor relative of another one. At this point, it became clear to us all that we should indeed apply for the specialist status ourselves, so for the second time, I set about constructing a bid. Disappointingly, our first attempt failed – but we were successful the second time, so Langley became 'Langley School and Performing Arts College'.

Central to our bid was the development of a new programme – the 'Young Arts Leader Award' (or YALA), which is now known quite simply as 'The Arts Award'. The original award was developed by Langley's exceptionally talented Head of Arts, Terry Clarke, in conjunction with the Arts Council, and comprised the following key elements:

- Developing skills in an area of the Arts
- Visiting and reviewing arts events
- Creating a portfolio of evidence
- Researching careers pathways in the Arts
- Leading an arts-related project in the community

Crucially, the award carried GCSE equivalence. The QCA (Qualifications and Curriculum Authority) gave the silver award a half-GCSE equivalence, and the gold award, a full GCSE equivalence. The award was thus another example of how pupils at the time were able to gain GCSEs in a number of different ways. In the case of our Arts award, even a cursory glance at the framework shows that pupils were gaining a completely different set of skills to those traditionally gained through GCSEs – skills which would transfer to many other areas of life – as well as the ability to appreciate the value and beauty of the Arts in their own right, as summed up Metro Goldwyn Mayer's strapline 'Ars gratia artis' - 'Art for Art's sake'.

Needless to say, the Arts Award was a great success, and soon spread to other schools, both locally and nationally. In many ways, it was a 'Duke of Edinburgh's award' for the Arts. As with the DofE award, it had (and still has) three levels – bronze, silver and gold. Indeed, today, the Arts Award is an 'Approved Activity Provider' for the Duke of Edinburgh's Award, allowing young people to do an Arts Award as part of the DofE programme itself. I stated earlier that this book is not setting out to give forensic analysis of the different forms of curriculum design. However, I believe it is worth underlining at this point the value that a variety of qualifications can bring to a young person's life, especially for our VYPs, whose lives are indeed the focus of this book.

We noted earlier that for many young people, especially our VYPs, a diet of 'pure' exam-based GCSEs is not in their best interests, not least because some simply do not perform as well as their abilities would otherwise indicate when the outcome for success is based on exams in 8 or 9 subjects taken in one sitting. The pupils at Langley really enjoyed the Arts Award. From Year 7 onwards, we used it as a framework to integrate the Art, Music and Drama curriculum, giving them the option from Year 9 onwards to spend more time in this area to pursue either a half or full GCSE in the award. This ability for schools to offer courses assessed in a variety of different ways during the 1990s and early 2000s was, I believe, a key factor in helping to keep young people, especially our VYPs, both in school and engaged in their studies. The full extent of this was to become abundantly clear to me as I took on my next challenge, headship of Campion School.

'We, are, the Campions…'

(misquoting Queen, 1977)

We looked at Campion School earlier on through the lens of pupil exclusions. In this chapter, I want to revisit the school, but this time to examine it through the lens of its curriculum, and the impact that this has on pupils, especially our VYPs. We saw previously that it had become to a certain extent a 'dumping ground' for pupils excluded from other local schools, and as such, had a very high proportion of challenging and vulnerable young people. As such, behaviour was very poor and exam results were very low. It had become both unpopular with parents, and of huge concern to the Local Authority, who were very worried that it would be judged to require Special Measures at its next inspection.

When I became Headteacher in 2004, our first job as a team was therefore to restore order. There are many reasons for which pupils behave badly, including an inappropriate curriculum, but until there is a culture of clear expectations around behaviour driven by the school's senior leadership team, even really good teachers armed with a really exciting curriculum will struggle. Indeed, although it may seem extreme, as Headteacher I took almost every single act of poor behaviour as my responsibility and 'my fault'. As we noted earlier, this led to what would now be considered a frighteningly high level of exclusions – both fixed-term and permanent – but we refused to compromise on our standards. Armed with around 50 copies of Sue Cowley's excellent book 'Getting the Buggers to Behave – 2', (Cowley, 2002) we worked as a staff at establishing a new set of norms, and over time, behaviour improved out of all recognition. With this great reduction in managing daily crises of behaviour, we were able to focus on improving teaching practice. However, solid behaviour management and much-improved levels of teaching skills were not enough in themselves to ensure the full engagement of all our pupils, and so once again, I tackled the issue of curriculum development to strengthen this vital area of the school.

Arriving at the school, it appeared that there had been little curriculum development for several years. Pupils generally only sat GCSE courses – in other words, those that relied fully on a set of exams being taken all at once. The needs of those for whom this approach didn't work had no real alternatives – their needs were catered for simply by reducing the number of subjects they studied to between five and seven, instead of the eight or nine taken by most. Whilst there is some merit in allocating more time to core subjects like English and Maths, I considered it certainly possible to do more than just this. So, for what was now to be the third time, I turned to the specialist college programme for a solution.

One of the programme's driving principles was to ensure that in any given geographical area, there was a spread of different specialisms. The thinking behind this was to enable parents to choose a school with a specialism that suited their child. Thus, if their child was keen on sport for example, they would apply to go to the local school that had a sports specialism. In practice, whether or not this was actually possible depended on the popularity of the school and its admissions policy. Given that the first three categories of priority were typically pupils with a statement of special needs, geographical distance and having a sibling in the school, this supposed choice was somewhat of a lottery. However, a key criterion for any new specialist college bid was that it would broaden the range of options in any given area. By 2004, Leamington Spa already had Sports, Languages, Technology and Performing Arts colleges, all of which limited our own options. In the end, I decided to risk bidding for an almost unique specialism – Arts and Enterprise.

In my previous two specialist college bids, I had been helped enormously by being able to look at the successful bids written by other schools. There was generally a strong level of collegiality around bid-writers at the time; whilst the process of designation itself was competitive (only a certain number of schools were given the designation in any specialism nationally at any one time, meaning that there were 'winners and losers'), once the designation had been awarded, sharing the bid upon which it had been based to help future schools achieve designation was seen as perfectly reasonable. For my part certainly, I had happily shared both my successful Language College and Performing Arts bids with several other schools. However, at the time, I could only find one other school nationally that had achieved 'Arts and Enterprise' status and to my great disappointment, that school refused to help us in any way, even though to do so would have posed little, if any, risk to their own continued success.

I mention this not out of any notion of 'sour grapes', but simply to draw attention to a key issue that impacts on provision for our VYPs, which will discussed in much greater detail later on. Undeterred by this rather less than gracious response, I put the bid together and fortunately, we were successful on our first attempt. This gave us the funding and the resources to put in place a number of initiatives which broadened our curriculum, especially at Key Stage 4 (14-16 Year olds), when disaffection can really raise its ugly head. Over the course of the next three years, we established a number of key developments which enriched the curriculum considerably, with four of them providing alternative qualifications to GCSEs.

First on the list was the introduction of the Young Arts Leaders' Award (YALA). Inspired by my experiences with at my previous school, Langley, I immediately set about introducing it at Campion, again integrating our arts provision at Key Stage 3 and giving this award as a GCSE option at Key Stage 4. As expected, this proved to be both a popular and successful choice. At Campion however, we were able to enrich the course in a very unexpected way. One of our teaching assistants had encouraged, or in all honesty nagged me, to visit a centre in Leamington called 'Hybrid: Arts'. This centre focussed on teaching digital music production, dance and DJing to pupils that had been expelled from other schools, with incredible success. Using resources from the specialist college programme, we managed to establish our own branch of Hybrid:Arts at the school, both as a course in its own right and as part of YALA.

The second part of our specialism was however just as important. A very common criticism of schools, certainly at the time, was a failure to prepare pupils for 'the real world'. Typically, what was meant by this was a need for pupils to have basic financial awareness, employability skills and some experience of 'the world of work'. An easy win in this respect was the introduction of a range of ASDAN courses. ASDAN, or the 'Award Scheme Development and Accreditation Network', had devised accredited courses for a number of years in areas not covered by traditional GCSEs. A good example was their 'Certificate of Professional Effectiveness' (COPE) which 'did exactly what it said on the tin' – helped pupils develop a series of transferrable skills which would enable them to succeed in their working lives. Assessed through a portfolio, it was approved by QCA to be the equivalent of either a basic 'E' grade or higher 'B' grade GCSE. A common criticism of these courses (and indeed several others, as we shall see later on) was that they were 'too easy' and that allowing pupils to follow them is a 'soft option'. However, at risk of making a somewhat barbed comment, recent UK political history would suggest that at least two of our recent prime ministers would appear to have severely lacked any personal effectiveness whatsoever, with extremely serious consequences for our country.

Our final set of initiatives in this area was to launch two new directly vocational options, the first of which was a GNVQ in horticulture. This proved immensely popular with a number of our pupils. Not only were our pupils able to learn the science and practice of growing flowers and vegetables, but they were also able both to establish a business selling them at a number of local events, and display their products at the locally-run 'Royal Horticultural Show', at which one year they won a 'silver-gilt' award. This course too carried either 2 or 4 GCSE equivalence, depending on how many modules they studied. Last but by no means least, we converted an old classroom into a hairdressing salon, employed a highly talented tutor, and introduced hairdressing onto the curriculum. This course, which also carried GCSE equivalence, not only gave pupils interested in this career-path practical hairdressing skills, but also the business skills they needed to run their own salon. This again proved to be a very popular option.

In addition to the introduction of this range of practical, vocationally based options however, we also wanted to open our pupils' eyes to the reality and possibilities of international business, and with this in mind, we also introduced Mandarin Chinese as an extra-curriculum activity. I had been convinced from the mid-1990s that Mandarin would become a key business language and that in this respect, even a basic appreciation of Chinese language and culture would be of great benefit to our young people. Fortunately, Warwickshire had just signed a Memorandum of Understanding with the province of Shenzhen to develop cooperation between schools in our two countries, and this gave us the ability both to employ a Chinese assistant, and to set up an exchange programme with Tsinghua Experimental School in Shenzhen. Whilst this particular set of activities didn't lead to any formal qualifications, it certainly enriched the learning of our pupils and opened their eyes to a world of which they had had no prior knowledge.

Taken as a whole, our curriculum developments in the Arts, in developing personal effectiveness, in vocational diversification and indeed in offering Chinese all worked to give our pupils much more to 'buy into'. It was particularly effective at re-engaging our VYPs - as time went on, our horrendous level of exclusions dropped as those most at risk of exclusion were able to benefit from a much more varied diet both in terms of content and assessment. It would be fair to say that our programme was proving successful and when Ofsted inspected us in 2006, we were delighted to be judged 'Good' in all areas, but 'Outstanding' in Leadership and Management.

Our final initiative during my time as Headteacher of Campion was to relaunch the sixth form that had sadly been shut down a number of years earlier owing to the difficulties in which the school found itself. The importance of a sixth form to improve pupils' aspirations was acknowledged by Andrew (now Lord) Adonis – a leading force in the development of academies. Under the 'Building Schools for the Future' scheme, which was launched in 2004, the only academies being opened were those replacing schools that had been deemed to be failing. At the time however, a condition advocated by Lord Adonis for receiving funding for a new building under BSF was that it should include plans to establish a Sixth form, in recognition of the impact this can have on motivating VYPs to remain in education post-16. Campion's Sixth form achieved exactly that purpose – in the first years of its relaunch, it catered well for pupils, many of them VYPs, who would not normally have considered progressing to post-16 education. This is an extremely important point when looking at strategies to help VYPs succeed; by providing a good range of subjects and assessment methods up to age 16, their chances of wanting to stay on post-16 are greatly increased – another theme that we will explore in more detail shortly.

Chapter 5 – Developing the curriculum through the Academy programme.

Abstract:

This chapter celebrates the curriculum freedoms initially allowed through the 'Academies' programme, and is illustrated through several personal experiences as I took up the leadership of Archbishop Sentamu Academy. The end of the chapter introduces the reader to Michael Gove's 'English Baccalaureate' or EBac, which I discuss with reference to the concept of 'Baccalaureates' in general. I also give a brief account of the work of the American educationalist E.D. Hirsch, upon whose theories Gove is believed to have based the EBac. Finally, I explain the difference between the concepts of 'Equality of Opportunity' and 'Equity'. I argue that Gove's EBac appears to have been driven by the former , but that in choosing this approach, he actually reduced levels of equity in schools, to the detriment of our VYPs.

'Welcome to the Jungle'

Guns N' Roses, 1987

Before launching into an analysis of the curriculum opportunities offered by the government's academy programme and their impact on our VYPs, it is probably a good idea to 'draw breath', and sum up the opportunities for curriculum diversity that schools had enjoyed from around 1990. Prior to that time, (although it is true that GNVQs were introduced in 1987), the main qualification open to pupils at age 16 was an exam-based GCSE. By the early 2000s however, we have now seen how a number of so-called 'alternative qualifications were being offered in schools, examples being our old friend Mode 3 languages GCSE offered by SEG, the YALA Arts Award, GNVQs in a number of subjects, and ASDAN awards accrediting a range of skills. This range of alternatives was however to expand further. For example, the Institute of Financial Studies offered a half-GCSE equivalent in basic financial skills, the IMI (Institute of Motor Industries) offered course in car mechanics, and an innovative company called TLM (The Learning Machine) offered an extremely useful course in the practical use of ICT applications. Alongside all of these, Functional Skills in Literacy and Numeracy were also offered as alternatives to GCSE English and Maths. Importantly, all of the qualifications mentioned here carried 'GCSE equivalency' at either foundation level (GCSE grades D to G), or higher level (GCSE grades A* to C), which was vital to schools in terms of the performance tables against which their effectiveness was, and still is, judged.

No account of the opportunities for curriculum innovation would be complete however without discussing the key role that BTecs played in this area. Business and Technology Education Council diplomas (to give them their full name) were introduced in 1993 and ran alongside the GNVQs we looked at earlier. Like GNVQs, they gave pupils the option to study more vocationally based subjects, such as Business Studies, Health and Social Care and Leisure and Tourism. As with GNVQs, they were available at three levels – foundation, intermediate and advanced, and carried GCSE (or in the case of the higher levels, 'A' level) equivalence. For schools however, the 'game-changer' was BTec Level 2 Science.

Previously, it had indeed been possible for schools to offer a GNVQ in Science. However, uptake had been low, possibly at the time due its novelty and concerns about perceptions of its value as a viable GCSE alternative (Learning, 1999). BTEC Level 2 Science qualifications on the other hand rapidly gained more popularity in schools. There are a number of possible reasons for this, including a perception that they had a more hands-on, practical approach than the equivalent GNVQ Science course (Independent, 1997). Another possible reason is that whereas one third of the GNVQ programme was assessed through a terminal exam, BTecs (until 2016) were fully assessed through a portfolio of coursework. Whatever the explanation however, this meant that for the first time, a significant 'core' subject could be taken without pupils having to sit terminal exams. We noted earlier (based by this point on around 20 years of my own experience), that VYPs preferred this type of assessment to terminal exams. It was not just my experience however – by the mid 2000s, BTecs were being offered by many schools, particularly those serving deprived areas.

Importantly, these vocational qualifications were becoming an increasing feature of Sixth-form provision, thereby providing a clear 'pathway of progression' for those pupils who previously would never have considered staying on to higher education. It is perhaps no surprise that a report entitled **'Vocation, Vocation, Vocation'** produced by the Social Market Foundation in January 2018 discovered that 26% of university applicants entered Higher Education with at least one BTec qualification (Gicheva, 2018). This phenomenon was found to be particularly strong in specific regions, including the West Midlands, the North East, the North West and Yorkshire and the Humber – in other words, some of the most socially-deprived regions of the country – from which almost 50% of pupils entered university with a BTec qualification. Whilst BTecs and GNVQs ran alongside each other for a number of years, the last GNVQs were awarded in 2007, meaning that the main vocational qualification delivered in schools from around 2008 onwards was the BTec. Taken together, the cornucopia of qualification diversity available by the early 2000s was to be key in the development of the academy programme, to which we shall now turn.

The academies programme was launched in the early 2000s by the Labour government under Education Minister David Miliband. If the Specialist College programme was seen as a cost-effective way of boosting school improvement and accountability measures, academies were seen as a solution to the problem of very poor outcomes for pupils in schools serving the most-deprived communities. As we saw in chapter 2, under the programme, sponsors were given to the opportunity to run struggling schools in return for an investment of £1million (although this figure was to reduce and ultimately disappear completely over time). As part of the deal, academies were given a brand-new building under the 'Building Schools for the Future (BSF) programme and were also expected to launch a sixth form, as we mentioned in the last chapter. The programme was designed to bring both inspiration and aspiration to young people in some of our most deprived communities, in an effort to improve educational outcomes. It was not without its critics, both from within the education community itself and the wider political spectrum, and I don't intend to enter into that particular debate in this book. Suffice it to say that in 2008, the exciting opportunity arose to lead one of these new academies in Hull.

Archbishop Thurstan School had served the community of East Hull faithfully for many years. Based in a very old building on Hopewell Road, it had a wonderfully kind, committed and caring staff working tirelessly to motivate pupils who, by the 'Income Deprivation Affecting Children Index' (or 'IDACI') scale, lived in the top 1% most-deprived community in the country.' The IDACI scale is the standard measure used to assess the relative poverty of a particular community, or 'local Layer super-output area' (LSOA) to use its official term. England is divided into around 35,000 LSOAs, and these are 'ranked' for their relative deprivation by the IDACI scale, considering factors such as household income, employment and educational levels. In 2008, taken as a whole, the pupils at Archbishop Thurstan came from the 33rd. most deprived LSOA in the country. This meant, of course, that the school had a very high proportion of VYPs. In spite of the school's valiant efforts, exam outcomes were low, and it needed a real 'shot in the arm' to improve.

The Academies programme offered just that. Sponsored jointly by the Church of England and what was then Hull's Primary Care Trust, and armed with the promise of a new building, new sixth form and huge injection of funds, the project offered real hope to a community that had suffered greatly for generations. Reading through the application pack, I was tremendously excited by the opportunity to lead a school in such a poor area of the country and was convinced that it had the right backers in place to support it. In March 2008, I was delighted to be appointed Principal of the now re-christened Archbishop Sentamu Academy.

At the 1996 Labour Party conference, Tony Blair stated that his three top priorities on coming to office were 'education, education, and education'. By 2008, it appeared to me that the task of the academies programme was to solve some of education's most intractable problems through 'innovation, innovation and innovation'. In order to achieve better outcomes for these pupils, leaders at the time had a free hand to put in place whatever curriculum they thought would best serve their needs best. For academy principals, it was a dream come true. Having analysed the specific challenges faced by our communities, we had the freedom, funding and facilities to devise an education that would inspire a generation of young people, many of them VYPs, for whom up until that point, education 'simply hadn't worked'.

And so, we got to work. As was the case at Campion School, our first task as a new team was to ensure that standards of behaviour were high so that teachers were actually able to teach. Being completely new to the area, I wasn't quite sure what to expect from the young people themselves, having read some horror stories about the area, and so during my first week at the academy, I walked around with one of my vice-principals whilst becoming familiar with the academy, just in case I came across a situation where a little support might be needed. Overall, I need not have worried – the majority of pupils were kind, funny, loyal and genuinely supportive of each other, their major failing as a whole being simply not expecting enough out of life. However, as can quite often be the case, there was indeed a minority of highly disruptive pupils who were more than capable of spoiling the whole of the school experience for the majority of pupils. The difference here was that our highly disruptive pupils also had highly disruptive parents – bringing the former into line meant getting the latter on board. A few examples, amusing in hindsight, make this clear - the first one not even putting me in any physical danger.

I had made it clear to the whole school community that from Day One, I expected pupils to stand up whenever I walked into a classroom. This was not out of some desire to be treated like a demi-god, but simply so that I could speak to the class quickly and easily, should the need arise. They were very willing to do this, with the exception of one boy, whom we will call 'Nick' (not his real name). When I asked him why he had refused, he informed me that his father had told him not to stand up for anyone. To resolve this, I told him to go to my office, at which point he stood up and promptly obeyed, much to the amusement of his classmates. Checking out his story subsequently, it turned out to be completely true. A lengthy phone-call with the father ensued, after which grudgingly agreed he would instruct his son to comply.

The second example however was a little more hair-raising. This wasn't an isolated case, and over the first year of my time at the academy, I had to deal with a number of highly aggressive parents. Those who had been in prison for violent assault or murder didn't worry me too much – I'd figured that if any attacked me, they would be straight back 'inside' and that this would act as sufficient incentive for them to keep their fists to themselves. Quite apart from this, as someone who wears glasses and is about as physically intimidating as a three-legged sheep, I also hoped that they just wouldn't think that assaulting me was worth their time and effort. That said, the aggression of a small number did take me by surprise. One such parent, having become incandescent with rage about some perceived injustice perpetrated on his son, threatened to 'throw me through the effing jeffing window' if I didn't effing jeffing do whatever it was he wanted (to this day I still can't remember what it was), and then went on to smash his fist into the bookcase about 2 centimetres from my left ear. 'My goodness', I thought, 'he'll be breaking his effing jeffing fist soon if he isn't careful…' Fortunately, he eventually ran out of steam, and I lived to fight another day.

The most amusing incident of this nature however took place after I had sent a boy home for having had an eyebrow piercing, which were not allowed. Unbeknown to me, he immediately phoned his father to tell him about this (using his mobile phone which we had also banned, along with the piercings). As a result of this, about 20 minutes after excluding the boy, I heard someone shouting up the stairs. I walked into the corridor to see what was going on, and saw a very large, very angry and very noisy parent running towards me at full tilt. Fortunately for me, in what turned out to be a final act of defiance, the boy in question had decided not to go home after all and on hearing his father storming up the stairs to point out to me the flaws of his son's carefully considered sanction, broke cover from the corner in which he had been lurking for the previous 10 minutes and threw himself in front of his father shouting 'Don't hit Mr. Chubb, Don't hit Mr. Chubb'. This selfless act of heroism was impressive and doubtless, saved me a beating. All of that said, it wasn't long before our newly introduced behaviour policies ushered in an atmosphere of calm. I realised just how far we had come when one of our rugby teams lost a match at home to a rival team - the pupils themselves behaved impeccably, but a small number of our parents started a brawl with parents of the opposing team.

Having established calm, we were able to develop the curriculum that we believed would achieve the aims of the academy programme, bringing aspiration, hope and success to a community that had known little of any of this for generations. This was without doubt helped by the generously funded 'Building Schools for the Future' scheme, introduced by Prime Minister Tony Blair in 2004. The scheme set out to rebuild much of the country's secondary estate through a programme which was designed to bring inspiration to a new generation of pupils through iconic design and, by state education standards, fairly lavish specifications. In total, Hull's share of the programme was £450 million – our new building alone was to cost £35 million with a further £1 million set aside for a state of the art computer network to assist us with our curriculum plans.

Thus, in addition to getting to grips with a whole new community of pupils, parents and staff, 2008 also saw us become immediately involved in designing our new building, due for opening in September 2011 complete with new Sixth Form. Fuelled by the generous level of funding, and the conviction that we should have facilities that would give our pupils the best possible chance to succeed no matter where their interests lay, we designed a building with a fully-working theatre, comprehensively-equipped Motor Vehicle Technology workshops, suites of Apple Mac computers and a professionally fitted-out gym – in addition to the usual range of classrooms, laboratories, workshops and playing fields.

Although our Sixth Form was not due to start before going into the new building, having the freedom to innovate enabled us to make an earlier start. Within a year of my taking up post, it became crystal clear that a significant number of our most at-risk young women were going to leave the academy at 16 with no prospect of any further education. To resolve this, we found a former rent-office nearby (complete with bullet-proof glass!), purchased it, and by September 2009 had turned it into a small Sixth Form block, offering Post-16 Health and Social Care to a group of 17 young women, most of whom completed the course. Our partnership with Hull's Primary Care Trust (PCT), one of the original sponsors of our academy, even enabled us to procure an unlikely teaching aid in the form of 'Stan'. Stan was an (almost) living, breathing cyborg, who was subject (or perhaps, rather, subjected) to the care of these students. Thanks to the technology inside him, it was possible to take his blood pressure, his pulse, give him food and drink, inject him and, I believe, even carry out some basic operations on him – and then see the results of these various clinical interventions on his health. Our partnership with the PCT also gave our sixth-formers access to very useful work placements and overall, our first Level 3 course (A-level equivalent) in Health and Social Care was a great success. Buoyed by this, the following year we introduced Business Studies for a further 16 young men and women, using academy funds to buy them all suits in the process. Although seeing them walk along the local Preston Road was a little like a scene from Tarantino's 'Reservoir Dogs', this course too was a great success, with both these courses forming the backbone of our nascent Sixth Form in our new building.

Having spent 2 years designing the building however, we almost didn't get it. In 2010, the newly elected Coalition government ushered in an era of austerity, and one of the first acts of a fresh-faced Michael Gove in his role as Education Secretary was to axe the whole BSF programme. Fortunately for us, Hull's scheme just made it – I believe that the funds had been placed in the necessary bank accounts just 4 weeks before his announcement. Many places were not so fortunate however, and the outcry against this particular policy reversal was the first of many that would become a feature of his tenure in the role.

With our Sixth Form already underway and the design of our new building complete, we were riding a wave of enthusiasm. This was heightened in early 2011 when we were judged 'Good' in all areas by Ofsted. In September 2011 we moved into our new building. It was vast, and we had to get to know it quickly, so on the first training day, our Senior Vice-Principal had the brilliant idea of organising a game of staff hide and seek. Over the space of about 2 hours, we found every area where pupils might be able to hide, which stood us in good stead for their arrival the following day.

Needless to say, our pupils were absolutely wowed by their new school, whose overall shape could perhaps best be described as a post-modern cathedral. The BSF programme was criticised (in many ways quite fairly) for its expense, but there was no denying the impact it had on our pupils, who were all-too used to feeling undervalued at every turn of their lives. In our old building, it is true that on account of our long-standing links with a school in Beijing, we had managed to introduce Mandarin Chinese - a subject which has proven both popular and successful with many of our students to this day.   The new facilities however enabled us to run an extremely diverse curriculum, with pupils able to find pathways they really enjoyed, whether in the field of Sport, Art, Music, Performing Arts, Mandarin Chinese, a more traditional set of subjects, or even Motor-Vehicle Engineering.

As a self-confessed 'petrol-head', this last option was particularly dear to my heart. It proved immensely popular with many of our pupils too, and gave one of them the fantastic opportunity to put my life in serious danger. The MVE teacher at the time thought it would be a good idea if the pupils were able to work on real cars that people drove, as well as the series of cheap insurance write-offs that we had already purchased for our pupils to repair.   Naturally, I thought I should volunteer for this, and so I allowed one of the worst-behaved and truculent lads in the academy to service the brakes of my then-ageing Nissan X-Trail – admittedly under the supervision of the teacher.   Impressively, the lad resisted the temptation to cut the brake hoses, and carried out an excellent repair through his efforts. Showing him trust and giving him the opportunity to excel in an area of interest to him was typical of an approach that, during a period of several years, meant we had extremely low levels of fixed-term exclusions and almost no permanent exclusions whatsoever.

It was no surprise then that the vast majority of our young people excelled in this environment. Our new curriculum contained a significant number of BTEC and other 'alternative' qualifications as options, meaning that our pupils could all find a pathway that suited them, bringing success to both them and the academy. For some, this involved a traditional diet of GCSEs including a triple science qualification, whilst for others, it led to a mix of GCSEs and more practical or vocational GCSE-equivalent courses. For those pupils who performed far more poorly in exams, there was even the option for all of their work to be portfolio-assessed, by replacing GCSE English and Maths with 'Functional Literacy and Numeracy'. Over the next few years, we coupled this highly diverse curriculum with a system of 'multiple early entry' for English and Maths exams, which gave our pupils both the practice and the confidence to tackle real GCSEs in real exam conditions early on in their school careers.

The years between 2011 and 2016 were arguably the highlight of our academy's success. Our highly diversified curriculum and system of 'multiple entry' for English and Maths enabled us to personalise the learning of our pupils far more than was ever the case previously. Exam outcomes went from strength to strength, and importantly, the proportion of our pupils who went on to further education at age 16 also increased. In the early days, our own Sixth Form appealed particularly to those pupils who lacked the confidence to attend one of the city's much larger establishments. Typically, these were pupils who would otherwise have left school at 16, many of them being our VYPs who are the focus of this book. Thus, our own Sixth Form played a key role in delivering a government objective of keeping more young people in education until age 18. All of this was well-reflected in our Ofsted inspection of February 2014, in which we were judged to be at least 'Good' on all accounts, but 'Outstanding' for both 'Pupil Behaviour' and 'Leadership and Management'. Little did we realise at the time however that the ice of accountability upon which we were skating at the time was so thin, and about to crack wide open.

The initial warning shot across the bows of our highly diverse , personalised and successful curriculum was fired from the cannon of one of Gove's first curriculum initiatives, the so-called 'English Baccalaureate'. The concept of a baccalaureate is that by requiring pupils to pass a particular combination of subjects, the 'wrapper' of the baccalaureate itself confers additional value to the pupil. Gove's baccalaureate attempted to confer this additional value to a combination of so-called 'academic' subjects, all examined through terminal GCSE exams.   Thus, under his initiative, those students who achieved at least a C-grade pass in English, Maths, Double or Triple Science, History of Geography and a modern foreign language would be granted the so-called 'E-bac'.   Even the most casual analysis of this throws up a number of significant objections, and the E-bac remains to this day, in my view, one of the worst thought-out, indeed stupid, pieces of curriculum legislation ever introduced. As such, it's worth spending some time unpicking its most obvious weaknesses.

Most obviously, by including only GCSEs in its 'wrapper', it is making the assumption that the ability to demonstrate knowledge and skills through passing exams is inherently of more value than other methods, such as on-going coursework. Is this really the case? Whilst it is certainly true that for some people the ability to pass exams is important in later life (for example those who follow a profession such as medicine, law or accountancy), for the vast majority of people, exams end either at age 18, or 21 if they attend university. Secondly, by including only a limited range of subjects, the E-bac by definition devalued all other subjects that weren't included. By contrast, the French baccalauréat (taken by pupils at age 18) falls into three main categories or 'filières'. Firstly, there is the General Baccalauréat (Baccalauréat Général), designed for students who wish to pursue higher education. This is perhaps the one closest to Gove's 'E-bac', and is focused on academic subjects like languages, humanities, sciences, and social sciences. In addition to this however, there are also the Technological Baccalauréat (Baccalauréat Technologique) and the Vocational Baccalauréat (Baccalauréat Professionnel). These two paths respectively are more specialized for pupils who want to work or continue short technical studies in fields such as management, health or engineering in the case of the former, or who may wish to pursue further study in a related vocational field in the case of the latter. It can be seen therefore that the French system attributes value to a wide range of pupil interests and aptitudes - each type of baccalauréat is designed to cater to different educational and career paths, by offering a range of options for students based on their interests and career goals. In contrast, by offering only one version of baccalaureat – the E-bac – Gove devalued at a stroke the study of all those subjects not included in his particular baccalaureat 'wrapper'.

More invidiously, by setting up the E-bac as some sort of notional 'gold-standard' (a notion which many, including me, strongly refute), Gove was setting up precisely the sort of 'perverse incentive' against which, as we shall see, he railed in other areas of practice. Crudely, the introduction of the E-bac gave schools a vested interest in promoting a qualification to which many were not suited, none more so than our VYPs. As we shall see in our chapters on assessment policy, 'what gets measured gets done', and the introduction of the E-bac was the first step in Gove ensuring that 'what got done' was in line with his particular philosophy of education. So, what was this?

Gove appears to have been heavily influenced by the writer E.D. Hirsch, an American educator and education theorist (Abrams, 2012), (Jonathan Simons, 2015). Hirsch advocates for a curriculum that emphasizes the learning of key facts, which aligned with Gove's vision of arming children with a body of essential knowledge to aid their learning. According to Hirsch, this body of knowledge, summed up as 'cultural literacy', was essential for citizens to be able to function effectively in their country. Additionally, Hirsch's work highlighted the disparities in cultural knowledge among students from different backgrounds, which resonated with Gove's aim to provide equal educational opportunities for all students. Finally, Gove saw the structured approach to education proposed by Hirsch, whereby children learn facts in an organised manner, as a way to renew teaching as a vocation and benefit children from all social groups.

Whilst there is evidence to suggest that Hirsch's theories were effective in helping primary school children make progress in areas of New York (Green, 2013), basing the E-bac on these principles was, to my mind, a huge mistake and, at the very best, a flawed application of Hirsch's principles, if you agreed with them in the first place. Much could be written on this. For the sake of our narrative however, I will limit myself to the following three points: Firstly, there is the general point that simply 'copying and pasting' any educational initiative from one country to another is liable to be problematic as doing so fails to take account of differences in culture and practice, especially if this is implemented without consultation from those charged with delivering the reforms (as was the case here). Secondly, if the aim of a policy is (laudably) to promote equity, then working out 'what equity looks like' is important before putting in place policies that promote the equality of opportunity which will lead to the desired greater levels of equity. At worst, Gove's reforms could indicate that the distinction between the two concepts was never thought through, or perhaps even realised in the first place. At best however, the notion of equality of opportunity that drove the introduction of the E-bac was based on a very narrow definition of equity, one in which pupils from a far wider range of backgrounds than had previously been the case were given a better chance of accessing a (by Gove's definition) 'top' or 'Russell Group' university.

But is educational equity really defined solely by a person's ability to access a so-called 'top' university? I would argue that this is emphatically not the case, and that a better definition of equity would be to ensure that young people of all backgrounds had equality of opportunity to access a career pathway of their choice. As we will see in our chapters on assessment, by imposing the E-bac on schools and with it, a perverse incentive for schools to adopt it, Gove thereby set in motion changes in schools that actually *reduced* equity for all, as schools were not as easily able to offer curricula that were as personalised as desirable to achieve this. Once again, this was especially the case for our VYPs. From these two points, it could be fairly argued that to achieve improved levels of equity, Gove and indeed his successors would have been far better placed speaking with, and taking advice from, experienced leaders in this country who understood the barriers faced by young people, rather than, or at the very least in addition to, an American academic, no matter how distinguished. I will argue in subsequent chapters that this tendency for 'top-down control' rather than 'bottom-up consultation' has been both a major feature and problem of the last 10 years, and that addressing this concern is key if we are to restore the fortunes of our VYPs.

By the time the E-bac had been introduced however, our growing success as an academy, including encouraging pupils into both our Sixth Form and from there to university, gave us the confidence that we had hit upon a formula which was, demonstrably, improving the life-chances of our young people without any help from Mr. Gove. Armed with this confidence, we avoided any attempt to implement the E-bac, and instead focussed on developing and refining our curriculum in the ways which we could see were proving effective.

Chapter 6 – Developing our own 'Baccalaureate'.

Abstract:

In response to Gove's (in my view) highly flawed 'English Baccalaureate', or 'EBac' as it has become known, this chapter outlines how we developed and attempted to launch our own Modern Baccalaureate ('Modbac'). It argues that young people should be assessed on a far broader range of skills and competencies than the purely 'academic' set of exams of which Gove was a proponent, and sets out a framework for achieving this. Acknowledging that the award never achieved any widespread take-up, the chapter goes on to show how we nonetheless used the Modbac framework and the success of our 2014 inspection to bid for, design and open one of the largest Alternative Provision academies in the country – ASPIRE Hull.

'Get bac'

(misquoting the Beatles, 1970)

Rather than simply reject Gove's (to our mind) philosophically flawed E-Bac however, we thought that we could usefully design a different baccalaureat based on our own observations and experience in promoting equity for all our students. With this in mind, a team of use set about designing what became 'The Modern Baccalaureate', or 'Modbac' for short. The framework, which at the time was endorsed by (amongst others) Sir Mike Tomlinson, Sir Tim Brighouse, Mick Waters, Professor Guy Claxton, The RSA and the Curriculum Foundation, aimed to enable students to be ready for further study, the world of work and active citizenship – in short, to be 'equipped for life'. A full description of the award can be found in Appendix One, but for the sake of our narrative, the following is a brief summary.

Our 'Modern Baccalaureate' had three parts:

- A 'core' of between 5 and 8 qualifications including English and Maths GCSE, and at least one science award;

- An 'honours' section comprising seven other areas of experience as follows:

   1. Internationalism / Language study;

   2. An extended project;

   3. A community service award;

   4. A personal challenge;

   5. An IT award;

   6. A Personal Finance and / or Enterprise award; and

   7. Preparation for, participation in and reflection on, a period of Work Experience.

- A selection of 'skills development' awards, that included areas such as Personal Learning and Thinking Skills (PLTS), Adult Literacy and Numeracy skills, and wider key skills such as Team Building and Leadership.

In contrast to Gove's E-Bac, our Modern Baccalaureate allowed students to follow different pathways, according to their interests and abilities, which were 'validated' by on overarching award (see below). That is not to say that all students achieved the same level or study the same subjects, but rather that they worked within one overall framework. The aim was to eliminate the implied hierarchy of value attributed to 'academic', 'technical' and 'vocational' education, and through this, to enable all pupils to follow a pathway which they could see as coherent.

A common criticism of allowing pupils to study for qualifications that do not lead to 'traditional' exam-based GCSE assessment is that in doing so, we are 'selling our pupils short', 'dumbing down' their curriculum' and / or 'lacking in aspiration. This is both a lazy trope and a dangerous trap. A lazy trope, because it attributes greater value to one particular set of skills (in this case, amongst others, the ability to memorise large quantities of facts and reproduce them under exam conditions), over another set (for example, the ability over time to demonstrate the skills needed to strip down and rebuild an engine or to undertake a lengthy project such as designing and launching a website). A dangerous trap, because imposing on school curricula this traditional hierarchy of qualifications espoused at least implicitly by Gove and others has the effect of demotivating large swathes of pupils, and in particular, our VYPs.

'Modbac' was designed to counter precisely this problem. The award was able to be gained at Level Two, Level One and Entry Level, representing GCSE grades A*-C, D-G and pre-GCSE respectively. The individual components of the award could be gained at any stage in a pupil's career, the aim being to give pupils early success and through this, to encourage them to aim for higher levels as they progressed through the academy. As such, the award was carefully designed to encourage students to aim as high as possible in all their subjects, across the entire ability spectrum. For example, at Intermediate level (Level 2), whilst 'C' grades gave students access to 'pass' and 'merit' awards, B, A and A* grades were needed to get to 'Distinction' / 'Distinction*'. Our framework therefore aimed both to encourage early success and reward students' higher aspiration. A good example of this was how pupils who took a GCSE exam 'early', for example Maths during Year 10, could 'bank' that grade but aim for a higher grade at the end of their Year 11 studies.

The award had other significant advantages. The 'core' section acknowledged the value of qualifications which had a smaller (for example half) 'GCSE equivalency', such as Extended Projects, Wider Key Skills, and Short Course GCSEs, whereas the 'honours' section was designed to accredit development in a wider set of skills which would prepare pupils effectively for further study (for example through the 'extended project' and 'IT' elements), the world of work (through a high quality work-placement), and 'life in general' (for example, through the personal finance award and the requirement to undertake a 'personal challenge'). Additionally, the 'core' and 'honours' elements were independent of each other. Thus, a pupil who had struggled with more formal qualifications could still demonstrate excellent levels in skill in the other areas of the programme. An example of the final certificate, which included a QR code so that the externally awarded qualifications were independently verifiable, can be seen in fig. 1 below.

With hindsight, my efforts to have this recognised at a national level were hopelessly naïve. A few academies bought into the idea, but the award could not gain traction. Our baccalaureate was not the only one being developed at the time, but attempts to join forces with these other frameworks failed. It was scant consolation that none of these alternative baccalaureates actually succeeded in shifting the needle of government curriculum policy. And yet, in spite of the disappointment that our framework wasn't recognised as an alternative to the E-bac, it was nonetheless to make a huge contribution to our next development as an academy, as we will now see.

Fig:1 – sample Modern Baccalaureate certificate

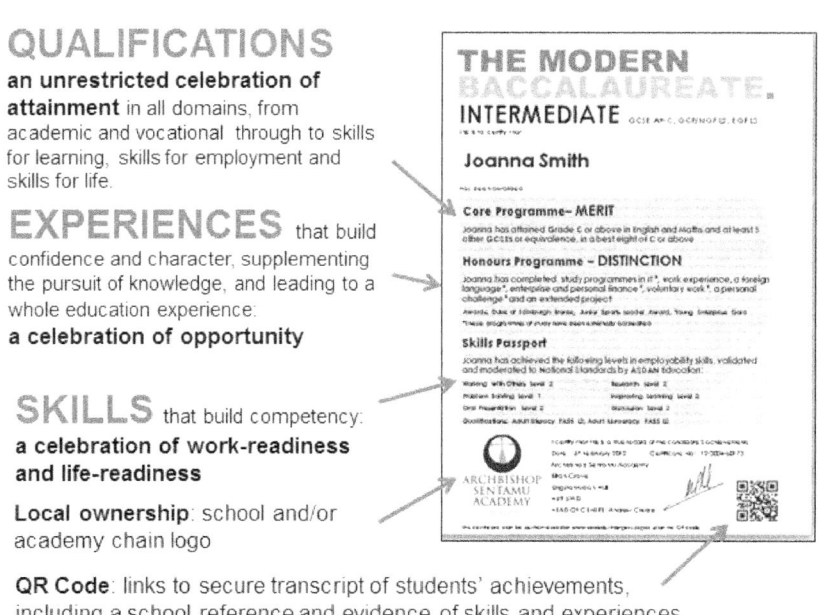

QUALIFICATIONS
an unrestricted celebration of attainment in all domains, from academic and vocational through to skills for learning, skills for employment and skills for life.

EXPERIENCES that build confidence and character, supplementing the pursuit of knowledge, and leading to a whole education experience:
a celebration of opportunity

SKILLS that build competency:
a celebration of work-readiness and life-readiness

Local ownership: school and/or academy chain logo

QR Code: links to secure transcript of students' achievements, including a school reference and evidence of skills and experiences

'We are Fa-mily…'

Sister Sledge, 1979

Four years in to our development as an academy, we were riding high. We had put a new and exciting curriculum in place, launched a successful Sixth Form and moved into a brand new building. Exam results were rising year on year, behaviour was vastly improved, and exclusions were extremely low - all the more so considering the levels of economic deprivation which can so often lead to high levels of pupil disengagement. These successes had all been recognised by Ofsted in our 2011 inspection, who noted the following:

'Archbishop Sentamu Academy provides a good quality of education. Within its first two years, it has developed some outstanding features and established a strong ethos reflecting its Christian values. Outcomes are mainly good, and students' confidence in their safety is exceptionally strong. Systems for care, support and guidance are highly effective and the academy works very well with its partners to promote the progress and welfare of its students. As a result, achievement and enjoyment have rapidly improved for every group of students. The academy promotes equal opportunity outstandingly well. Its motto, 'Aspire, Serve, Achieve', is increasingly meaningful to a great many students, who do their best to help their academy.'(ibid)

We were very pleased with this overall summary, but as we come to the end of this section of the book on curriculum, the following comments from the report are noteworthy:

'By adapting the curriculum to students' needs and interests, and offering effective extra help, they have ensured better engagement and rising aspirations. Students' attainment by the end of Year 11 has risen more rapidly than the national rate and shows no signs of slowing down. The number of students not progressing to further education, employment or training (NEET) has dramatically reduced. Time lost from learning due to persistent absence or exclusions has dramatically reduced. The new sixth form meets the needs of its small first cohorts and is growing well. The specialism has a positive influence on students' knowledge about health and enterprise.

Promising work is being done to improve literacy, numeracy and other skills across the curriculum.' (ibid)

In short, it appeared that we were developing a winning formula. At the most basic level, a school's ethos and success are underpinned by three key factors – strong behaviour and pastoral systems, an engaging curriculum and excellent teaching. These three factors are like a three-legged stool – the weaker any one of the legs becomes, the increasingly wobbly is the stool. The inspection of 2011 noted that teaching was good, although there were still areas in which improvement was needed. However, the strength of our both our pastoral care and curriculum at the time provided the atmosphere in which we could continue to provide this improvement. A key aspect of our first three years as an academy was the piloting of small 'Alternative Provision' centres off-site. The curricula were designed to engage and retain small numbers of pupils who were either at high risk of exclusion owing to their behaviour, or who simply did not want to attend school for a variety of reasons. In either case, they were highly vulnerable. Although we were greatly encouraged by the success of our first three years of operation, including by the results of our pilot projects to cater for our most vulnerable pupils, we knew that we were facing a real challenge just around the corner.

From the outset, it had been agreed that our academy would take a large number of young people from a nearby school that was closing, and which had an awful reputation for behaviour. All in all, we were required to take 150 of their pupils in Years 7-9 over a relatively short period of time. Whilst we were by that time extremely skilled as an academy in managing challenging behaviour, an influx of 150 badly behaved young people all at once was always going to be an immense challenge. Short-term plans to integrate them from September 2012 were put in place during that year, but we could see that we could have a real need for a significant amount of additional 'alternative provision' of our own fairly soon thereafter.

At this point, it's worth reflecting on the impact of long-term educational exclusion on our VYPs, and specifically, the concept of becoming a 'NEET' at age 16. 'NEETs' are young people 'not in education, employment or training', and in Hull, the figures were frighteningly high, as the following illustrates:

- At the end of September 2012, 9.7% of young people aged 16-18 were NEET (732 young people), in addition to 666 young people (9.6%) for the same period in the previous year;

- At the end of July Hull had twice the national average of NEET young people in this age group;

- There were similar numbers of males and females in the NEET group;

- Even for those lucky enough to gain a place at an existing Pupil Referral Unit (PRU), outcomes were low; fewer than 2.5% of students leaving a PRU at KS4 achieved 5+ A* to C including English and Maths (the key 'benchmark' at the time), and in 2012, not one of the 25 students in the KS4 PRU achieved a single;

- Only 40% of the NEET group obtained GCSEs grade A-C or above at the end of September.

- 46% of 2012 leavers were at risk of not participating in learning after compulsory education;

- 100% of young people on the Local Authority run 'Smart Moves' Alternative Provision were currently NEET (120 young people); and

- 20% of the NEET group were not available to the labour market for reasons of pregnancy, illness, and teenage parents.

Approximately 80% of these pupils were facing the following additional challenges:

- 204 (28%) were caring for their own child;
- 177 (24%) had learning difficulties;
- 103 (14%) were pregnant; 15 (2%) Looked After / In care;
- 48 (6.5%) were being supervised by YOT (Youth Offending Teams);
- 35 (5%) were care leavers; and
- 8 (1%) were themselves carers.

All in all, Hull demonstrably had a 'hard core' of young people locally who were unable to integrate mainstream education, who made poor life choices, and who, even if they possessed a number of level 2 GCSE or equivalent qualifications, lacked the skills to enter employment, training or further study. This was especially the case for those leaving the PRUs (the only Alternative Provision available at the time), all of whom, from that year's statistics, failed to achieve a positive destination. All of these VYPs were at great risk of becoming long-term NEET, and consequently faced a lifetime of exclusion, unemployment, crime and dependency, thereby adding to the existing levels of high unemployment already present in the area, and thus reinforcing the vicious cycle of deprivation.

This situation was bad enough, but the closure of the local school, from which we were going to accept 150 of their pupils, threatened to make the situation even worse for two reasons. First, exclusion rates from local mainstream schools (although not our own, where exclusions rates were very low) were rising to unprecedented levels, and as we have already noted, these same schools were becoming increasingly unwilling to give excluded young people from other schools a chance to re-integrate into mainstream education via the Fair Access Panel. This was compounded by the fact that both of the city's 'Pupil Referral Units' (PRUs) were full, meaning that there was no capacity in Hull for students to be given a short-term placement with a view to their turning around their behaviour. With the best will in the world, we fully expected to need more of these places with our large influx of potentially highly disruptive pupils. Second, we knew that within 12 months, the situation was going to be exacerbated further with the closure of the Local Authority -run 'Smart Moves' programme, which catered for a further 200 disenchanted VYPs aged 14-16 across the city.

Looking ahead, we could see that we were facing a potential crisis of provision for our VYPs. Fortunately for us, Education Secretary Michael Gove had by that time introduced his 'Free Schools' programme. Under this programme, organisations including (but not limited to) existing schools and academies were allowed to bid for funds to open new schools in response to local need. So, armed with our analysis of the challenges we knew we would be facing ourselves and a determination to improve the life chances of this group of VYPs, we decided to bid for funds to open our own 'Alternative Provision' academy to lever in far greater levels of resources, both for own pupils at high risk of exclusion, and also for those from other schools in Hull.

The project to open the 150-place ASPIRE academy was by all accounts both a highly ambitious project and a huge piece of work. Ambitious, because typically an AP academy would aim to house around 50 young people - our plans to accommodate three times this were described by most people, euphemistically, as 'brave', by which they really meant 'completely bonkers'. A huge piece of work, because running to 147 pages and over 50,000 words, the bid had to lay out in great detail our ethos, vision, curriculum, financial and governance plans, as well as how we would work with the Local Authority and other academies over admissions. Our load was lightened in one key area however, specifically our own Modern Baccalaureate. As stated above, this had failed to 'take off' at any level (let alone nationally); indeed with hindsight, I was hopelessly naïve to expect that it every would or could have done. We did judge however that it could provide a good curriculum framework for our new AP academy, and our bid was able to take advantage of all of that work. Fortunately for us, the DfE agreed and a year after submitting our Free School bid with 'Modbac' at its heart , ASA gave birth to its very first child – ASPIRE academy Hull.

ASPIRE was a great success right from the start. There is not the space here to explain how the brilliant Principal and his team managed to educate safely and successfully, year after year, over 150 of the UK's most challenging teenagers. Suffice it to say that the use of a whole suite of alternative qualifications was central to this success; if any proof were needed, ASPIRE demonstrated a central contention of this book, namely that a curriculum based around the needs of individual young people is far more likely to motivate them and bring about success, compared to one centrally imposed by government ideological diktat. This of course begs the question – if such an approach is allowed for pupils in Alternative Provision, why can't the same be true for pupils in 'mainstream' education? This is a theme to which we will return later on in the book.

Chapter 7 – Diving into the detail of ASA's curriculum.
Abstract

This chapter starts by turning back the clock to an earlier part of my career when I was both a young Head of Languages and also 'Head of House'. It looks at how I became convinced of the power of the Arts to secure pupils' buy-in for school, showing me the value early on in my career of the need in general for a highly diverse curriculum. Building on these experiences and the general curriculum 'Modbac' framework outlined in the previous chapter, I go on to describe here in more detail how providing courses including Arts awards, Motor Vehicle Technology, a Rugby Scholarship Programme and Mandarin Chinese enabled ASA to be established as a thriving, highly popular academy, even though it was attended by a very high proportion of pupils who would be considered VYPs.

'Waking up the neighbours.'

Bryan Adams, 1991

'Are you plugged in Phil?'

Check

'Are you turned up?'

Check

'..to 11?'

Check

'Your wig's slipped'.

A sweaty hand wiped away the remaining wisps…

'We're in A – that's A, not G – remember!'

We stood determined, brothers in musical arms, ready to rock. The crowd hushed, our drummer, a Y11 pupil, looked on with a mixture of nervousness and pity –

'Would this couple of ridiculous metal-head wannabees ruin his cred for ever?'

'Why on earth had he agreed, for the third year running, to be part of the House Rock Band?'

Plectra held high, our arms swung down on our respective axes, perfectly synchronised as the opening bars of 'Bat out of Hell' rang in the ears of the whole school, gathered together in the hall for the highlight of the year…

A month earlier, we had unfortunately received a real complaint. Practising in the 'temporary' science huts, which had already been there for at least 30 years, we'd made so much noise that a neighbour had rung up the headteacher to complain about the racket being made by his pupils. We apologised to the Headteacher profusely, but this was rock'n'roll! We had arrived! We were truly legends in our own lunchtime.

Phil and I had absolutely no talent, but were determined to make up for that pitiful fact with our twin weapons of volume and distortion as we practised, yet again, for the annual House Music competition, or, more specifically, the staff / student band. Arden school had the most revered, if not feared, Head of Music, who encouraged countless pupils to sing and play in a dizzying array of choirs, bands and orchestras. The House Music competition was the annual showcasing of this prodigious talent – the day was filled with stunning solos, dramatic duets, terrific trios – you get the picture. Each of the school's four houses put forward contestants for all the various categories, with points awarded to the winners. The final acts were the bands – eagerly anticipated by all, to see which teachers would make the biggest fools of themselves. I think that one year we actually came second, with our fine rendition of Guns'n'Roses version of 'Knocking on Heaven's door' (chosen because Slash's solo is so slow that even our arthritic fingers were able to cope with it – just about). But this year we were going for broke, 'No sleep till Solihull', with our amps turned up to 11. Phil had a new Les Paul for the occasion, whilst I had to make do with my Strat copy. Phil also had a bigger amp – 100w to my puny 80W version – but no matter – we were going to be awesome.

...*'And like a bat out of hell, she'll be gone when the morning comes..'*

is what should have been heard. Unfortunately, as happened to someone every year, the battery in the remote mike had died, meaning that our bat had well and truly flown away, along with any chances of our achieving rock glory, as the singer's tired vocal chords gave up the ghost.

'Get to the other mike!' – I pointed in desperation as, with only Phil hammering away at his power chords, the volume dropped temporarily to around 130 decibels. We were fast approaching the song's climax and with only one guitar, all would be lost..

'No, not that one – that's broken too – THAT one!'

Finally, the singer found a mike that worked, coughed, sputtered, and came in at the wrong part of the song. Phil and I frantically tried to turn things around..

'And like a sinner, before, the gates of heaven, I'll come crawling on back to you...'

And sure enough, crawling also straight into last place. The drummer just shrugged his shoulders, the head of music looked, well, ill – at least the pupils were kind-hearted enough to give us a good cheer.

'In fourth place, Eliot House'. The loyal pupils of Eliot House protested that *'we was robbed'*, but there we were, destined for another 12 months to the ignominy of being beaten by Fleming House's utterly unimaginative and totally safe rendition of 'Johnny B Good'. Not that I was bitter.

Teenagers can often be denounced as being lazy, ill-disciplined and / or uncaring. In my experience however, this often extremely unfair, as they are also capable of the most intense levels of work, loyally looking out for the peers and their leaders, keen to give of their best. They just need the right motivation. You might think that this capacity for work only applies those in areas in which they are interested – such as the Arts, or Sport, or anything else about which they may be passionate. Whilst that may indeed be true to a certain extent, I've also known many pupils produce pages of French or Fractions, German or Geometry, as long they also have an outlet for their real interests. They are quite capable of understanding that life isn't just a case of doing what you want - that there are ups and downs and 'boring bits' as well - as long as they can see that people care about their interests and passions as well as their exam results. Arden's house music festival was one great example of this, and working this out fairly early on my career stood me in very good stead for my time in Hull. Whilst providing a strong core curriculum was a key priority, I knew that in order to engage pupils fully, we would need to put in place a strong range of extra-curricular activities both for their own intrinsic value, and to help ensure that our pupils 'bought into' and worked hard in everyday lessons.

Arriving at ASA, I quickly realised that literally hundreds of pupils had a strong interest in one of two areas – the Performing Arts and Rugby League. The former was down to a legacy of excellent, inspirational teaching in drama, and the latter, the fact that one of Hull's two major Rugby clubs was situated within half a mile of our academy. I was keen to build on both of these strengths.

Our pupils' love for Performing Arts was perhaps best embodied by 'Rock Challenge', although this was really a misnomer – 'Dance Challenge' would have been a better name. Organised jointly by the Police and Health services, it gave schools the opportunity to compete with each other through a performance based on a theme of choice. Local winners went on to regional championships, and the standard was extremely high.   Archie's performances in this competition were stunning. Prior to my arrival, the school had managed to win the regional final in 2006, taking the performance on a tour in Australia to celebrate. By 2012 however, despite winning the local heat on several occasions, ultimate success had eluded us for some time.

'Rock Challenge' in many ways defined the spirit of ASA. Although there were auditions for the absolute key parts, a role was found for anyone who wanted to participate, whether as a performer, stagehand, costume designer, choreographer, steward or simply a general helper. In spite of the ferocious inter-school rivalry that characterised the competition, our staff always gave pupils from lower year groups the chance to perform, thereby eschewing the temptation to put forward only the top performers. In spite of, or perhaps because of this policy, we enjoyed great success, year on year. Our drama staff succeeded in finding themes that engaged the pupils, putting together powerful story lines with the most ambitious dance routines. Our art and design staff constructed the most fabulous sets, other staff sewed together the most amazing costumes, and our pupils practised endlessly, long after school and at weekends, to ensure the highest standards of performance. Tremendous friendships were forged during those times, and for many of our pupils, 'Rock Challenge' was their family.

There was, of course, the loss of a day or two of 'normal school' as dress-rehearsals were held in front of various year groups. Nonetheless, we felt that this was a small price to pay for the immense pride and joy that all those participating drew from the event. Every year, we were convinced that we would win, although it was generally a case of 'close, but no cigar'. In 2015 however, we had a particularly strong cast, getting through easily to the regional finals. For some unknown reason, these were held in the middle of the 'A' level exam season. As a consequence, the only way that some of our students were able to compete that year was to sit one of their formal exams in Scunthorpe, the location of the regional heat. This they willingly did, and so at 5pm, the whole cast stood in a circle outside Scunthorpe Leisure Centre, completely silent, preparing themselves for the competition later on.

That evening, their performance was stunning. The competition was stiffer than usual, not least because one of the schools was a local, professional, performing arts college. In spite of that, as the awards began to be announced, it looked like were in for a good night.....

'The winner for best soundtrack goes to...Archie!'

That was a good one to get in the bag. There were several categories of awards, and most schools received an award from at least one of them.

'The winner for best costume design, goes to…Archie!'

Good job! Our head of inclusion had spent months ensuring every button was sewn into place.

'The winner for best choreography goes to…Archie!'

I was delighted – our drama teachers had dedicated weeks of their lives to rigorous rehearsals, night after night.

'And the overall winner is….'

I dared to hope it would be us. As the seconds ticked by, I broke into a cold sweat, heart racing..

'Archie!'

The audience erupted, as rows of our parents leapt to their feet, cheering their 'bains', joined by an incredibly proud staff and Principal – writing this, I can still remember the electric bolt of adrenalin surging through me at that moment.

If the Performing Arts were one of our pupils' main passions, then Rugby League was certainly another, with *'Red and White or Black and White*?' being the key question in a city fiercely divided by two rugby clubs. As someone with zero talent for, and even less interest in the game, or any ball game for that matter, I nonetheless recognised that it lay at the heart of many of our young people's dreams. I don't wish to be unkind to East Hull in saying that it lacks many of the facilities you would hope for in any modern city – it just does. This realisation underpinned much of our early work as an academy – not only were we having to make up for the lack of educational opportunity suffered by the community for years, but also of *any* opportunity which could raise people's sights above the demands of daily existence. Fortunately, the location of 'The Robins' - Hull Kingston Rovers - just half a mile down the road from our new building helped us greatly as we sought to do just this. Given the general size of Hull KR's players – massive – I've never understood the choice of the gentle little robin as their mascot, other than the fact that, as with the team's colours, it's red. In spite of this dainty little bird however, the chance to play for Hull KR was and remains to this day the ambition of many of our pupils. And not just the boys

– over the years, rugby became increasingly popular with many of our girls.

This love of rugby was very clear from my earliest days at the academy, as staff briefings were dominated at least once a week by the all-important 'rugby report'.

'The lads played well', Tony informed us – *'they had real spirit against a team twice their size'.* This was generally the case. One of the many faces of poverty in our area was size, or lack of it, and our pupils got used to playing teams in which their opponents were far bigger than them.

'If anyone sees (insert here the name of Scally X,Y or Z) today, tell him 'well done' for not punching the ref when he made a bad decision' (instead of his usual practice of answering back any teacher with whom he disagreed)

'Also, if you see....'

and so it continued. I used to allow Tony to go on for up to 10 minutes – far too long really - but the reports were really colourful. They often ended with the immortal words:

'We was beat 252 – 16, but the lads played real well', to which I would always reply:

'Close Tony, close – thanks very much and please pass on my congratulations to the team!', after which morale-boosting result we would all go off and face the day.

Although Tony was of indeterminate age – but certainly close to 60 – his enthusiasm for the game never waned. In addition to coaching and inspiring hundreds of our young people over the years, he also used to organise a bi-annual trip to Australia, where rugby league is also highly popular. The challenge of course was that of finances – another area in which East Hull was lacking. Undeterred by this small obstacle however, Tony turned out to be the most incredible fundraiser, pulling together the necessary cash need to pay for an otherwise exorbitantly expensive trip. Helping him in these endeavours was his long list of 'mates', whom he somehow managed to persuade to contribute. I was never quite sure how, and didn't like to ask questions, instead preferring to find a way of helping with my own meagre talents. Putting aside my many failures as a guitarist in the past, I suggested to ASA's Rock Band 'The Excluded' that we played a set during a virtual horse-racing event that Tony ran at one of our fine local pubs. This basically involved people watching a dodgy horse race from the 70s, in which the horses concerned had all been given dodgy names, and punters putting a bet on one of them, not having a clue who might win. To cheer up anyone losing money, 'The Excluded' performed a small set – completely free of charge! – and people seemed to leave happy enough. Events such as these raised the necessary thousands of pounds however, thereby enabling the trip to Oz to go ahead.

Having been around 60 for at least 10 years, Tony's long-suffering wife eventually persuaded him to retire, and he was awarded to everyone's great pride the British Empire Medal, in recognition of his long and successful service to the young people of East Hull. We also named our inclusion hub after him, and the Elvin Centre remains to this day a symbol of the fantastic spirit of courage in overcoming adversity that is so characteristic of our community.

Tony's departure left a gap however, and one that we needed to fill urgently. Fortunately, at that point, I was approached by Hull KR's former Head of Youth, who offered to run a bespoke training programme. 'Embedding the Pathway' enabled budding sports people of all disciplines, but especially rugby, to receive high levels of coaching and game practice, as well as top nutritional advice. Importantly, inclusion in the programme was conditional upon good behaviour around the academy in general - any pupils who displayed a poor attitude in any other aspect of their school life would not be allowed to play in any of the league matches. This engendered a spirit of collective accountability amongst the players - on more than one occasion, a crucial game was played, and subsequently lost, on the basis that a key player had been sanctioned for a misdemeanour. Developing a successful team is a long process however, and over time, this refusal to compromise paid dividends, with each year group enjoying incredible success, both regionally and nationally. Interestingly, and perhaps unsurprisingly, these cohorts of 'rugby scholars' showed the highest levels of attendance, lowest levels of poor behaviour and best levels of progress overall of any particular 'cohort' of pupils in the academy, regardless of year group - an issue to which we will return in our section on assessment. By the time I finally retired in 2020, ASA boasted over 350 pupils on the rugby programme – or around 25% of all students. This included many girls, who could be easily identified at breaktime as they sat in the canteen, tucking into healthy snacks of fruit, nuts and decent sandwiches, and thereby putting to shame supervising staff such as myself as we patrolled with our bacon butties.

Over time, both of these initially extra-curricular programmes became a part of (to at least a certain extent) our formal curriculum. In the case of 'Rock Challenge'(and other shows), our pupils were able to use participation in these as part of both the 'Young Arts Leader' award (which, we will remember, carried full GCSE-equivalence), and also as evidence towards the 'Personal Challenge' section of our own 'Modern Baccalaureate'. The rugby scholarship programme went even further – by 2017 we had established a whole Y7 'stream' of pupils in the programme, who took most of their lessons together as a group. We were interested to see the impact of this grouping on achievement, and so we analysed their performance in terms of both behaviour and the amount of progress the made from their starting points. Interestingly, we discovered that on both counts, they were the top performing group of pupils. I don't know what happened to that group after I left, but at the very least, it demonstrated the impact that an initially extra-curricular programme could have on academic achievement.

In addition to these two particularly strong initiatives however, we can add a third – the study of Mandarin Chinese. At the time of writing this book in early 2024, relationships between the UK and Chinese governments are at a significant low point. However, I have always been convinced of the importance of learning the language and culture of one of the most populous countries in the world, which is also now the world's second biggest economy. In 1996, the introduction of Mandarin Chinese was central to my successful 'languages college' bid at Arden School, and in 2004, it formed a part of my successful Arts and Enterprise bid t Campion School. I was delighted therefore to discover in 2008 that a successful link with

China had been developed by Archbishop Thurstan School - the school that was to become Archbishop. Sentamu Academy.

In 2006, Hull's local council had taken part in an exchange with the Fengtai district of Beijing, which led to a formal Memorandum of Understanding being signed between the two areas. As a part of this, our school had an exchange visit with Da Cheng School, and that in turn was the starting point for an extremely fruitful collaboration. The success of any venture in China depends to a large extent to the strength of your 'Guanxi' – your contacts – and we had been fortunate enough to be linked with an individual whose influence stretched way beyond that of the Beijing School she represented. If you were going to choose an area of the country in which to introduce Mandarin Chinese, it probably wouldn't be East Hull. And yet as the years progressed, our pupils enjoyed real success in this language. The curriculum freedoms from which we benefitted between 2008 and 2015 gave us the opportunity to introduce Mandarin the right way – slowly. Building on the early success of the exchange at school leader level, we launched Mandarin language and culture first as an extra-curricular activity, with the assistance of a teacher from our partner school in Beijing. This gentle start enabled us to assess the likely challenges in offering a full GCSE, but within a few years, our first cohort was indeed doing just this. We made time for pupil exchanges, so that those studying the language also had the opportunity to visit the country. Many of our pupils didn't travel much outside of Hull itself, so one can only begin to imagine the impact of a visit to Beijing on their lives. Although I don't think any of them experienced the 'delights' of eating either Wolf or Sea Slug, as I did on one such trip, Snake was certainly on the menu, as were all sorts of other new foods. They experienced classes of 70 pupils, Chinese calligraphy, whole-school Tai-Chi and visits to the Great Wall, to name but a few of the activities.

On the basis of this success, we were subsequently invited by the Confucius institute to be a lead school in what became the 'Mandarin Excellence Programme'. In 2015, Chancellor George Osborne allocated Schools' Minister, Nick Gibb, £10 million to fund a programme to create 5000 competent Mandarin speakers. Under the programme, at least 20 pupils each year from Year 7 onwards would study Mandarin intensively, with a view to gaining a good level of competence by the time they left school. We were thrilled to join the programme, and had no shortage of pupils who at age 11, were prepared to come into the academy at 8:00 every day to learn Mandarin. Meanwhile, for those who had already been studying with us, GCSE results were strong and improving year on year, and eventually, we were able to offer Mandarin at Pre-U level in the Sixth Form. In 2016, out of 5000 centres world-wide, we were one of 5 schools to be awarded 'Confucius classroom of the year'. Our Mandarin programme had become a great success, even inspiring one of our alumni both to study and establish his own business in China.

All in all, by 2015, we had developed an extremely diverse curriculum which we knew engaged the vast majority of our pupils and enabled them to succeed. In addition to this level of diversity however, we had one other strategy – multiple entry for GCSE exams and in particular, the core subjects of English and Maths. We saw earlier that GCSEs are 'norm-referenced'. This has nothing to do with a person called Norman carrying out an administrative task, but rather describes a process by which standards are deemed to remain constant. Under 'norm-referencing', the percentage of pupils gaining a particular grade at GCSE remains pretty much fixed year-on-year. This is supposed to 'smooth out' any unexpected rise or drop in exam results owing to the exam being either easier or harder than would be expected. There is a glaringly obvious problem with this philosophy, as we shall see in the next section of this book, but for now, the above explanation will suffice.

One of the consequences of norm-referencing is that in any given GCSE exam sitting, the proportion of pupils able to obtain a 'C' grade or higher is limited to around 70%. In order to increase our own pupils' chances of success in these exams, we therefore developed a system of 'multiple entry', which became increasingly sophisticated. Pupils were able to enter both iGCSE (International GCSE) and GCSE exams, at different levels (foundation and higher) and for different exam boards, in different years. Under this system, at one end of the spectrum some of our highest-attaining pupils managed to obtain an English GCSE at 'C' grade in Year 8. This wasn't the end point for them however, but rather 'insurance' against any problems they might encounter later on in their school career. Given that at least 50% of our pupils were considered vulnerable – our VYPs – this 'insurance' was important. A common criticism of this sort of policy at the time was that it 'limited ambition', leaving pupils content to pass with a 'C' grade. That however was not our experience – rather, those pupils who achieved a 'C' or 'B' grade were keen to work towards achieving the top grades. Taken together, Ofsted agreed that our strategies were working well; our 2014 Ofsted report noting that:

'The academy's curriculum is outstanding and meets students' needs increasingly well. Arrangements to support the move from primary to secondary school, especially for those whose literacy and numeracy skills are not as well developed, are highly effective. The regular 'master classes' in communication and mathematical skills, for very able Year 6 learners, enable them to make very fast progress. Disabled students and those with special educational needs are well catered for. The number of academic courses is increasing, and the range of successful vocational opportunities is well matched to students' aptitudes. Alternative courses delivered off the academy's site are equally well targeted, and the quality of experiences and outcomes rigorously checked. These courses make excellent contributions to individual students' attendance, confidence and self-esteem..... The proportion of students attaining five or more GSCEs grades A* to C, including English and mathematics, is just above average. This means that, over time, students make good progress, given their generally well-below average starting points. As a result, their achievement is good.' (Swallow, 2014)

The report also commended the strength of our extra-curricular activities, noting that:

'Extensive sporting, musical and performing experiences, and an abundance of extra-curricular activities, make strong contributions to students' social development. Educational links with schools in China, visits to Auschwitz, Europe and Australia, enrich students' cultural awareness. Daily collective worship, projects with the city's Second World War Veterans' Association, and regular visits by local

and national church leaders, underpin students' spiritual understanding. Entrepreneurship is openly encouraged. All of this underpins equality of opportunity, and emphasises the academy's desire to tackle immediately any discrimination that may arise.' (ibid)

Earlier on, I referenced the 'Archie Family'. I was particularly pleased therefore with the report's following comments:

'Students typically describe the academy as 'one big family', and go out of their way to support each other. Parents say how well the academy looks after their children, giving them every opportunity to succeed. They are especially pleased with how adults respond to their concerns or views. The academy's mission statement 'Aspire, Serve, Achieve' is embodied in the excellent relationships between adults and students, and between students and their peers. For these reasons, bullying of any kind is rare. Students are confident that adults will always be at hand to help, should they experience difficulties.' (ibid)

A key feature of our academy was the high proportion of vulnerable young people – our VYPs – who attended. In April 2011, the Coalition government introduced the 'Pupil Premium' – additional funding for those pupils coming from severely disadvantaged families. A key priority for schools was to ensure that progress made by this group of pupils was at least as good as that made by their more socially advantaged peers. Their academic progress was scrutinised separately by Ofsted, and at the time, just under 40% of our pupils fell into this category. All of those pupils could be considered to be our 'VYPs', so we were delighted to read the following lines in the report of 2014:

'The academy knows its students exceptionally well, and successfully removes barriers to learning. As a result, all have an equal opportunity to succeed. Margins between the performance of students in receipt of pupil premium funding and their peers are closing. In many years the gaps are insignificant. In some, they have entirely closed.' (ibid)

I want to close this part of the book with an extremely simple observation. By 2015, we had developed a curriculum and exam-entry policy that enabled the vast majority of our pupils to succeed, a view fully endorsed by Ofsted. Not only had we achieved this for our own pupils, but on the back of this success, had launched the biggest Alternative Provision academy in the country which in turn, quickly became a great success in its own right. Finally, our VYPs had access to an education that transformed their life chances. These successes in turn combined to enable us to form our own Multi-Academy Trust, and in September 2015, three local primary schools joined ASA and ASPIRE to become the Sentamu Academy Learning Trust.

Part 2:

The development of school performance metrics policy

Abstract

This section of the book is more academic in nature, as I seek to explain (albeit as simply as possible) how changes in evaluating the success or otherwise of schools' exam results led over a period of years to the situation we now have – one in which schools have 'perverse incentives' to drive VYPs through a curriculum to which they may not be best suited. Central to this part of the book is the explanation of how the current 'Progress 8' metric puts schools in the invidious position of being forced to choose between making curriculum and exam entry decisions based on what is best for the pupil as opposed to what is best for the school, in terms of the published performance or so-called 'league tables.'

Chapter 8 – An introduction to school performance metrics.

Abstract:

This is a technical chapter, laying out the concepts of 'Attainment', 'Progress' and 'Value-added', and how government performance metrics of these concepts changed significantly in the 10 years between 2006 and 2016. It goes into considerable detail to explain in particular the concept of the 'Progress 8' metric which, it turns out, is severely limited as a measure of Progress! Crucially, this chapter argues that the exigencies of the current set of metrics (including Progress 8) can often militate against schools offering their VYPs the most appropriate curriculum for their needs.

'It ain't what you do, it's the way that you do it'.

(Bananarama and the Fun Boy Three, 1982)

This book starts by asking how, in a 2 year period between 2014 and 2016, the flourishing academy I was leading went from a judgement of close to 'Outstanding' to one of 'Inadequate'. A major part of the answer, I am suggesting, lies in the haphazard way in which government policies in the three areas of curriculum and assessment, school performance tables and inspection have been developed independently of each other, and without due consideration as to how a change in one area impacts all the others. In Part One, we looked at how developments in the type of qualifications offered to pupils led to a great expansion of courses, many of which, although assessed differently, had 'GCSE Equivalence', or in other words, judged to carry the same value as GCSEs for both schools and pupils. In this section of the book, we will see how school performance tables changed, and the impact that this had on pupils, especially our VYPs (a summary of the changes can be found in Fig. One at the end of this chapter).

Last year, I became aware of the concept of 'trigger alerts'. The idea is to warn people that they might find a particular film, radio show or book distressing, owing to a particular theme with which it is dealing. This section of the book carries its own 'trigger alert' on the grounds that it might appear we are going down a series of mathematical rabbit holes, with no hope of finding an exit. I would encourage the reader to persevere however, because understanding the concepts behind school performance tables is key to our central theme. Indeed, it is tempting to conclude that successive education secretaries have either not grasped the concepts adequately themselves, or conversely, having done so, used these concepts to support their own ideological ends. For a really detailed analysis of the issues, I would encourage the reading of an article that appeared in the British Educational Research Journal in 2017 (George Leckie, 2017). However, the following summary will hopefully suffice, and so with this in mind, we will don our diving suits and oxygen tanks, and explore the murky depths of government performance tables.

School performance tables matter. They matter to parents, because they set out to show the extent to which schools enable their pupils to make progress. And they matter to schools for two reasons. First, taking the above point, they can be used as a marketing tool to encourage parents to send their children to the school. Second, they are used by Ofsted as an inspection tool to judge the overall effectiveness of a school. In short, it is impossible to overstate the importance of these performance tables. Known informally as 'league tables', they purport to play exactly that role, enabling both parents and Ofsted to give an initial 'ranking' to schools. As we shall see however, these tables are often highly misleading. (In addition to the GCSEs and equivalencies taken in Y11, up until 2008, pupils also had to sit at age 14 'end of Key Stage 3' SAT exams in English, Maths and Science. These were dropped however in 2008, and for the purpose of this book, I have opted not to discuss this issue).

The first concept to understand is the difference between *attainment* on the one hand, and *achievement* on the other. The former is a raw indicator of a given level of expertise in any subject, such as 'C' grade GCSE. The latter is an indicator of the progress a pupil has made from a particular starting point (for example the outcome of a particular English or Maths test at the end of primary school) to a particular end point (such as a GCSE result in English or Maths). With this distinction in mind, let's look at the outcomes of 2 schools. In School A which we'll call 'Scrubwood School', the average GCSE grade achieved by its 100 pupils at the end of Year 11 was a 'C', whereas in school B (we'll call it 'Acacia Academy'), the average grade achieved was a 'B'. On the face of it, Acacia has 'done better' than Scrubwood. From an attainment perspective, the results are certainly higher. But whether or not it has indeed 'done better' than Scrubwood depends on the starting points of its pupils. In our imaginary scenario, further analysis shows that on average, pupils in Scrubwood ended primary school with 'Level 3s' in Maths, whereas the pupils in Acacia ended their primary education with 'level 5s' in Maths on average. In fact, Scrubwood School has done really well, indeed much better than Acacia Academy (for more reasons than our perhaps immediately apparent as we shall see when we look at the concept of 'Expected levels of progress' shortly).

The situation is further complicated when we look at the social background of the pupils in our two imaginary schools. It turns out that Scrubwood draws its pupils from a highly disadvantaged background, whereas Acacia's pupils come from economically more advantaged families. The correlation between levels of deprivation and achievement is very strong *(ibid. P 57)* – in general, the higher the levels of deprivation for any pupil, the lower their achievement is likely to be. Returning to our admittedly simplistic example, we can now see that the pupils in Scrubwood have now done *even better* than their peers in Acacia – not only have they made more progress from their individual starting points, but they have done so in spite of coming from a more socially-deprived background. From this, it should be clear that any meaningful set of performance or so-called 'league' tables should take all of these factors into account, all of which gives rise to our first set of problems.

Up until 2006, the acknowledged 'benchmark' by which schools were judged was the percentage of pupils who gained 5 or more GCSEs at C or above. There were at least three problems with this. First, remembering our example above, this original benchmark took no account of pupil *achievement,* i.e., the progress they had made from their starting points at the end of primary education. Second, they took no account of relative levels of pupil deprivation and third, there was no stipulation as to 'which subjects counted'. At this point, it is important to remember our GNVQs. A full GNVQ was given the equivalence of 4 GCSEs (shorter versions of GNVQs with an equivalence of 2 GCSEs could also be taken). This meant that, up until 2006, a pupil could be deemed to have met the benchmark having passed one full GNVQ and one other GCSE or indeed GCSE equivalent.

Whilst hindsight always gives us 20/20 vision, these problems were really not that difficult to spot and it would be reasonable to expect therefore that any revisions would have taken all of these issues into account. In 2006, Education Secretary Ed Balls addressed two of them. First, he stipulated that the success benchmark of '5 GCSEs or equivalent at 'C' grade or above' should include both English and Maths. Second, the concept of 'Contextual Value Added' (CVA) was devised. The easiest way of describing this is through a golfing analogy. In order for players of differing levels to be able to compete in the same game, golfers are given a 'handicap' score – the higher the 'handicap', the lower the level of skill. A 'scratch' or highly skilled golfer might be expected to complete an 18-hole round of golf using only 54 shots – an average of 3 shots per hole. Conversely, a player new to the game might have a 'handicap' of 30. On this basis, a golfer who completed the course making 84 shots would have performed as well as her or his more skilled counterpart who completed the course in 50 shots. Moreover, if this newcomer managed to complete the course using only 75 shots, they would actually have 'done better' than their 'scratch' golfing counterpart who completed the course in 54 shots.

CVA attempted to represent this principle by formally recognising acknowledged barriers to academic success. These included the following factors.

- Gender (girls typically performed better than boys overall);
- Age (the month of year in which pupils are born);
- The socio-economic background of pupils using the ICACI scale that we looked at earlier;

- Free-school meal eligibility (another key way of gauging levels of social deprivation);
- The numbers of pupils who were registered as having a 'Special Educational Need';
- Ethnicity (white boys and white girls are the two lowest-performing cohorts of pupils);
- First Language;
- Care status ('Looked After' children are particularly at risk of low achievement); and
- Mobility (as we saw earlier, moving between schools has been shown to be a very big barrier to achievement)

Whilst by no means perfect, CVA did set out to 'do what it says on the tin' – give a context in which the exam results of any given school could be better understood. On this scale, a school with an absolutely average set of pupils, who made an absolutely average amount of progress based on all the above factors, would be awarded a score of 1000. Scores lower than 1000 indicated increasingly poorer levels of performance, and scores higher than this, increasingly higher levels. With these 2 new measures in place, (CVA and the new 'benchmark' of 5+ A-C including English and Maths) more detailed comparisons between schools were possible, as we can see by returning to our 2 institutions, Scrubwood School and Acacia Academy. Let's say that in 2008, 45% of Scrubwood pupils achieved 5 or more GCSE grades at C or above, whereas at Acacia, that figure was 60%. Under the system for measuring school performance prior to 2006, Acacia would be deemed to have been more successful. But by 2008, CVA had also been established, and in that year let us imagine, Scrubwood's CVA score was 1035,whereas Acacia's was 985.

This clearly paints a very different picture. On the face of it, Scrubwood has outperformed Acacia – and that may indeed be true. However, in order to get the full picture, we would need to look at their respective curricula. The reader will remember that earlier on, we saw that GCSE equivalent qualifications (such as BTecs, the Young Arts Leader Award, ASDAN awards and so on) were *criterion referenced,* meaning that any pupil could pass them, as long as they reached the accepted standard (rather like in the case of a driving test). GCSEs on the other hand were *norm-referenced*, through which a maximum of around 70% of all entries was able to be awarded in any given exam-sitting. From this, it could be argued that the lower CVA score of Acacia reflected a curriculum that was more or wholly based on pupils taking GCSE exams, whereas Scrubwood's impressively high score could have been down to the fact that their curriculum included more GCSE equivalencies. Alternatively, and perhaps more probably, the difference between the two scores could have been down to a combination of factors including teaching standards, socio-economic background and curriculum policy.

Yet another possibility came to light when I took over as Principal of ASA in 2008. Prior to it becoming an academy, the Local Authority was advising the school to keep the number of pupils on the Special Educational Needs (SEN) Register as low as possible. There is not the space here to discuss the reasons for this, but suffice it say, a large number of pupils who should have been placed on the register were not on it. Apart from the obvious issues around ensuring their needs were met, an additional consequence was that the school's CVA score was artificially low – rectifying the SEN register so that it properly reflected the proportion of pupils in the school with special educational needs made an immediate and positive difference to the school's CVA score.

From all of the above, it can be seen that whilst on the face of it CVA gave more context to school results, a higher score didn't *necessarily* indicate a more successful school. Indeed, as we shall see when we discuss the Wolf report (2012) on vocational education in schools, Education Secretary Gove was suspicious that schools were 'gaming' the system – for example by entering large numbers of pupils onto courses that were perceived as being 'easy', and/ or worse, inappropriate – in a bid to increase their place in the relative ranking. Wherever the truth lay, by 2012, CVA had been scrapped – a decision we will discuss in more detail shortly – and from 2012 onwards, achievement was measured by the concepts of 'Expected Levels of Progress', 'Floor targets' and 'Average Point Score'.

'Expected Levels of Progress', or EP, judged pupils' performance in GCSE English and Maths based on the levels they had achieved in these two subjects at the end of their primary education in the Key Stage 2 exams (SATs). EP was the equivalent of '3 levels of progress'. This meant that if a pupil achieved a level 4 in English or Maths at the end of KS2, they were expected to achieve at least a 'C' grade in the corresponding GCSE five years later. This was important, because it underpinned a new concept, that of the 'floor targets'. To reach the 'floor target', a school had to ensure that at least 40% of its pupils achieved 5 or more GCSEs (or equivalents) including English and Maths at grade C or above. However, if a school's pupils didn't achieve this figure of 40% but *did* make greater than the median national progress in terms of 'Expected Progress' (i.e., more than 3 levels of progress in each of the two core subjects of English and Maths), then they would not be judged to have failed to meet the floor target. This in turn was also important, as failure to reach the floor target was a key issue of concern in Ofsted inspections.

It can be seen from this that the concept of EP has at least one flaw – it took no account of any of the factors that the proponents of CVA would argue had a crucial effect on pupil achievement – such as socio-economic background. There was however another problem. First, it became clear very quickly that nationally, pupils with a higher starting point (for example those achieving a level 5 in English or Maths at the end of KS2) actually made, on average, *more* than 3 levels of progress, whereas nationally, those with a lower score at the end of KS3 (such as those achieving a level 3) made *less* progress nationally.

In 2016, only 62% of pupils leaving primary school with a level 3 made EP in their English GCSE. For those with a level 4, the figure jumped to 73% making EP, whereas for those leaving with a level 5, the figure making EP rose again to 79%. For Maths, the differences were even starker. For those leaving primary school with a level 3, only 42% made EP nationally. For those with a level 4, there is an even bigger jump than for English, with 69% making EP, and for those leaving with a level 5, the figure rose again to 79% making EP. From this we can see very quickly that the floor target was harder to achieve for schools having higher numbers of lower-attaining pupils.

However, the situation is further complicated by the issue of sub-levels. Each KS2 level is broken down further into 3 sub levels - a, b and c, with c being the lowest level. A pupil achieving a level 3a (at the top of the level 3) at KS2 in English or Maths would have a GCSE target in the subject of 'D', whereas a pupil achieving a level 4c (at the bottom of level 4) at KS would have a corresponding target of a 'C' grade at GCSE. In other words, a very small difference in attainment at primary school (the difference between a level 3a and a level 4c) led to a much more significant difference in GCSE target grade (the jump from a 'D' grade to a 'C' grade being considerable). The same phenomenon occurred at the level 4/5 border – a pupil achieving a level 4a (the top of level 4) would still be given the target of a 'C' grade (as for the pupil who achieved a level 4c), whereas a pupil achieving a level 5c (the lowest level 5) would have a 'B' grade GCSE as their target.

Putting all of this together, we can see that the combination of 'Floor Targets' and 'Expected Levels of Progress' presented a real challenge to schools whose pupils have below average levels of attainment when they join in Y7 at age 11. Not only were they less likely to reach the floor target of 40% 5+ A-C grades (including English and Maths) itself, but they were also statistically less likely to make the target of '3 levels of progress' in English and Maths – in effect, a 'double whammy' for schools with high levels of low-attaining pupils. Returning to the central theme of this book, we can see that EP in effect penalised schools with low prior attaining intakes – especially with those who 'just' achieved a level 4c (a key benchmark by which primary schools were judged) and rewarded those with high prior attaining intakes. Moreover, as we noted above, no account was taken of pupils' socio-economic background, in spite of the fact that this was known to be a key factor in pupil achievement. It follows therefore that this system of measuring pupil performance at GCSE gave a 'perverse incentive' for schools to select high prior attainers at the expense of their lower prior attaining peers, since the former require fewer resources to reach their target grades.

The third measure between 2010 and 2016 involved assessing the average points gained from the total of the subjects they passed. This particular statistic involved allocating a number of points to each grade, and then dividing up the total number of points gained by all pupils and dividing it by the total number of pupils in the school. Under this system, an A* was worth 8 points, an A 7 points, a B 6 points ,and so on down to a G grade, which was worth 1 point. We need to remember however that at this point, there was no limit on the number of subjects that could be included. Thus, it would be perfectly possible for a pupil to take English, Maths and two BTecs (each of which were worth 4 GCSE equivalents), thereby gaining points for 10 GCSEs. Let's now return to our two fictional schools – Scrubwood School and Acacia Academy to examine the implications of this.

Scrubwood is a school with a highly disadvantaged pupil intake, a factor which we know limits pupil attainment significantly. In order to help engage their pupils, many take English, Maths, and 2 BTecs (worth 4 GCSEs each), giving them a total of 10 GCSEs. If they achieve an average of a B grade in each, their average point score would be 50. In Acacia academy however, most pupils only take 8 or 9 GCSEs each. If they achieved an average of a B grade, these pupils' average point score would only be 40 or 45. Whilst these are only examples, it hopefully makes the point that up until the introduction of 'Attainment 8' and 'Progress 8', schools had the flexibility to match their curriculum to the individual pupil much more closely. This was particularly important for our 'VYPs', who typically responded better to a mix of assessment methods which included portfolio work. Whilst 'average point score' was not included in any assessment as to whether or not a school had met the so-called 'floor target', it did at least give the option for schools to provide a countermeasure if performance with respect to the former was poor. More importantly, it enabled schools to ensure that as high a proportion of its pupils as possible achieved at least 5 good GCSE grades or equivalent – a key benchmark from the pupil's point of view for being accepted onto a 'Level 3' (i.e. 'A' level or BTec equivalent) programme of study post-16.

That, however, was not the end of the story of assessment developments between 2010 and 2016, as during this period in which 'Expected Progress', 'Floor targets' and 'Average Point Score' reigned as the academic measures by which schools were held to account, Gove made another change. On the 29th. September 2013, he announced that whilst a pupil would be allowed (quite fairly) to keep the *highest* grade that they achieved in any particular subject, the school's performance would be judged on the aggregated scores of the *first* grade pupils achieved. Readers will remember that many schools at the time, including the academy which I led, had implemented a system of 'multiple entry' in the core exams of English and Maths, to give pupils the best chance of achieving a good grade.

As we saw in part One, this was particularly important for pupils who might just miss a 'C' grade. GCSE grades can be taken at either foundation level (grades G-D) or higher level (C to A*), as the following example illustrates. For those pupils 'on the C/D borderline', the choice between whether to enter them for a foundation or higher paper was critical. In order to give them the best chance of passing, schools would typically enter them in Y10 for a foundation paper – if they succeeded to gain a 'C' grade at the end of Y10, then they would be entered for the higher tier in Y11, with a correspondingly more stretching curriculum. If they failed to achieve a 'C' grade however, they could retake the exam in January of Y11 , and again in the Summer. Whilst this system had its detractors, including Gove himself, it certainly motivated our own pupils to try as hard as possible to get the best grades in those subjects.

The decision to legislate that only the first exam would count in school performance tables placed headteachers in an impossible situation. Effectively, Gove was forcing us to choose between what experience told us was in the pupils' best interests (the opportunity to sit the exams more than once) and our position in the school performance tables – the latter being a key consideration in Ofsted inspections. It was made all the worse by the fact that at that point, along with other schools who adopted this strategy, we had been preparing our pupils for the forthcoming 'January resits'. Quite apart from my total aversion to Gove's new policy, I felt that to tell these Y11 pupils that this option would now be denied to them would be an act of betrayal. As we reflected on the implications of this new policy, our senior team including the heads of English and Maths all agreed that we had to persist with what was best for our pupils. The decision was unanimous- we would carry on as before. I remember at the time thinking that this would probably lead to my having to 'carry a particularly large, heavy and unpleasant can' at some point. This was indeed to be the case. Before we get to looking at the implications of this decision however, we need to look at a final piece of legislation to bring us right up to date.

In 2013, Gove also announced that as of 2016, the progress made by pupils would be judged by two key metrics – Attainment 8 and Progress 8. In order to understand this fully, we need to revisit Gove's 'English Baccalaureate', or E-Bac. As we saw earlier, a key plank of Gove's curriculum reforms was his view that so-called 'academic' subjects (typically assessed through an exam-based GCSE) were of intrinsically higher value than so-called 'vocationally' subjects, such as those examined more through portfolios of evidence such as BTecs. In his thinking, to deny all pupils the opportunity to pursue a 'rigorous academic' curriculum would constitute a lowering of ambition for them, on the grounds that to do so would be to deny them the opportunity to attend a top university. I argued in chapter 7 that this thinking was fundamentally flawed; in effect by pushing schools to make these subjects compulsory in the interests of equality, he actually succeeded in 'switching off' large numbers of the very pupils he was trying to help, thereby reducing equity. These issues notwithstanding, the introduction of the 'Attainment 8' and 'Progress 8' metrics were the next steps in his mission to drive his policies.

The first key factor to understand is that under 'Attainment 8', pupils' performance as represented in the national school performance tables would be judged on the results of 8 exams, as shown by the following table given by the DfE:

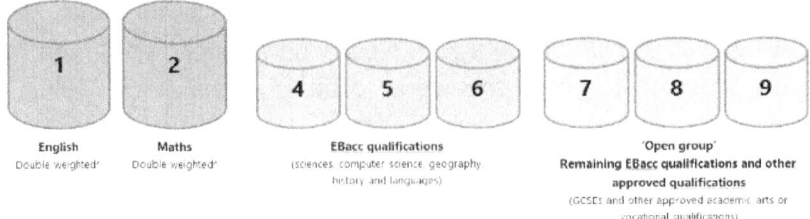

English
Double weighted'

Maths
Double weighted'

EBacc qualifications
(sciences, computer science, geography,
history and languages)

'Open group'
Remaining EBacc qualifications and other
approved qualifications
(GCSEs and other approved academic, arts or
vocational qualifications)

'Higher score of English Language OR English Literature
double-weighted if a student has taken both qualifications

From this, the influence of Gove's view on the curriculum can be clearly seen. Firstly, the relative importance of English and Maths was increased by doubling the weighting attributed to each of these subjects. Thus, the scores from 8 subjects effectively became the scores of 10 subjects, with the points achieved in English and Maths accounting for 40% of a pupil's total score. Secondly, the 'E-Bac pot' only included science or computer science in Pot 4, History or Geography in Pot 5, and a modern foreign language in Pot 6. If a pupil failed to take a subject in any one of those pots, they could not achieve any points *for the school* in that area. We noted above that in only allowing schools to count the results of the *first* GCSE entry in their performance tables, Gove had already forced Headteachers to choose between the best interests of the *pupil* (as expressed by being given more than one chance to bank a good GCSE grade in, typically, English and / or Maths) and the best interests of the *school* (as expressed by the fact that only allowing a pupil one bite at any given exam 'cherry' would almost certainly lead to a better overall score for the performance tables).

With the introduction of 'Attainment 8', this invidious pressure to make schools adopt a curriculum in the interests of the school, rather than the pupil, continued. A particular challenge for us in this respect was the issue of RE. As a Church of England School, a key requirement is that all pupils studied RE as an exam-based subject. RE however was not included as an alternative in 'Pot 5' – the Humanities pot. There seems to be absolutely no justification for this omission, and the consequence for our academy was that if we were going to be able to 'earn points' from pupils taking a humanity in 'Pot 5', then they would actually be required to sit *two* Humanities, not just one. 'Pot 6' required pupils to take either a modern foreign language (or Latin or Greek), and the final 3 pots were 'open choices'.

On the face of it, these three open choices provided some sort of counterbalance to the requirements of the other five. However, regrettably they had to be subjects examined through GCSEs – many of the 'equivalences' (such as our Young Arts Leader Award, Institute of Financial Studies Award or ASDAN awards to name but three) were deemed no longer to 'count' for the school. 'Attainment 8' therefore became Gove's way of enforcing compliance with his curriculum policy. In a final twist, schools were also assessed on the percentage of pupils who actually achieved 'C' grade passes or higher in each of the subjects making up his 'English Baccalaureate'. Whilst this did not carry the same weight as the other measures, schools were expected to show that they had targets to increase the proportion of pupils both sitting and passing the EBac year on year.

'Attainment 8' by itself of course had no notion of 'value-added' built into it – it was a straightforward measure of the levels reached by pupils in eight subjects. As we have seen earlier, this sort of measure is not terribly helpful for anyone trying to understand how successfully any given school educates its pupils – broadly speaking, pupils who leave Primary School with higher levels of attainment than average will, equally, leave secondary education with higher levels of attainment than average (or indeed significantly greater than average, given the fact that pupils attaining higher levels in the Key Stage 2 exams actually make *more* progress than their lower attaining peers, as we saw above). To mitigate this obvious problem and introduce a notion of 'value-added', the concept of 'Progress 8' was introduced alongside 'Attainment 8'.

The idea of Progress 8 was to measure the progress made by pupils between the Key Stage 2 SATs taken at the end of the Primary Phase, with the results achieved at the end of their GCSE exams in Year 11. Under this system, a pupil's Progress 8 score is defined as their Attainment 8 score, minus their 'estimated' Attainment 8 score, the latter being defined as the average Attainment 8 score of all pupils nationally with the same prior attainment (the levels they achieved) at the end of their primary education. The greater the Progress 8 score, the greater the progress made by the pupil compared to the average of all pupils with similar prior attainment.

From this it can be seen that the Progress 8 score for a school is the average of all its pupils' scores, calculated each year on the basis of their actual results. (As a result, the Progress 8 score for a school as a whole can't be predicted, as the average scores on which the measure is based can't be known until the exam results are issued). For Progress 8, the average score of all secondary school pupils nationally is 0. Since its introduction, Progress 8 scores nationally have, as one might expect, ranged significantly. For example, a score of -1 means that on average, pupils are making one grade less progress than the national average between Years 7 and 11, whereas a score of +1 indicates that they are making on average one more grade's progress. The minimum standard expected or 'floor target' is -0.5 – any school achieving less than this attracts the negative attention of Ofsted. Conversely, a score of + 0.5 or greater indicates that a school is making well above average progress with its pupils.

Those reading astutely will notice that even though Progress 8 purports to measure 'value -added', it takes no account of the fact that nationally, lower attaining pupils make less progress than higher attaining pupils (as we saw above in our discussions on the concept of 'Expected Progress'), nor does it make any allowances for pupils' socio-economic background. There is in fact a third objection which we will examine when discussing in a later chapter the impact of Progress 8 on Ofsted judgements. By now however, I imagine that many readers' heads are hurting. So, returning to our diving metaphor, we will resurface, take several deep breaths, and try to sum up the impact of the many changes in assessment and school performance policy over the past twenty or so years.

Fig. One: Changes in performance metrics for schools, 2000 to present day

Year	Performance Measures	Subjects included	Floor Target	Value-added measure
Pre 2006	KS3 SATs taken at age 14. 5+ A-C GCSEs at age 16	Any	None	None
2006 - 2010	KS3 SATs (abolished in 2008) 5+A-C including English and Maths. Multiple entry allowed	English, Maths, any others including equivalencies	30% 5+ A-C including English and Maths	CVA
2010 - 2016	5+ A*-C incl. En & Ma -New A* grade introduced for GCSEs and 'equivalencies' in 2010. Average Point Score From 2015, only first GCSE result counted	English, Maths, any others including equivalencies	≤ 40% achieving 5 + A* to C including En & Ma % making 'Expected Progress'	EP had limited effect in this respect
2016 – Now	5+ A* to C incl. En & Ma. (Between 2017 and 2019, GCSE scale changed from A*-C to 9-1) Attainment 8 score Progress 8 score	Subjects contained in the 8 'Pots'	≤-0.5 P8 score	P8 has limited effect in this respect.

Chapter 9 – Metric Madness!

Abstract

This chapter looks in further detail at the concept of 'Perverse Incentives' for schools to act in their own interests, rather than those of their pupils. We examine briefly the Wolf Report which was instrumental in Gove's decision to change school performance metrics, and assess how reasonable his fears in this respect actually were. The chapter examines how the pressures created by changes in these metrics have created a new set of 'Perverse Incentives,' include that of 'off-rolling' pupils to improve a school's performance table outcomes. The government definition of this concept is however challenged, and I argue that care is needed before schools are accused of adopting such practices.

'Won't Get Fooled Again'

The Who, 1971

Having worked through the various changes in the metrics judging school performance, it is well worth making an initial assessment of their strengths and weaknesses. It may be rather a sweeping statement to say that 'what gets measured gets done', but that is, after all, the point of a target. When you take into account the fact that the careers of teachers and senior leaders can often depend on their perceived relative success of meeting government targets, it is therefore not unreasonable to assume that changes in the targets for which we are accountable leads to changes in our behaviour. With this in mind, we will now consider how changes in school performance measures influenced my own behaviour as a leader, and how this in turn impacted the experience of the VYPs for whom I was ultimately responsible.

From 2004 to 2008, I was leading a school with relatively high levels of deprivation, and certainly the highest levels in Leamington Spa. During that time, the main measure of school performance was the percentage of pupils gaining '5 A-C grades'. It is easy to level two criticisms at the system in which this was the main measure. On the one hand, there was, arguably, not enough of an accountability incentive to pressure schools into ensuring their pupils achieved the highest possible grades in the core skills of English and Maths. On the other hand, there was no measure of 'value-added' – either in terms of progress from their starting point at the end of primary school (flawed as this measure is) or from the point of view of socio-economic background of their pupils. As such, it would be safe to say that this measure was at best a very crude measure of a school's performance.

But what of its impact on our VYPs? As I discussed in an earlier chapter, my immediate priority as Headteacher was to restore good levels of behaviour in the school. Unfortunately, during the first two years, this involved a very high level of both fixed-term (temporary) and permanent exclusions. However, the introduction of a more varied curriculum, including courses in more practical subjects such as horticulture, hair and beauty and digital media studies, the level of exclusions dropped. At the very least, there was certainly a strong correlation between broadening the range of subjects offered and a fall in the exclusion rate. The 'headline measure' of '5+ A-C grades' (including equivalencies such as the courses mentioned above) enabled us to offer these courses to the benefit of pupils and to the school. This being the case, it is my view that in this respect at least, government performance measures worked to the benefit of our VYPs, who typically would opt for at least one of these alternative qualifications.

On the other hand, the failure to include English and Maths as two compulsory subjects in the '5+ A-C' measure is perhaps more controversial. Critics of this situation would argue that it gave schools too much of a 'free pass' as in effect, a pupil could achieve 5 or more GCSE grades (and thereby be deemed to have met the key 'headline measure') without passing either English or Maths. Needless to say, we worked extremely hard to ensure our pupils passed those two key exams even in the absence of being held fully to account for this. If we take the view however that 'what gets measured gets done', it could be argued that the measure in place between 2004 and 2008 ran the risk of 'selling pupils short' on achieving good passes in these key exams.

During this same period, the notions of 'perverse incentives' and 'gaming' began to raise their heads. As these were to become key issues for debate in the following years, it is worth spending some time looking at them now. In the field of education, a 'perverse incentive' is an aspect of government policy that encourages schools to act the interests of the organisation, rather than those of its pupils. Schools who take decisions based on these 'perverse incentives' are deemed to have engaged in 'gaming the system'. To illustrate this, let's return to our imaginary school Scrubwood, who, for the sake of argument, appointed a new headteacher in 2004.

Up until 2004, Scrubwood had been languishing in the (albeit highly misleading) performance tables, with typically around 30% of its pupils achieving the headline measure. This was in direct comparison to its nearby rival Acacia Academy, where around 65% of the pupils achieved the measure. This situation meant that increasingly fewer parents were opting to send their children to Scrubwood, meaning the school was suffering from 'falling roles' – whereby more pupils left in Year 11 than joined the school the following year in Y7. This in turn was leading to a drop in core government funding and ultimately, risked the closure of the school.

A newly appointed headteacher was naturally keen to turn this situation around. She took the view that a key plank of her strategy would be to enter all pupils for the GNVQ in ICT that was available at the time. This would enable all pupils who passed to gain 4 of the 5 GCSEs needed to meet the headline measure straight away. Readers will remember that unlike GCSEs, GNVQs were *criterion-assessed,* meaning that anyone who met the required level could pass, thereby gaining the 4 GCSEs. Our new headteacher introduced this course into the Year 9 curriculum, and within two years, around 80% of all pupils had passed the GVNQ. Of these, 90% gained at least one more GCSE at 'C' grade or above. Consequently, within the first three years of her headship, 72% of all pupils a Scrubwood were achieving the headline figure – a huge improvement on the performance of recent years, and one which even outstripped the achievements of neighbouring Acacia Academy. Even more fortuitously for the headteacher, following the introduction of CVA in 2006, Scrubwood enjoyed a spectacular headline 'value-added' score of 1043, owing to the fact that the achievements now took into account the fact that its pupils, many of whom had special needs, came from a highly impoverished socio-economic background. By contrast, Acacia Academy's CVA score of 1005, although still positive, looked somewhat mediocre.

At this point, leaders in Acacia academy began to cry 'foul', claiming that Scrubwood had used a perverse incentive to 'game' the system. This claim was, however, debatable. In entering all its pupils for the GNVQ, it could indeed be argued that Scrubwood had used a GCSE equivalent in a way not originally intended. On the other hand, in enabling 72% of its pupils to achieve 5 or more GCSEs, it was giving far more young people the basic passport to higher education, as well as an extremely useful qualification in the process. But what about the subjects that were 'sacrificed' to make way for this qualification? Well, at the time, ICT was a core lesson in many schools. By introducing the qualification to pupils in Year 9, our canny Headteacher was using time already being spent teaching ICT to accredit pupils' work. This meant that by Y10, although the qualification was worth 4 GCSEs, it could be delivered in the time needed typically to teach two GCSEs. She judged that all her pupils should gain a qualification in ICT anyway, so in effect, the GNVQ was only taking one other option slot. Moreover, by raising success in the headline measure by such a degree, pupils at Scrubwood became prouder of both themselves and their school, leading to improvements in attendance, behaviour and achievements in other subjects. In short, the introduction of the GNVQ in ICT was the catalyst in a turn-around of Scrubwood's fortunes.

Whilst this account is fictional, I suspect that readers of this book working in education will recognise that such a story is perhaps not that far from reality. Regardless, it is an example of how over the years, changes in education policy have led to very significant changes in the behaviour of schools to meet their accountabilities, particularly when, as we shall see, the stakes of the accountability regime increased dramatically.

This situation was addressed at least in part by Education Secretary Ed Balls in June 2008, when he included the key subjects of English and Maths in the headline measure, which at that point became '5+ A-C grades including English and Maths'. On the face of it, the inclusion of English and Maths into the headline measure of school performance was a reasonable policy, including for our VYPs, as it required schools to demonstrate how well their pupils had achieved in two 'core skills'. It was not without its critics however, with some arguing that it represented a move towards centralisation (Nelson, 2008). Whichever side you took however, it was certainly a significant move in tightening school accountabilities.

The years between 2008 and 2010 were, in my view, those in which national education policy was best aligned with meeting the needs of our VYPs. During that period, schools had the freedom to run a whole series of qualifications with GCSE equivalencies, including GNQs, BTecs, ASDAN awards and the other courses we discussed earlier on in this book. Headline measures by which schools were held to account included both the scores from all these qualifications (for which there was no limit) and CVA, which took into account the socio-economic background of pupils. At the same time, the requirement for schools to fulfil the headline measure of 5+ A-C including English and Maths dealt with the criticism (whether or not it was actually justified) that schools had no incentive to ensure that pupils passed exams in these core skills. From 2010 however, the arrival of the Coalition Government was to bring about a series of changes that would impact severely both on schools' freedoms and the lives of our VYPs.

In 2011, newly appointed Education Secretary Michael Gove commissioned Dr. Alison Wolf to carry out an independent review of vocational education to consider how it could best prepare 14- to 19-year-olds for successful progression into the labour market and / or higher level education and training routes (Wolf, 2011). In the forward to the report, Gove draws attention to Dr. Wolf's views that far too many 14-16 year-olds were following courses of little value, and that they were only doing them because they 'counted' in the school performance tables.

The 196-page report was wide-ranging, and covered several areas outside the scope of this book. However, it is worth noting that it was indeed critical of what was claimed to be an increasing practice of schools entering pupils for vocational qualifications of questionable value, and which did not enable them to progress to Further Education and employment. Her report makes implicit reference to her 2002 book *'Does Education Matter?'* (Wolf, 2002). Chapter 3 of that book, entitled *'a great idea for other people's children' (ibid)* points to a view that low level vocational courses are somehow seen as being automatically the best, even the default 'offer' for 'less academic' pupils *(ibid)*. In the 2011 report itself, we read on p114:

'There of course remains a risk that some schools will, as has happened in the past, effectively write off some of their least academically successful students, and park them in vocational courses irrespective of whether these 'count'.' (ibid, P69)

Discussion of the full implications of the Wolf report certainly merits a book in its own right. A significant amount of the criticism levelled at schools was where they had introduced NVQs – National Vocational Qualifications – which are indeed designed to be delivered at the workplace. It could indeed be argued that Dr. Wolf's concerns of her 2011 report - that these were not appropriate for delivery by schools - were a fair criticism *(ibid, P69)*. However, the vocational options being delivered by many schools at the time of the report were not these NVQs, but rather the BTECs and other options that we have discussed earlier. Indeed, in contrast to Dr. Wolf's contention above, at Archbishop Sentamu Academy, we found the opposite to be true; giving pupils the opportunity to study vocational options designed for delivery within a school-based context certainly did motivate our pupils, and encouraged many who previously would not have considered progressing to Post 16 education the motivation to do so. Indeed, far from 'writing off' some of our least academically successful students, the option for them to study at least one vocationally oriented subject was the key to their success.

In spite of the undoubted success of our strategy however, the die had been set and by 2016, most of the 'alternative' qualifications mentioned in this book no longer 'counted' in the performance tables. The notable exceptions were BTECs, but even here, the rules had shifted considerably; whereas before 80% of the assessment was portfolio-driven with 20% being assessed through terminal examinations, from 2016, these two proportions were reversed, with around 80% of the course being assessed through formal examinations. This in effect took away the advantage that BTECs used to offer to those pupils who, for whatever reason, failed to demonstrate their full potential through formal exams. Whilst this undoubtedly impacted most negatively on our VYPs, it also affected other more 'typical' pupils. Quite by accident, I was speaking with the extremely bright son of a friend the day I wrote this chapter. He was talking about his experience of school – which in all honesty probably resembled our fictitious 'Acacia Academy.' Totally unprompted, he was bemoaning the fact that he had to sit so many exams at the same time, telling me that he would have really liked to have had had at least some of his courses examined through portfolio work.

Whilst this is of course a purely anecdotal example, it hopefully illustrates the fact that exams simply aren't the way that many people demonstrate all that of which they are capable. This brings us right back to our discussion of equality and equity – it is my contention that in endeavouring to provide his own narrow definition of 'equality of opportunity' by legislating for schools to deliver a 'formal, academic curriculum', Gove actually reduced the equity of those people who, prior to his reforms, were able to access further and subsequently higher education through a mix of GCSE and 'equivalencies'. In short, in trying to prevent schools engaging in what he described to Parliament as a *'Race to the Bottom'* (Gove, 2013), he actually made it harder for those actually at the bottom – specifically our VYPs – to improve their prospects. I realise that this is a bold claim, and I will endeavour to substantiate it in later chapters.

As we saw in the previous chapter, the period between 2012 and 2016 saw three main changes to school assessment policy – an increasing emphasis placed on the English Baccalaureate or 'E-Bacc', the introduction of 'Expected Progress' as a concept, and the policy which dictated that only the first exam sat by a student in any subject would count in the school performance tables. We will now consider the impact of each of these policies on our VYPs.

The impact of the EBac on VYPs was probably, at least at first, minimal, as initially, schools were not judged on the percentage of pupils that passed that particular combination of subjects. This was fortunate for us, as in the first year of its introduction, only 3% of our pupils achieved it. Personally, as I stated earlier, I considered it to be a really stupid and damaging piece of policy (a view I hold to this day), and with the support of our governors, refused to make any change to our successful curriculum model to accommodate it. The policy therefore had no impact on our particular VYPs. However, as the years progressed, schools were expected to show they had plans to increase the percentage of their pupils achieving the EBac. Even if there were no formal 'floor targets' for this, the government did however have other ways of 'nudging' schools to comply. For example, anyone submitting a Free School application or a bid to become a 'Teaching School' would be expected to show 'ambition' for its pupils on this measure.

The change to measuring 'Value-added' through the concept of 'Expected Levels of Progress', which compared pupils' progress from the end of their primary education to the end of their compulsory education at age 16, probably also had little impact on VYPs, again at least at first. As we saw in the last chapter - whilst it was at best of limited value in terms of measuring progress, it didn't change our own practices at all in terms of our determination to enable all our pupils to succeed in these two core skills. Gove's final piece of policy in this period however, namely the decision to count only the first entry of any exam in the school performance tables, was very different. We saw in the last chapter how Gove's decisions to effectively end the practice of 'multiple entry' for (in particular) English and Maths forced schools to choose between what was in the pupils' best interests, and what was in the schools' in terms of their position in performance tables. I explained that, with the agreement of senior leaders and governors, we decided to continue our policy of 'multiple entry' for English and Maths as, alongside improvements in teaching, it had led to very significant improvements in the exam outcomes in these subjects - a fact that was noted by Ofsted in our 2014 inspection. Whilst this policy change had no impact on our own VYPs at first therefore, within three years we were forced to change it, as we will see later. Thus, I would argue that this particular policy did indeed in the medium and longer term have a damaging impact on our own VYPs.

As an aside at this point, I have to state the utter exasperation that I (and I believe many others) feel when a politician imposes his or her personal ideology on practices which the profession finds to be effective, but with which the politician takes personal exception. Gove was particularly prone to this. He abolished CVA on the totally unprovable basis that it 'lowered expectations' for socio-economically deprived pupils. He then introduced the EBac because he believed that his personal choice of what constituted a 'rigorous academic curriculum' should be followed by all pupils in the interests of equality, the philosophical and practical weaknesses of which view we have already discussed. His fight against multiple entry was the third salvo in a battle against schools whom he believed were 'gaming' the system, rather than acting in the best interests of their pupils. If the imposition of his ideology was exasperating however, the disdainful attitude he displayed towards caring, highly qualified and extremely hard-working education professionals was, to my mind, simply insulting.

The final changes in policy relating to the assessment of school performance were the introduction of the 'Attainment 8' (A8) and 'Progress 8' (P8) measures in 2016. As we have already seen, these measures imposed a de facto restriction on pupil choice, and therefore, arguably on their success, as we generally work harder at things that we enjoy. We have already seen how this particularly affected our VYPs, as the majority of them benefitted from taking courses assessed through a mixture of assessments, including portfolio-based work. With the introduction of A8 and P8, these courses were no longer available to them and as such, I would argue that this policy too worked against the interests of VYPs.

If we now stand back for a moment and look at the sweep of legislative change in the 10 years between 2006 and 2016, we can see the following themes emerging:

1: There has been a general trend from a very broad, single headline measure (5+ A-C GCSEs or equivalencies) to a far more tightly defined range of measures under A8 and P8.

2: There has been a movement to measure 'value-added' more precisely. However, with the exception of the period 2006-2010 when CVA was used for this purpose, value-added measures have been based solely on prior attainment. As it has been shown that pupils with lower prior attainment actually make less progress nationally than those with higher prior attainment, we have noted that these measures are at best limited in comparing the rates of progress that different schools enable their pupils to make.

3: There has been a clear centralisation of curriculum policy, and with this, an increase in the distrust shown by government towards schools, as accusations of 'gaming the system' began to be levelled at schools during this period.

Overall, I find this an unhappy picture. Before ending this chapter however, there is one more issue that we need to address – the practice of 'off-rolling'.

In our second chapter, we looked at a number of ways in which some of our vulnerable young people – our VYPs - were denied access to a secondary school. This included, amongst other strategies, 'Fair Access Panels' being slow to admit excluded pupils into a new school, pressure being brought to bear on the parents of disruptive pupils to 'find another school' before their child was expelled, or simply dropping a non-attender off the roll after a few weeks. It is fair to say that these practices had been employed by many schools, to a greater or lesser extent, over a number of years. However, by around 2015/16, the practice had gathered momentum and the practice of 'off-rolling' began to hit the press more regularly. Ofsted defines Off-rolling as: *'The practice of removing a pupil from the school roll without using a permanent exclusion, when the removal is primarily in the best interests of the school, rather than the best interests of the pupil. This includes pressuring a parent to remove their child from the school roll'* (Owen, 2019). The problem with this definition is that it is open to interpretation, as the following will illustrate.

Readers will remember that in 2014 we opened our Alternative Provision (AP) Academy – Aspire, to give young people who had either been expelled already, or who were at serious risk of this, an opportunity to rebuild their lives through a highly personalised education. When a pupil starts at an AP academy, they are typically 'dual-registered', meaning that they remain on the roll of the school from which they transferred, and thus remain that school's responsibility – including for their exam results. However, there is nothing legally to prevent an AP academy having them 'single-registered' on their roll – i.e. assuming total responsibility for the child (including for their exam results. The key date for school performance tables is the pupil census taken in January of Year 11 – if a pupil is not on the roll of the school at that point, even if they have been for their whole career up until that point, then their exam results do not count in the school performance tables. If this is so, then what is there to stop schools simply transferring their 'difficult' pupils to the roll of an AP academy in Y11?

The answer lies in whether or not the move of roll is in the pupil's interests, or those of the school – and that is a matter of judgement. Aspire accepted pupils (including our own) from Year 7 onwards. The hope was always that they would only remain there for a limited amount of time – for two reasons. First, we wanted a so-called 'revolving door' to give as many pupils as possible the opportunity to benefit from the provision – the demand for places always greatly outstripped the supply given that the provision was for the whole of Hull, not just our own pupils. Second, we wanted as many pupils back in mainstream education as possible, as it is there that pupils will find the widest range of opportunity which, in an ideal world, we obviously wanted them to experience. Under these circumstances, dual registration was clearly the appropriate strategy.

It quickly became clear however that the longer a pupil remained at Aspire, the less likely was their return to a mainstream school. We would of course have said that this was in no small measure down to the excellent education they received there, but as time went on, it became clear that for some pupils, the smaller, tightly-controlled environment simply suited them better – which of course was fine. Under these circumstances, there appeared to be little benefit in keeping them on the roll of their original school, and many transferred totally to Aspire's roll. We argued that single registration in this case was most definitely in the interest of the pupil – knowing that they wouldn't have to return to their original school was a source of security and helped them to thrive in their new environment.

However, with the introduction of Progress 8, schools were under increasing pressure in the school performance tables. As we saw in earlier chapters, assessments were almost totally exam-based, limiting the ways in which pupils could demonstrate success. Although P8 is supposed to be a 'value-added' measure, we also saw that this is at best debatable, as pupils who come in with lower levels of attainment also make lower levels of progress. Schools with a high proportion of these pupils faced ever-increasing challenges to achieve a positive P8 score, and it is against this background that 'off-rolling' gained momentum as a practice. At this point, the situation became very murky indeed. At ASA, the removal of multiple entry for GCSEs, the removal of GCSE equivalencies as courses and the introduction of the curriculum requirements of Progress 8 had all made our pupils' lives far harder, as well as our own in terms of the school performance tables.

So, with all this in mind, we began to look at the possibility of transferring more of our pupils to the roll of Aspire. We estimated that for at least 10-15 % of our year-group (around 20-30 pupils), pursuing a curriculum based on the exigencies of Progress 8 was most definitely not in their interests. For those pupils, it would have been far better to have allowed them to follow a curriculum which included subjects whose results did not 'count' in the performance tables, but which would have nonetheless been of benefit to them. We could of course have moved them to our own AP academy Aspire at the start of Y10, 'single registering' them with Aspire, and losing our accountability for them in terms of their exam results. Such an approach would, in my view, have been fully justified providing that the moves had been carefully planned on a pupil-by-pupil basis.

However, by that time Aspire was completely full, so we considered another approach whereby these pupils would indeed be on Aspire's roll, supported by them and following a highly personalised curriculum, but spending much of their time at ASA. Under this model, the pupils would have some of their teaching delivered by Aspire staff, and some by ASA's. The dilemma was this – by remaining on ASA's roll, the performance criteria of Progress 8 would have required us to drive these pupils down a road to which we knew they were not suited. But to move them to Aspire's roll and enable them to follow a curriculum to which they were far more suited involved a very significant risk with respect to Ofsted, who by this time were highly attuned to any practices that had the appearance of 'off-rolling' (Roberts, 2019). Having just come out of 'Special Measures', and with Leadership and Management in the academy now being judged 'Good', the very last thing we wanted as an academy was another run-in with Ofsted.

Sadly, we decided that on this occasion, we could not act in those pupils' best interests. These pupils were, of course, our VYPs. In hindsight however, we almost certainly dodged a bullet, as around that time, a number of academies were beginning to be criticised for exactly this practice. I have chosen quite deliberately not to highlight, reference or comment on any of these cases, as I have no more knowledge of the detail of any of the examples of this beyond that which was written in the press. I will however comment on the words of a DfE spokesperson about this issue. In essence, the official said that any school 'off-rolling' pupils on the basis of their academic results was, quite simply, breaking the law. Given the severity of the accusation, I find this a very lazy charge, as it 'lumps together' what are in effect three different practices - simply dropping a pupil off roll without ensuring they are enrolled anywhere else (which is certainly illegal), encouraging' a pupil to 'find another school' before they are expelled (which may well be morally questionable, but not illegal) and moving a pupil to the roll of an AP academy. Here, the charge of 'off-rolling' would imply that it is better for a pupil to remain on the roll of a school to whose curriculum they are inherently not suited, rather than to be moved to the roll of an Alternative Provision (AP) academy, where they are much more likely to thrive. As such, the statement provides a strong disincentive against pupils being moved to AP academies, even though to do so could well be in their best interests.

More generally, government ministers, the DfE and local councils alike are displaying a breath-taking naivety if they expect schools **not** to look at how any school might improve its performance measures as and when they develop. In 2013, it was my decision to act in the interests of *pupils* and **not** to change our curriculum in the interests of *performance tables* that was, in large part, the reason we were put into Special Measures by Ofsted in 2016. At the time, I believed that a reasonable Ofsted team would understand and even applaud such a principled stand. However, it turned out that I had been totally naïve, and far too over-confident in my own powers of persuasion. With inspection being such a battleground and indeed a fight for survival, it is no wonder that school leaders look for any and every way in which the performance metrics for which they are accountable can improve.   This is an issue to which we will return in more detail in the next section.

Returning to the central theme of this chapter – specifically, the impact of the 'Progress 8' regime on our VYPs, I think we can now note the following points:

1. Under Progress 8, schools are accountable for the extent of success their pupils demonstrate in filling each of the 8 'pots' of qualifications;
2. Typically, our VYPs will not perform to the best of their ability within these constraints;
3. Although purportedly a measure of value-added, we know that statistically, pupils who are lower-attaining when they arrive at secondary school make less progress nationally than their higher-attaining peers. Many of these will be our VYPs. This being the case, schools with higher numbers of lower-attaining pupils on entry are at proportionally higher risk of a lower P8 score;

4. Lower P8 scores (as we shall see in our next chapter) put a school at greater risk of criticism and intervention from Ofsted;
5. Single-registering pupils in an AP academy runs the risks of a charge of 'off-rolling';
6. Faced with all of the above, schools may well feel that they have a 'perverse incentive' to require VYPs to study a curriculum to which they are not best suited, in the interests of the school.

My conclusion for this chapter therefore is that the performance measure of Progress 8 most certainly works against the interests of our VYPs. Indeed, there is a huge irony that, in order to avoid charges of acting in the best interests of the school and the pupil (for example by placing the pupil on the roll of an Alternative Provision Academy or at least letting them follow an alternative programme, even if this doesn't 'count' in the performance tables in the same way as a more 'traditional' programme), schools are effectively having to do precisely that – require our VYPs to follow a curriculum based on filling the Progress 8 'pots' to mitigate as far as possible what could be low P8 scores. With this somewhat depressing thought in mind, we will now turn to look at the third area of education policy – Ofsted.

Part Three – the Development of Policy around Ofsted

Abstract.

This section of the book looks at how changes in Ofsted policy over the years has impacted the interests of our VYPs. A key issue raised is that when coupled with the changes in performance metrics outlined in previous chapters, the increasingly higher levels of accountability brought in through Ofsted has in many cases actually worked against schools' efforts to improve outcomes for our VYPs.

Chapter 10 – The Links between School Performance Data and Ofsted.

Abstract:

This is another chapter which is fairly technical in nature, in which I discuss the differences between criterion referencing, norm-referencing, and norm-referencing linked to comparable outcomes, demonstrating that with respect to the latter, it is mathematically impossible for all pupils to achieve a good grade in their GCSEs, a policy which impacts our VYPs disproportionally. The chapter also deals with Gove's failure to understand that, in requiring all schools to be 'Good' (i.e., better than 'average'), he was in fact asking for something which, again, was mathematically impossible.

The role played by Ofqual in developing these performance criteria is also discussed, and this in turn is related back to the development of government curriculum requirements which have all but eliminated the possibility of pupils studying courses assessed through criterion-referencing (which unlike GCSEs, all pupils can pass if they reach a particular standard). These factors are then brought together to explain how much harder it now is for our VYPs to demonstrate success in their studies. The point is made here that Ofsted have to inspect within the remit they are given; this chapter discusses how changes in this respect have impacted on schools, drawing in part on my experiences when I was training to become an inspector myself. It also sets the scene for a fuller discussion on the impact of Ofsted on our VYPs in Part Four, when we look at potential solutions to the problem of how schools can better serve our VYPs.

'Rock the Boat'

(The Hues Corporation, 1973)

A central contention of this book is that education policy on curriculum, metrics as expressed in performance tables, and inspection practice has been developed in a somewhat haphazard fashion, and that a consequence of this is that the most vulnerable young people in schools – our 'VYP's – are increasingly at risk of losing out. To illustrate this, we saw in the last chapter how the current 'Progress 8' metric leaves schools with little option other than to force as many pupils as possible down a curriculum pathway made up of qualifications which fall into all of the 8 'pots' which 'count' in the current iteration of the performance tables. We noted that these are basically all GCSEs, with the vast majority of 'equivalencies', many of which can motivate our VYPs, no longer counting. To fully appreciate why this 'matters' so much to schools, we now need to look at our third area of education policy – the inspectorate Ofsted.

Just as whole libraries have been written on the relative merits of different curriculum models, so have countless articles been produced on Ofsted. I do not intend to 'compare and contrast' the many and various views expressed elsewhere, but rather, paint a picture from my own experiences, both as a school leader going through inspection, and as a trainee inspector in my own right. In both this and the following chapter, I will illustrate the links between school performance data and Ofsted inspections, and then use these observations to look at their impact on our 'VYPs'.

I can still remember the interview for my application to undergo Ofsted training. The inspector asked me the most basic question: 'What is the aim of Ofsted?' I think I mumbled something about 'holding schools to account' and 'helping schools to improve' – both of which are wrong. The stated aim of Ofsted is to give information to parents, so that they can make informed choices about which school their child will attend. This of course poses an immediate problem, as for many parents, there will be no choice if the 'most popular' local school their children could attend is over-subscribed, or indeed if there is in effect only one school in the area at all.

Putting this (admittedly quite serious) issue to one side however, it is worth spending a few moments looking at what Ofsted actually measure. This has changed over the years, but the current categories are:

- Quality of Education,
- Behaviour and Attitudes,
- Personal Development; and
- Leadership and Management.

There is then an overall judgment of one of four words: - 'Outstanding', 'Good', 'Requires Improvement' or 'Inadequate'. Schools that receive a judgment of 'Inadequate' are deemed either to have 'Serious Weaknesses' or, in the most serious cases, to require 'Special Measures', the latter judgement being given when the inspection team believes that the leadership of the school does not have the capacity to improve itself. In either of these two cases however, a judgement of 'inadequate' for a local-authority maintained school leads to an 'academy order', and the running of the school will be handed to a Multi-Academy Trust (MAT). If an academy judged 'inadequate' is already part of a MAT, then it could be 're-brokered' to another MAT.

Ofsted arrives at its judgement of a school through a combination of 'pre-inspection' analysis of performance data and other documentation, and then a series of lesson observations and interviews with pupils, staff and governors over either a one-day period (if the school currently holds a judgement of 'good' or better) or two-day full inspection. The relative weight attributed to school performance data versus what inspectors observe in classrooms has varied over the years. This is important, as at various points in the history of the inspectorate, judgements have been 'linked'. For example, in 2016, 'teaching and learning' could not be judged to be 'good' overall, even if good teaching was observed during the inspection, if the school performance data indicated otherwise.

This may on the surface seem reasonable – but we need to remember the statistical evidence that nationally, pupils with lower prior attainment also make lower progress than their higher attaining peers. Thus, in a school with lower-attaining pupils on entry, I would argue it is perfectly possible for good teaching to be the norm, even if levels of progress appear to be lower than average. The thinking behind this was perhaps best illustrated by an exchange between Michael Gove and the Education Select Committee in 2012. In this exchange, he was asked the following question:

Chair:
if 'good' requires pupil performance to exceed the national average, and if all schools must be good, how is this mathematically possible?

Michael Gove:
By getting better all the time.

Chair:
So, it is possible, is it?

Michael Gove:
It is possible to get better all the time.

Chair:
Were you better at literacy than numeracy, Secretary of State?

Michael Gove:
I cannot remember. (Gove, 2012)

Gove's failure to understand the mathematically impossible goal that all schools must be better than average perhaps explains some of the thinking behind the Ofsted schedules that were in place at least until recently. To illustrate this point further, we need however to take a closer look at the definitions of 'progress from starting points' that we looked at in the last chapter, and which form a key part of the judgements that Ofsted make on school performance. Here, we can begin to see how the various strands of educational policy begin to cause problems when taken as a whole.

We saw in chapter 11 above that, although Progress 8 purports to measure 'value -added', it takes no account of the fact that nationally, lower attaining pupils make less progress than higher attaining pupils (as we saw above in our discussions on the concept of 'Expected Progress'), nor does it make any allowances for pupils' socio-economic background. This in itself is bad enough in terms of the availability of information on which inspectors have to make judgements. Previously, a positive 'CVA' score could, as we saw, mitigate significantly low attainment scores for a school. Faced with a lack of 'official' data in this respect however, schools such as ASA suddenly had an uphill battle to persuade inspectors that 'Value-added' was high, even if attainment appeared to be low. However, as we will now see, the assessment principles underpinning the Progress 8 metric exacerbated these two factors, causing in effect a 'triple whammy' for schools in this respect.

Readers will remember that exams taken at 16 and 18 are assessed in one of three ways – by coursework, by exams, or by a mixture of the two. Examples of the former would be the old-style Science BTEC at both level 2 (GCSE-equivalent) and Level 3 (A-level equivalent). An example of the latter would be a typical Maths GCSE or A-level, in which all assessment is carried out through exams. Courses combining an element of both methods include the most recent BTEC courses, where grades are awarded on a combination of traditional exams and portfolios of coursework, or up until quite recently, GCSE Science which included an element of assessed practical work, coupled with traditional exams.

To understand the system fully however, we looked at the concepts of criterion-referencing and norm- referencing. Under the former, students are given a grade according to the standard they reach. Thus, theoretically, if all the nation's pupils were taught extremely well in a subject assessed this way, then they could all pass. Up until relatively recently, all BTECs and a suite of other so-called 'equivalent' qualifications were assessed in this way. GCSEs however are based on the principle of 'norm-referencing'. Under this system, only a certain percentage of pupils nationally are ever allowed to achieve a particular grade, no matter how hard they work. Although the system does allow for small annual variations of up to around 3% nationally, broadly, this means that around 35% of all pupils will achieve a grade lower than the current minimum pass grade of a level 4 in any given subject, no matter how brilliantly they have all been taught, or how hard they have revised. Ofqual, the government's exam regulator, claims that this is to ensure that pupils aren't unfairly penalised by a particularly 'hard' exam, nor advantaged by a particularly 'easy' exam in any given year. Thus norm-referencing places a cap or limit on the number of pupils able to achieve exam success.

However, this restriction is increased further when we look at a third concept involved in our exam system, that of 'comparable outcomes' used to set the threshold scores for individual GCSE grades (for example 80% for a 9 – the top grade – or 65% for a 6 – a good middling grade). From 2016 onwards, Ofqual based these 'grade thresholds' on the results that all the pupils sitting their GCSEs achieved nationally five years previously, when they took their SATs exams in the last year of their primary education. In other words, if the nation's pupils performed particularly well at primary school in 2011, the thresholds for the various grades awarded in 2016 would reflect this by being higher than in previous years.

Thus, when combined with the notion of comparable outcomes, norm-referencing doesn't just place a limit on the number of pupils able to achieve any given grade, it bases that limit on the national average success rate for Reading, Writing and Maths achieved by that very same year group across the country when they were in Year 6. The aim is to avoid so-called 'grade inflation'. The crucial point to understand here however is that in setting these restrictions, Ofqual was effectively making it impossible for all schools to demonstrate improvement. This can be illustrated by the following theoretical scenario:

Let's imagine that in 2011, all the secondary school leaders in the country had attended a conference organised by Gove, at which he pointed to the high standards now being achieved by pupils nationally at age 11. The secondary headteachers all agreed to work doubly hard to ensure these achievements were replicated in their own schools, and for the next five years, they did so. Indeed, they worked so hard, that year on year, progress of the nation's teenagers leapt forward. All the headteachers were very excited when their pupils sat their exams in 2016, believing that the fruits of their labour would be evident to all in the form of a much higher rate of exam passes. To their dismay however, the results were similar to those of previous years – what had happened? The cause of their misery was the immutable principle of comparable outcomes, which meant that, in spite of all their hard work, the percentage of pupils gaining each particular GCSE grade was still limited. Although the pupils did indeed perform better nationally in 2016 than in previous years, the principle of 'comparable outcomes' meant that in effect, the thresholds for achieving each grade had been raised correspondingly, to take into account the higher levels of progress they had made at the end of their primary education in comparison to previous years. In this way, it had in effect become impossible for all schools to improve.

But that is not all. Whilst grade boundaries are altered to take account of any change in the perceived level of difficulty in the papers for that year, KS2 SAT grade boundaries (upon which primary school performance is judged) are not linked to performance in any previous exams - any pupil who reaches the standard can gain any given grade. Theoretically, it is therefore possible for every primary-school pupil to achieve a minimum pass grade, or indeed any grade. This is in direct contrast to GCSE outcomes. Thus, whilst it is theoretically possible for every primary school in the land to show improvement in the performance of their pupils, it is not possible for secondary schools to do so, as *their* performance criteria is based on norm-referencing linked to the outcomes obtained at age 11 in the KS2 SAT exams. In short, the system used to judge school performance simply isn't fair, with secondary schools being the losers in this respect. Ofqual, perhaps not unsurprisingly, categorically refute this view on their website, claiming that their approach to maintaining standards does not prevent schools from improving their own results even when national results remain steady, and saying that they will consider evidence from exam boards if results are significantly higher or lower than predicted (Jadhav, 2017). They then quote research from Cambridge assessment which supports their view that norm-referencing based on comparable outcomes does indeed enable individual schools to improve (Benton, 2016).

At this point, we do risk going down another 'rabbit hole'. The research paper referred to here (*ibid*) would appear to conclude that the extent to which the system of comparable outcomes limits rises in exam success nationally is, well, limited. However, the author of the research paper notes that: *'Nonetheless, it is certainly true that the regulator is actively attempting to keep any such rises under control' (ibid).*

This, to my mind, highlights the central flaw of the argument presented in the paper. The author argues that there is little evidence that grades have varied that much since the introduction of comparable outcomes (although he does reference a couple of exceptions) in comparison with any so-called 'grade inflation' prior to that point. However, from 2011 onwards – the point at which comparable outcomes were introduced - the DfE's accountability regime forced schools into making rapid improvements in GCSEs, as many needed to move away from BTEC courses and other equivalencies completely. And it is during that period precisely that, to repeat the researcher's own words: *'it is certainly true that the regulator is actively attempting to keep any such rises under control' (ibid).*

This same paper then goes on to quote Glenys Stacey, the Head of Ofqual at the time, writing in September 2012 to the then Head of Ofsted Michael Wilshaw, pointing out that the 'comparable outcomes' approach does indeed make it less likely that schools as a whole will be able to evidence improvement with better exam results year-on-year, and that this has implications for Ofsted in terms of the extent that exam results are a significant part of the inspection evidence-base. To labour the point – the system of norm-referencing based on comparable outcomes can thus be seen to work directly against the expectation that all schools will continue to improve their pupils' exam results.

If we now come out of this particular rabbit hole and blink our eyes, it is worth reminding ourselves again why all of is this is so significant. Up until the introduction in 2016 of 'Progress 8' as the main measure of school performance, the consequences of norm-referencing were mitigated by the fact that pupils were able to take both GCSEs and equivalencies, the latter being criterion referenced (meaning that anyone who reached the standard could pass). Moreover, even the norm-referenced GCSEs could be taken more than once, improving both pupils' chances of passing and schools' chances of demonstrating success. In short, up until 2016, schools were free to allow their pupils to follow the pathway best suited to them, without fear of 'bombing' in performance tables.

As teaching improved, this improvement was clearly acknowledged in criterion-referenced subjects as there was no limit on the number of pupils who could pass – they just had to meet the relevant criteria. These freedoms were of course incredibly important in particular for schools in areas of high social deprivation, in which families are far less well-placed to support their children in exam preparation compared to those in more affluent areas. We saw however that from 2015 onwards successive changes in government policy stripped away all those freedoms:

- For the 2015 series of exams, functional skill equivalents in English and Maths were withdrawn from performance tables;
- From 2016, school were only allowed to account a pupil's first entry in any subject, and BTEC assessment was changed to include a much higher proportion of assessment exams taken under formal test conditions;
- From 2016, with the introduction of 'Progress 8', schools were only allowed to count one 'equivalency' in their performance tables, with all other subjects needing to be full GCSEs;
- From 2018, the practical 'coursework assessed' element of the science exam was removed; and
- From 2019, the relative weighting of the practical 'speaking' element of the languages' exam was reduced from 25% to 10%.

This is why the changes mattered so much. By 2018, almost all examinations taken by pupils at 16 were norm-referenced, based on comparable outcomes.   This had the effect of creating an educational dystopia – a GCSE exam version of the 'Hunger Games'

- in which every year, around 35% of pupils would be destined to achieve a grade lower than a 'basic pass' (i.e., a grade 1, 2, or 3) in any given subject. I can remember speaking to my last group of Y11 pupils during the 2017/18 academic year in exactly these terms, imploring them to take advantage of all the additional classes and support we gave them, to ensure that they ended up within the top 65% of pupils who would gain a good grade, and I am sure that this encouragement was being replicated in schools across the land. Returning now to Ofsted, it is my contention that the systems that are now underpinning school performance data, particularly that of norm-referencing linked to comparable outcomes, makes it almost impossible for every secondary school to demonstrate good levels of improvement.

If the data systems themselves give a less than secure basis on which to make judgements, then the process of 'lesson observations', which form a key part of inspections, is even more subjective. For many years, inspectors would go into lessons, observe for, typically, 25 minutes or so, and then give a 'judgement' on that lesson – ranging from 'outstanding' to 'inadequate'. This particular system was widely criticised for fairly obvious reasons, the main one perhaps being that a 25-minute section of one lesson did not necessarily display 'typicality' of practice, and that a judgement based on that was in fact fairly meaningless and highly unfair on individual teachers. Consequently, the outcomes of lesson observations during an inspection are now judged 'in the round', rather than individually. Whilst this may have removed an element of unfairness with respect to individual teachers however, this 'rounded' judgement is still based on a series of 25-minute observations which, arguably, still fail to present a picture of typicality. The situation becomes more concerning when you consider the vagaries of individual inspectors. Here again, I am speaking from my own experience, but it is experience borne out of my own training to become an inspector, five full inspections and two monitoring visits in my own school, and three inspections of other schools in the MAT of which was CEO.

I never wanted to be an Ofsted inspector, but most certainly wanted to ensure that I really understood the system. When I undertook my training in 2014, it was on the back of a government drive to attract more 'serving practitioners' into the system, believing it would bring more credibility to a much criticised organisation. As a consequence of this drive, 'my' cohort of trainees was full of serving headteachers and other senior leaders. This should have given us great confidence, and so it was that we approached our first task – assessing a pre-recorded Y9 Geography lesson. At the end of the task, we all had to 'grade' the lesson, giving reasons for our gradings. Given the levels of expertise and professionalism in the room, you might have expected a fairly consistent level of judgement. However, the assessment of the lesson covered the whole range – from 'outstanding' to 'inadequate'. I have to say that I was astonished by this, (and also quietly smug that I had personally 'got it right'). Over the course of the next months, I finished my training, but never completed my 'sign-off' inspection. This was because the government changed the rules during my course, effectively requiring inspectors to sign up for formal amounts of time to inspect rather than just 'when it suited them'. I was too busy planning our Multi Academy Trust at the time, and was not prepared to commit to a set number of inspections. I did find the training useful, but my overriding memory was that of the first task we all undertook. Whilst it is true that the training was meant to standardise our judgements as a group over time, this initial vast discrepancy in judgement made me seriously question the reliability of 'one-off' lesson observations at all.

Straight away, it is clear that the stakes of an Ofsted inspection are very high. A judgement of anything less than 'Good' often puts the headteacher's job (and possibly those of the school's senior leaders) in immediate jeopardy. The drive to return to a judgement of 'Good' is gruelling; teachers know this, and so it can be harder subsequently to attract staff. Additionally, schools placed in Special Measures are banned from taking on Newly Qualified staff, so ironically, the worse the Ofsted judgement, the harder it can become for the school to recruit staff at precisely the time when, in an era of teacher shortages, this is most needed.

Statistically, schools in deprived areas (as measured for example by the proportion of pupils eligible for Free School Meals) are far more likely to be judged less than 'good'. Indeed, in 2018-19, they were twice as likely to be judged either 'requiring improvement' or 'inadequate' compared to schools in the least deprived areas (Walker, 2023). Headteachers are of course aware of this. Back in 2004 when I took on my first headship, I was excited by the prospect of being able to take on the challenge of restoring the fortunes of a struggling secondary school. It never once crossed my mind that in doing so I could be out of a job within a couple of years. Buoyed with the success of this first headship, I approached my leadership of Archbishop Sentamu Academy with the same level of optimism. Whilst I was aware that failure to make improvements could have cost me my job, 'football manager syndrome' for headteachers hadn't quite taken hold by that point, so again, I felt (probably naively) pretty fearless. However, rolling the clock forward to the present day, I would not be so confident, as we will see in the next chapter. Suffice it to say that whilst I was Head of ASA between 2008 and 2018, since that point there have been no fewer than four headteachers, three of them within the last three years.

Chapter 11 – ASA's Journey into 'Special Measures'

Abstract:

This chapter illustrates further the issues I raised in chapter 10 through an account of ASA's disastrous 2016 inspection, pointing out in particular the very strong link between school performance data and Ofsted outcomes. It opens up the account of our journey into Special Measures, and the impact that this had on the whole school, including, of course, on our VYPs.

'The Wall'

Pink Floyd, 1979

It would be fair to say that aspects of what follows here could be seen as highly subjective, especially with respect to my views on the role that school performance data plays in terms of 'confirmation bias' for Ofsted inspectors. However, it is worth emphasising that my comments are based on my experience of 6 full Ofsted inspections in 4 different schools over a period of around 15 years.

If you have visited an optician recently, you may well have been asked to look into a machine and focus on the image of a hot air balloon. As you are doing that, the machine clicks and whirrs and, apparently, gives the optician a pretty good idea of what your prescription should be. The tests that follow ('tell me, which is clearer – is it A.....or B?) merely confirm this initial computerised assessment of your vision, possibly with a few minor tweaks to produce your final prescription. In my experience, school performance data in each of the six inspections I have experienced works exactly like the clicking and whirring machine at the optician – it gives inspectors a solid (in their view) assessment of how well the school is performing, with all the observations and interviews of the inspection itself then being used to back up this initial assessment, albeit with some possible tweaks.

Ofsted would of course refute this. In particular, the most recent inspection framework is supposed to take the quality of the curriculum and observed teaching more into account, to enable, in theory at least, a potential 'decoupling' of school performance data and what is observed during an inspection. In other words, without going into too much detail on the intricacies of the Ofsted inspection handbook, it should be possible for a school with relatively low performance data still to be judged as 'good' if inspectors see good teaching and learning during the inspection, and are also happy that the curriculum offered to pupils is of good quality.

I can't comment on how well this theoretically more nuanced model has worked in practice – first, I haven't experienced an inspection under that framework and second, the pandemic undoubtedly brought its own anomalies to the inspection process, making comparisons with recent inspection outcomes arguably less robust. Personally however, I would suspect that the link between performance data and final Ofsted outcomes remains strong, not least because of the effort involved in justifying an inspection outcome that looks 'abnormal'. As a minimum, it is still certainly far harder for a school with relatively poor performance data to achieve a judgement of 'good'. Bearing in mind everything we have said up until now about lower-attaining pupils making less progress, it is still harder for schools with proportionally higher levels of socially disadvantaged pupils (our VYPs) to achieve good, as the same article in the journal SchoolsWeek, referenced in the previous chapter, makes clear *(ibid, P83)*

Returning to my own experience of Ofsted however, the link between performance data and overall outcomes was very clear, and very tight. The first encounter was in 1999, when I was Head of the Languages department at what was then Arden School and Language College. The performance data for our department was particularly strong, and it was therefore no surprise that many of the lessons were graded outstanding, with the Languages Department as a whole highly praised. The school (and thus our department) benefitted from being located in a socio-economically highly advantaged area, and it was no surprise therefore that pupils were judged to be academically highly successful. This is not in any way meant to detract from the quality of the teaching there – it was indeed very good – it's just that as we have seen, pupils who have higher attainment on entry make better progress nationally.

My second encounter with Ofsted was at Langley School in 2001, where I was a Deputy Headteacher. Although generally in a more advantaged area, its catchment area served communities with pockets of deprivation. Performance data at the time (based on the '5+ GCSEs at 'C' grade or above) was generally good overall, and it was no surprise when at the end of the inspection, was school was also judged to be 'Good' overall. When I moved to Campion School in 2004, I was fortunate that the performance data metric was still '5+ A-C at 'C' grade or above. By 2006, we had managed to show significant improvement on this measure so even though we were below the national average, our rapid improvement over a two-year period was praised by inspectors. Based on this data, leadership and management was judged to be 'Outstanding' and the school overall, 'Good'. Had the inspection occurred in 2008 however, I'm not sure we would have had such a glowing report, as by then, the metric had changed to '5+ A-C including English and Maths'. At the time, whereas well over 50% of pupils were achieving the old metric, fewer that 30% of pupils were achieving the new one. This meant that, in 2008, the school was identified as one of Education Secretary Ed Balls' 'National Challenge' schools, in which pupils were performing poorly in either English and / or Maths (in our case, Maths was the weakness). Happily, however, the school continued to improve after the 2006 inspection, and it has remained a 'good' school to this day.

My experience with Ofsted continued at ASA when in 2011, we had our first inspection. At the time, as described in chapter 11, a range of performance measures were in place, including 'CVA' which took into account pupils' socio-economic background. During our first three years, our exam results improved well, and even though the metric of '5+A-C including English and Maths' was still relatively low (certainly below the national average), pupils were scoring well in the overall range of GCSEs and equivalencies that were permitted at the time, and were demonstrating good levels on 'value-added' on the CVA metric. It was therefore no surprise that overall, our academy was judged to be securely 'good' on all counts, as extracts from that report will illustrate. The opening statement noted that :

'Archbishop Sentamu Academy provides a good quality of education. Within its first two years, it has developed some outstanding features and established a strong ethos reflecting its Christian values. Outcomes are mainly good, and students' confidence in their safety is exceptionally strong. Systems for care, support and guidance are highly effective and the academy works very well with its partners to promote the progress and welfare of its students. As a result, achievement and enjoyment have rapidly improved for every group of students. The academy promotes equal opportunity outstandingly well. Its motto, 'Aspire, Serve, Achieve', is increasingly meaningful to a great many students, who do their best to help their academy' (Susan Bowles, 2011)

In terms of pupils' academic achievement, the report noted:

'The quality of students' learning is good. Good behaviour and positive attitudes to learning are expected and nearly always shown... Students' attainment is average and improving across the board. The academy has narrowed the gap between boys' and girls' attainment. All groups do at least as well, overall, as similar students in other schools, because the academy adapts provision well to their needs and provides determined support at the first sign of underachievement. However, attainment in English and mathematics is still below average. When all subjects are taken into account, the progress students make is outstandingly good. In the key subjects of English and mathematics, progress has been satisfactory, but is improving well. Every group of students makes at least good progress, including those with special educational needs and/or disabilities. Higher prior-attaining students, whose progress has been in line, were the exception. This year, more students are on track to attain GCSE grades B, A or A* than in previous years' (ibid).

These comments reflect the breadth of the metrics in place at the time – the fact that our English and Maths scores were below average was balanced the fact that when all subjects were taken into consideration, progress was good. Indeed, when the whole report is read, once again, we see that the overall judgements followed the school performance metric. This experience was repeated in our inspection of 2014 – as we saw in Chapter 2, exam results had continued to improve year on year and even though by this time 'CVA' was no longer there to acknowledge the challenges we faced owing to our pupils' socio-economic background, the overall points score achieved by our pupils was very high. This being the case, even though performance in English and Maths was not as high by comparison, overall judgements were extremely favourable, and we narrowly missed a judgement of 'Outstanding' overall. Once again, the Ofsted judgement had closely tracked the performance data. All of which brings us to our disastrous inspection of 2016.

To recap quickly – in 2013, Gove had determined that only pupils' first entries would count in the school performance tables from 2015 onwards. As I explained in chapter 11, we had found that by giving pupils the opportunity to sit key exams in English and Maths more than once, their chances of success improved dramatically. We decided that we would continue with the policy, as we judged it to be in the best interest of our pupils, even though we realised it paint a falsely negative picture of our academy.

The first consequence of our decision was our position in a new table of '55 similar schools'. This particular performance measure, introduced in 2013, placed schools into rough groups based on their pupils' combined average prior attainment on entry and then 'ranked' them from 1-55, with 1 being the 'top' school on this particular measure. Our decision to carry on with multiple entry for pupils in English and Maths meant that whilst our position in this particular table up until that point had been broadly in the top half, in 2015 it was 55 – we were right at the bottom. It is important to note that nothing else had changed. Leadership and staffing of these two key departments was stable, we had continued to do our very best to improve teaching practice, and the final results for pupils in these two subjects continued to be broadly in line with those of previous years. The only change was in the metric itself. What this also showed however was that we were probably one of the only, if not the only, school to persist with our early-entry policy – certainly at least in comparison to the other 54 schools in our group. We were in trouble.

I will never know whether or not it was our position in that table, or the anonymous letter sent to Ofsted by a member of our staff, that triggered our inspection of May 5th. 2016. I expect that it was the awful picture painted by the new metric which put us 'on Ofsted's radar', and that it was the letter which gave them the excuses for the inspection being carried out as a 'no-notice emergency'. Whatever the case, the events of the next two days were probably the most miserable of my life. The inspection itself was highly partial in terms of the evidence looked at by inspectors, and highly flawed in terms of the process that was followed. Rather than go into those issues in detail here, a full copy of the subsequent complaint can be found at Appendix Two.

For the purposes of this chapter however, it is sufficient to note that once again, although this time to our great disadvantage, the various judgements contained in the report closely reflected the results of the new metric which assessed schools' performance on the results of pupils' first entry in English and Maths. So, what would a fair outcome have looked like? Over the previous 8 years, we had worked with a school improvement company, all of whose consultants were serving Ofsted inspectors, to ensure that the improvements we believed we were making were validated externally. The process for doing this was two-fold. Firstly, we submitted ourselves to an annual 'consultative review' which followed the Ofsted schedule, and this was followed up with any support that was deemed necessary to address areas of concern.

The reviews themselves were rigorous and were, needless to say, highly unpopular with staff. The support we received afterwards however was extremely helpful, and helped ensure that we remained focussed on improving the quality of our provision. Having worked with us for 8 years, their overall judgement was that at that particular point, we were somewhere between 'good' and 'requiring improvement', mainly down to (at the time) staffing weaknesses in Maths and Science. I completely agreed with this, and at the time of the inspection, making improvements in those two areas were our top two priorities. What I hadn't expected however was this company's response to our 2016 inspection. In a highly unusual move, they too wrote a letter of complaint – addressed in this case to the Regional Schools Commissioner – with a view to trying to obtain a re-inspection for us. A copy of that letter can be found at Appendix Three. In the event, neither my complaint to Ofsted nor Incyte's complaint to the Regional Schools' Commissioner were upheld, and the judgement remained. Once again, we saw the inextricable link between raw performance data and an inspection outcome – this time very much to our great disadvantage.

At this point, it would have been normal for directors to have resigned, heads to roll (almost certainly mine), a new leadership team to have been put in place and a series of 6-weekly follow-up inspections by Ofsted to have been instigated. In the event, none of these took place. Almost immediately after the inspection, I wrote a very large action plan, submitted it to Ofsted, and then waited. I expected it to be returned with all sorts of corrections and comments but heard nothing, so waited some more. Finally, just before the summer break, we received word that the plan had been approved without any further additions requested. Perhaps unkindly, I remember thinking at the time that it had somehow got lost, and that the inspector reviewing it must have signed it off just before getting on a plane for their holidays.

Wherever the truth lay, we breathed a half-sigh of relief and, completely exhausted, broke up for the Summer. When the results for that year's GCSE results came through three months later, we were delighted to see that our 'Progress 8' score had risen that year from -0.94 to   -0.17. It is true to say that 2015's score was artificially low – a product of our decision to carry on with our policy of 'Early Entry' in English and Maths outlined in previous chapters. However, a score or -0.17 was actually not bad. It was above a new threshold of -0.3 which had been established as an indicator that a school might be deemed by Ofsted to be 'coasting', and we discovered that several secondary schools with a P8 score of between 0.0 (average) and -0.3 were actually being judged as 'Good', not least those in socio-economic areas which were highly challenging. These observations all gave us great encouragement that a monitoring visit in the early part of the new academic year could lead to our being removed from Special Measures. We just needed that visit to take place.

Chapter 12: ASA's Journey out of 'Special Measures'

Abstract:

This chapter chronicles the dramatic events that followed our judgement of 'Special Measures'. It chronicles our peremptory removal from the DfE's 'Mandarin Excellence Programme, the DfE's underhand attempts to break up our Trust behind our backs, the failure of Ofsted for over a year to conduct the normal monitoring inspections to which we were entitled, and how we fought and won each of these battles.

' Livin' on a prayer'

Bon Jovi, 1986

After much deliberation, I decided to include an account of 'what happened next' in the book as it shows yet again how the various strands of government policy conspired to make things worse still, not better, as we worked incredibly hard to tackle the challenges confronting us. Sadly, the combined impact of events once again meant that our VYPs were not as well catered for as they would have been in the absence of the Ofsted judgement, as we will now see.

Returning from our Summer holidays, and buoyed with the relative success of our GCSE exams, we fully expected a monitoring visit from Ofsted within weeks, but by the end of that first term, none had occurred, the only contact being one telephone call as I shall explain below. We were of course running on adrenalin the whole time, redoubling our efforts to meet the demands of our highly ambitious action plan – but – nothing. No further contact from Ofsted whatsoever. By the end of the Easter term of 2017, we were still waiting. We believed that were making good progress against our plans, but nobody came to check, so we waited some more. May came and went, along with the anniversary of the inspection – but still further contact. You could be forgiven for wondering why, after such a damning initial report, we were keen for inspectors to revisit.

The answer of course is that we really wanted to show them how much we had improved – not just for our own sakes and the sake of our pupils, but because when a school is in Special Measures, they are barred from employing Newly Qualified staff. In an area where it is traditionally hard to recruit anyway, the failure of Ofsted to at least give us *the chance* to show them that Special Measures were no longer required meant that a vital source of new staff was cut off from us for a whole year – making our job of improving even harder. Worse, this lack of a visit was giving rise to an even greater threat as we shall see shortly. However, June and July also passed and so, by the end of that academic year, with still no word from Ofsted, the summer break arrived with our staff even more exhausted than was the case in the previous year.

At this point, it's worth spending some time drawing out the impact of a 'Special Measures' verdict on a school. For me, the most heart-breaking aspect was the impact it had on our pupils. This was best summed up by a group of our highly talented drama students, who, in an end of year review of their time at ASA, produced the following line in one of their pieces: 'Ofsted came and told us we were shit'. As we have already noted, ASA served the top 1% most deprived community in the country. By the time of the 2016 inspection, we had spent almost 8 years raising the self-esteem of our community's children – with considerable success. That single-word summary judgement of 'Inadequate' destroyed much of that work overnight.

Our community was used to 'hard knocks', and the judgement of 2016 – no matter how much Ofsted might have wanted the opposite to happen – merely reinforced their view that they were 'no good'. The reaction of our parents was both heart-warming and heart-breaking. Heart-warming because, when the report was finally published and 'hit the press', the comments from parents to the Hull Daily Mail were overwhelmingly positive. Most didn't believe the judgement, commenting that they were very happy with the school. This of course was in itself heart-breaking as it merely underlined to me how much we had let them down. Alongside the hugely negative impact on our community, however, was the impact on our staff. I will never be able praise highly enough the immense commitment of all who worked at ASA. Cooks, cleaners, teaching assistants, teachers, leaders – we had built a family which, in spite of all the inevitable ups and downs, worked tirelessly to improve the lives of our pupils and their families. To sum up all their efforts as 'inadequate' was, quite simply, as crushing and brutal as it was unfair. That was only the start of the issue however, as what was to unfurl simply added insult to injury.

Being in Special Measures feels like being 'kicked when you're down'. The initial judgement is the punch that knocks you over, and the first kick is the ban on appointing newly qualified staff. During the period of 2016-2018 however, we received three more kicks. The first one was completely unexpected, and involved direct ministerial intervention on our Mandarin programme. At the time of writing this book, relationships between the UK and Chinese governments are at a significant low point. However, as I pointed out earlier, I have always been convinced of the importance of learning the language and culture of one of the most populous countries in the world, which is also now the world's second biggest economy. In 2006, a group of local politicians had taken part in an exchange with the Fengtai district of Beijing, and following the signing of a Memorandum of Understanding, a number of schools in the city organised exchange visits. Archbishop Thurstan's stood the test of time, thanks to the outstanding work of the Deputy Head who was to become ASPIRE's highly successful Principal in 2014.

We had been fortunate enough to be linked with an individual whose influence stretched way beyond that of the Beijing School she represented, which in turn led to an increasingly fruitful partnering. I have already outlined how the greater curriculum freedoms we enjoyed between 2008 and 2015 gave us the opportunity to introduce Mandarin the right way – slowly. Building on the early success of the exchange at school leader level, we launched Mandarin language and culture as an extra-curricular activity, with the assistance of a teacher from our partner school in Beijing. This gentle start enabled us to assess the likely challenges in offering a full GCSE, but within a few years, our first cohort was indeed doing just this. We made time for pupil exchanges, so that those studying the language also had the opportunity to visit the country. It is sad to note that many of our pupils don't travel much outside the city, so one can only begin to imagine the impact of a visit to Beijing on their lives. Although I don't think any of them ate wolf (disgusting), as I did on one such trip, snake (also highly unpleasant) was certainly on the menu, as were all sorts of other new foods. They experienced classes of 70 pupils, Chinese calligraphy, whole-school Tai-Chi and visits to the Great Wall, to name but a few of the activities, and over time, our pupils started to enjoy great success in beginning to master the language.

On the basis of this success, in 2015 we were invited by the Confucius institute to be a lead school in what became the 'Mandarin Excellence Programme'. The Chancellor George Osborne had given the Schools Minister, Nick Gibb, £10 million to fund a programme to create 5000 competent Mandarin speakers. For our part in it, we committed to at least 20 pupils each year from Year 7 onwards studying Mandarin intensively, with a view to gaining a good level of competence by the time they left school. We were thrilled to join the programme, and had no shortage of pupils who at age 11, were prepared to come into the academy at 8:00 every day to learn Mandarin. Meanwhile, for those who had already been studying with us, GCSE results were strong and improving year on year, and eventually, we were able to offer Mandarin at Pre-U level in the Sixth Form.

By 2016, out of 5000 centres world-wide, we were one of 5 schools to be awarded 'Confucius classroom of the year'. Our Mandarin programme, thanks in no small part to our brilliant teacher, was an unqualified success. However, in 2016, shortly after our judgement of Special Measures, we received the most unwelcome news that, at the stroke of a ministerial pen, ASA had been removed from the programme. There was no direct communication – as I sought to ascertain the reasons for this, it appeared that it would simply have been too embarrassing for the DfE for us to remain on one of their flagship programmes. I will of course happily stand corrected if anyone from the Department wishes to tell me otherwise.

The DfE's decision was as non-sensical as it was crushing – carrying on with the programme would actually have helped improve the academy at a time when morale was low. Depriving our young people of such a fantastic opportunity for no apparent reason infuriated me, so I sought the necessary funds from another source, completely ignored the DfE's directive, and just carried on with the programme. I judged that once we were out of Special Measures we would be able to re-join the programme anyhow (which did indeed turn out to be the case), and didn't want to lose momentum in the intervening period. Ironically, this decision came to support the country during the pandemic. By 2020, one of our pupils had gone on to study Mandarin and Politics at Goldsmiths, becoming completely fluent in the language. As a consequence, he became involved in direct negotiations with the Chinese to procure a large shipment of PPE, translating for our Business Secretary, and ensuring that the delivery took place. That specific contribution notwithstanding, I am pleased to say that Mandarin teaching has carried on to this day at ASA, and is an area in which pupils and staff can take great pride.

If this first 'kick' had threatened however to destroy a part of our curriculum (a highly successful part, of which we were justifiably very proud), the second 'kick' to come from the DfE however threated to destroy our whole Trust. An important part of our vision as a new academy in 2008 was to create a family of schools in our local area, working in partnership with our local primary schools in particular. There were many reasons for this, but three stood out. First, I wanted to be able to understand better the challenges faced by our primary colleagues. It is well documented that one of the greatest threats to pupil progress is at point of transition to another school – including the move to secondary education. Working closely with our partner primary schools seemed an obvious way to reduce that risk. Second, I wanted to know if there were any ways in which we could share our incredible new facilities with younger children in the area. Third, headship is hard, and East Hull is a tough patch – I judged that by working together, we could support and encourage each other. With these broad aims in mind, in 2011 ASA formed the Association of East Hull Schools (AEHS), along with six other primary schools.

The AEHS was born shortly before the era of Multi-Academy Trusts (MATs) which now dominate the educational landscape. Adopting the motto 'Starting with the end in sight', we did just that, working out how best to ensure that a local child's educational journey from age 5-16 and beyond was as seamless as possible. We shared our curriculum plans, organised sporting competitions for local pupils, and organised weekly visits to ASA through our 'Funky Friday' programme to help pupils feel confident about coming to 'big school'. I have always had a huge respect for primary school teachers, not least because I'm married to one. Whilst dealing with stroppy teenagers has always very much been my meat and drink, I didn't have a clue about how to deal with an upset 6-year old, let alone design a programme for nursery-aged children. Indeed, my only memory of working with primary children up until that point was going into my wife's class one day and causing some poor child to cry when I told him he couldn't read aloud for the second time as it was someone else's turn. As such, working with my primary colleagues was an eye-opener – I learned much from them. So, having worked together in this way quite successfully for two or three years, we began discussions around forming a MAT as a natural development of our work. In addition to our AP Academy Aspire, two of our local Church of England schools also joined quite quickly, as did one of the other schools in the AEHS. All this led to the formation in September 2015 SALT - The Sentamu Academy Learning Trust, and for the next three years, I was to be both Principal of ASA and CEO of SALT.

As we moved into 2015 / 16, other local schools began to consider the move to our Trust too. The years 2014-18 were key years for Hull, as the tectonic plates of the educational landscape began to coalesce into firm groupings – to this day, Hull has one of the highest proportions of 'academised' schools of any area in the UK. The process was not necessarily that smooth. Many headteachers, quite understandably, were nervous about losing their independence to the strategic aims of a MAT. In spite of this understandable nervousness, the move to joining a trust was, by 2016, pretty inevitable, and final decisions were being considered by individual governing bodies. It was precisely in the middle of that period however that ASA, our main academy, went into Special Measures. The jaws of defeat, not victory, clamped firmly down on our plans; any hope of further growth was effectively canned. It wasn't just our future growth that was threatened, however.

For several years, the DfE's solution for a school judged inadequate was to force it to become an academy and join an academy trust, assuming it could find one that would take it. But what if the failing school were already an academy, and what if, moreover, that academy were deemed to be the lead academy of the Trust, as was the case for ASA? To deal with this scenario, the concept of 're-brokerage' was introduced around 2016. Under this policy, existing Trusts could be forced to relinquish a 'failing' school to another Trust. If this school was the lead school however, the DfE was able to force the Trust itself to be broken up or transferred wholesale into another Trust. And so, it was deemed to be for us. As the lead academy in our trust, ASA's failure - my failure – led to the DfE determining to break up our whole Trust. Discussing the situation with my executive team we concluded however that this particular threat could well be time-limited - following the logic of the decision, as soon as ASA was removed from Special Measures, the need to re-broker the trust would disappear. In all honesty, we had no idea if this theory was correct or not, but it gave us a goal to aim for and the hope that we could survive. Undaunted however, we continued to plan the further development of our Trust whilst also working flat-out to bring about improvements at ASA.

Yet again, we found ourselves again in direct conflict with the DfE. During the Christmas term of the 2016 academic year, officials approached the leaders of each our five academies and offered them an alternative Trust to join. This all happened 'behind our backs' – although I was the CEO of the Trust, I was never informed that any of these conversations were taking place, and certainly wasn't involved in any of the negotiations. The process wasn't however straightforward. Owing to an existing agreement between the Church of England (C of E) and the DfE, academies with a C of E designation can only join trusts run by the Church of England itself, or those in which the C of E has representation at 'company member' level. In practice, this limits the options for C of E academies considerably.

Our two primary C of E academies were given the choice of leaving SALT to join one such Trust, and to our relief, they turned it down, choosing to stay with us. Our third primary academy, which was not C of E, decided to join another Trust. We were extremely disappointed, but wished them well and were delighted for them when they had a successful Ofsted inspection themselves shortly afterwards. ASPIRE, effectively birthed by ASA, also chose to stay, although it was worried about being forced to join another Trust. That just left ASA itself. Towards the end of that term, another local C of E trust was approached with a view to our joining. However, they declined. I have always imagined that we were simply considered too much of a risk for them. So, by the end of that term our Trust was still intact, albeit one academy down.

This of course was all happening whilst we were still awaiting ASA's first monitoring visit from Ofsted. I explained above how we had to wait over a year for that first visit and that in December, we did indeed have a call. However, having thanked the inspector for telephoning, I asked her if she was aware that the DfE were trying to re-broker us. She replied not, and said she would call me back. It transpired later on that Ofsted had agreed not to revisit academies that were in the process of being re-brokered by the DfE. Needless to say, I found it quite ironic that an academy deemed to be in serious need of improvement should be denied this element of support which it would normally have received.

Believing we had seen off attempts to completely split up the Trust, the last week of the Christmas term of 2016 brought more surprises. I had been interviewing a candidate for a senior position in our Maths department and had offered him the job. Fully expecting him to accept the offer, I was genuinely astonished when he informed me that prior to the interview, he had been warned by his then current employer against accepting the job, as his Trust at the time was due to 'take over' our own. He asked me if I knew about this – I replied not, saying that it was news to me. Fortunately, he accepted the job anyway. Needless to say, I was both angry and upset that a deal to take over our Trust had been brokered without my knowledge and before I had been made aware of it. I was even more angered by the fact that the Trust involved was using this knowledge in an attempt to stop one of its own employees leaving them, especially as it was in a subject (Maths) to which it was very hard to recruit. In response to this information, I wrote both to our directors and to our Diocese setting out the reasons for which I thought the take-over was a bad idea. The full account of my objections can be found at Appendix 4, but in essence they boiled down to the following four points:

1. Re-brokering would mean we would lose control of our ability to place our most challenging pupils into Aspire, which would make our progress to 'Good' even harder;
2. We felt it was completely unfair and indeed unnecessary to re-broker us when we had just achieved some much better exam results;
3. We had real doubts about the capacity of a Trust to help us if they were trying to block the move of one of their staff to us in the subject in which we most needed to improve; and
4. We viewed this move to try to stop their teacher moving as a form of 'insider dealing', which we found morally objectionable.

I have no idea how much of the content of the letter attached at Appendix 4 was relayed to the CEO of that trust. In any event, the offer was rescinded, and so 'we lived to fight yet another day'. Two years later, I was to learn that attempts were made at ministerial level to remove me from my position during the summer term of 2017, but that these too were rebuffed. And so began another academic year. By September 2017, we should by rights have had at least three monitoring visits, so it was with great relief that, finally, we had our first one 16 months after the inspection of 2016. Our HMI was pragmatic, supportive and principled, and confirmed that we were making good progress against our plans.

Our second visit took place in February 2018 against a backdrop of the worst snow we had experienced in a decade. Every school hates snow, because with snow comes snowballing, and managing that situation with 1500 young people keen to throw it at each other is, at best, challenging. We had devised a 'safe snowballing' policy which worked as well as any, but needless to say, we were less than delighted at having our second monitoring visit under those conditions. However, by the end of the first day, the HMI was happy to convert the visit to a full inspection, and by the end of that second day, she confirmed that Special Measures were no longer needed. Although we were judged still to 'require improvement', both leadership and management and pupil behaviour were judged to be good. The irony was not lost on us - the leadership team now judged to be good was identical to the one which, under two years previously, had been judged so hopeless that it was unable to improve itself. We were of course extremely heartened by this news, not least because the timing of the inspection enabled us to appoint newly qualified staff again. Our Trust was also now safe from forced re-brokerage. However, if the immediate crisis was over, we were, in the immortal words of Jon Bon Jovi, only 'half way there', with events following that far more successful inspection demonstrating we were, very much, 'livin' on a prayer'.

Chapter 13 – Attempts to welcome a 'SNoW School' into our Trust.

Abstract:

*In this chapter, we see how ASA's position of being judged to require 'Special Measures' almost prevented another Alternative Provision academy joining our trust. Ashwell was a local '**S**chool **No**body **W**anted (a so-called '**SNoW**' school) which needed, and was being given, support from our own highly successful ASPIRE academy. Once again, we see how the DfE worked behind our backs in an attempt to block the move of Ashwell academy to our Trust, and once again, we explain how we managed to fight and win this particular battle. Apart from the 'David versus Goliath' narrative, this episode is used to illustrate how government policy on Ofsted almost stopped the pupils (**all** of whom were VYPs), from **the** most highly deprived school in the country, receiving the support they needed. The chapter ends with some of my reflections on leadership in this situation, and how I eventually managed to retire, that event having been delayed twice owing to the fact that nobody wanted my job.*

'Don't stop me now…'

Queen, 1978

This book is all about the ways in which government policy over the past decade has often worked against the interests of the most vulnerable young people in society – our VYPs – and this section is about the specifics of how policy in relation to Ofsted outcomes impacts them. In the last chapter, we saw how government policy on dealing with Ofsted failures almost led to the break-up of the Trust I was leading, even though exam results which came out just months after the inspection indicated that at the very least, weaknesses had already been addressed and were bearing fruit.

Ironically, it was the very policy of re-brokerage that prevented the normal policy of HMIs supporting schools in Special Measures being applied in our case. Indeed, when HMIs finally arrived, every indication was that the Trust did not need re-brokering. As such, this is a good example of a new policy being applied unthinkingly, and actually working against an older policy which was still in existence. Had the new policy prevailed and our Trust been split up, there would without doubt have been a very negative impact on the VYPs in our Trust. As I hope is now clear, the establishment of the highly successful ASPIRE was a key part of a very long-term strategy to enable us to provide effectively for our VYPs; wresting control of ASPIRE from our own leadership would have made that task all the harder. However, even though we had beaten the DfE in this round, we were soon to be on the back foot once again.

Ashwell academy was a small 'Alternative Provision' (AP) academy for around 30 highly vulnerable pupils in Hull that had fallen on extremely hard times. In 2017, in light of ASPIRE's continued success as one of the largest AP academies in the country, we were approached by one of the governors of Ashwell for support. ASPIRE's excellent Principal was more than willing to help, and over the next few months, was able to support the transformation of the academy's fortunes. After around 6 months, the relationship had become so successful that Ashwell asked if they could join our Trust. By this time, ASA was out of Special Measures, and so we thought that there would be little objection from the DfE. How wrong we were. Just as we had started initial negotiations with Ashwell, I received a call from a local colleague who informed me that the DfE had been trying to persuade other local Trusts to accept them.

As had been the case with their attempts to re-broker our own Trust, this process was being conducted behind our backs, so I contacted the DfE official responsible and asked him why he was doing this when Ashwell was already being very able supported by us, and indeed wanted to join our own Trust. The hapless person muttered something about being deeply disappointed that people had divulged this information to me, at which point I questioned his naivety in thinking he could behave in this way without somebody telling me about it. Frustratingly for the DfE, but happily for us, it transpired that we were the only Trust willing to work with Ashwell - no other Trust wanted to take them on. Realising that we were the only option to avoid a closure of Ashwell, the DfE reluctantly agreed to the plan.

Needless to say, we were delighted, and began negotiations with them to secure some additional funding that was needed to remediate the quality of the buildings. At this point, my experience of haggling in Beijing's major silk market came to good use. The term 'silk market' was actually a misnomer – in truth you could buy almost anything there apart from a house – and you could probably do that too if you looked hard enough. Containing a labyrinth of booths, I worked out that, on average, the starting price for any given item was, on average, around 6 times the price you would end up paying. The trick was simply to walk away, at which point the sales assistant would grab you and implore you to buy the 100 grams of finest green tea or whatever item in which you had shown even the vaguest of interest.

On the basis that human nature is pretty much the same the world over, we adopted this approach with the DfE ; having secured their (albeit very reluctant) agreement for Ashwell to join the trust, we then refused to admit them unless we were given sufficient funding to bring the site up to at least some sort of reasonable standard. We didn't do this out of greed, and it was no idle bluff - we simply didn't have the sums of money needed to effect the necessary basic repairs. Happily, a pot of money was miraculously found, and in April 2019, Ashwell joined us, renaming themselves 'The Compass Academy' in the process. Three years later, they were judged 'Good' by Ofsted at their first inspection.

Unpicking this whole episode, we can see that, once again, a blanket application of one aspect of government policy - this time one linked to Ofsted inspection outcomes - threatened to work against the interests of our VYPs. At the point at which our Trust was approached by Ashwell, ASA was out of Special Measures, and although it still required improvement, leadership was judged to be 'good'. However, the interpretation of government policy at the time by the DfE appeared to be that taking on Ashwell would somehow dilute our efforts to continue to improve ASA's overall performance. In reality, taking on the challenge of Ashwell had absolutely no impact on ASA's overall capacity whatsoever. It is true that it made more demands of ASPIRE, but by that time, ASPIRE was very successfully established and was well-able to provide the support needed. As we noted earlier, Ashwell academy actually had the most socio-economically deprived cohort of pupils in the whole country, bar none. It was certainly true to say that all of their pupils were highly vulnerable. Thus, had the DfE had their way, government policy would have led to the academy effectively being closed. This in turn would have meant that our local area would have lost 30 places for some of the most vulnerable young people in the country, which would have been a tragedy.

I have done my very best throughout this book to avoid talking about the impact on my own health and well-being of the many and various battles I faced. Leadership is inherently tough, and if you take it on, you can't feel sorry for yourself when 'things don't go as planned', especially when this is down to mistakes of your own making. This being so, I have never shied away from accepting responsibility for my own errors of judgement. Objectively however, I do think it is fair to make the following observations as we conclude this section of the book. Our patron, Archbishop Sentamu, used to have a card on his office door with the line *'My job is safe, nobody wants it',* and this proved to be the case for me – twice. The first time was just before the inspection of 2016. Governors understood that leading both a large secondary school and a new Multi-Academy Trust was really too much, and so we advertised for a 'Head of School' to lead ASA. We had very little interest, and so I just carried on with both jobs. My suspicion is that even in 2015, aspiring headteachers could see that it would be very difficult for schools in highly deprived areas to demonstrate success in the new world of 'Progress 8', and that accepting such a challenge could well be a 'career-ender'.

Having led the academy out of Special Measures however, we tried again in 2018 and finally appointed a new Principal, freeing me up simply to focus on the MAT. In spite of this, I was nonetheless, in all honesty, deeply unhappy. It is true that, three years after our damning inspection, I did feel able to face my other colleagues in the city without quite as much shame – I had survived after all. But ultimately, I simply did not believe in the curriculum that we were having to force pupils through at ASA, as it was being driven by the demands of 'Progress 8' and not their individual needs. This weight, combined with my exhaustion from fighting the DfE at every turn for the previous three years, led to me tendering my resignation in March 2019. Believing that I had brought as much as I could to the Trust, my plan was to retire the following Christmas, giving the Trust around 9 months to find a replacement. I genuinely thought this would be sufficient – CEO posts come up rarely, and even though we were a relatively small Trust, I believed there would be plenty of takers. However, I was completely wrong – the field of applicants was very small in spite of offering a generous salary, and the Board were unable to appoint anyone.

It is worth reminding ourselves that at this point, three of our Trust's five academies were ranked in the top 10 most deprived academies in the country (ASA, ASPIRE and Compass), with, as we have already seen, Compass actually having the most deprived pupil profile of any school or academy in the whole of England. As we have noted throughout this book, government education policy is not kind to leaders of schools serving deprived communities and my own experience would indicate that this has an adverse impact not just on the recruitment of teaching staff, but also of people willing to assume the responsibility of ultimate leadership of these institutions. Once again, this works against the interests of our VYPs, whose schools desperately need the strong leadership which would appear to be easier to obtain in schools serving more affluent communities. For whatever reason though, in 2018 we still had not solved the problem of who would take over the Trust, and this was to prove my final challenge. In the final event, the solution to finding new leadership for the Trust was found quite close to home. In the meantime, however, I needed to carry on. Fortunately, by 2019 I had been able to reduce my contract to around 0.8 full-time equivalent. This gave me the breathing space to continue for a little longer, and so I agreed to stay on until August 2020 – at which point I was finally able to retire, completely exhausted.

Chapter 14: Merging with another Trust and its impact on our VYPs.

Abstract:

In this chapter, I illustrate further the government's policy on dealing with academies in Special Measures, again with a focus on the impact of these policies on our VYPs. I chronicle the events leading up to our ultimate merger with York's HOPE academy trust, and the consequences of that for ASA. I outline in more detail the developments of Ofsted since 2012, arguing that the confrontational approach adopted by Sir Michael Wilshaw led to a deteriorating relationship between the education profession and the government – a situation that has further impacted negatively on our VYPs.

'I can't get no…. satisfaction'

The Rolling Stones, 1965

I had first met Brian in 2010 when his school was being rebuilt. He had kindly agreed to let me see how it was progressing, as we were at that point still in the process of designing our own new building. Being the proud owner of a 4-wheel drive car at the time, I agreed to take us to the building site to look at progress; he was happy to accept my offer until he got into it, at which point he discovered that my family were not as proud of my car as I was. We had just returned from our summer holiday and amongst the general detritus associated with teenage girls, he had to fight for space with a crab shell, a range of old sandwiches in varying stages of decay and enough general sustenance to satisfy a foraging fox. In spite of this severe risk to his health, we remained good friends, keeping in touch over the years. We became CEOs at roughly the same time, and in 2019, I learned that finally, like myself, he was planning on retiring at about the same time as me. Armed with the information that both the HOPE and SALT academy trusts would need new CEOs by the end of 2020, we began to talk about the possibility of our trusts merging to form a new one.

For some time, I had been on the horns of a dilemma. ASA had come out of Special Measures in February 2018 following its second HMI visit. Leadership and Management had been judged to be 'Good', and we had managed to put the nightmare of the 2016 inspection behind us. However, I was completely exhausted, and the advert to replace me following my impending retirement didn't generate any suitable candidates. This, combined with the general and perpetual challenge of recruiting staff, led me to consider the possibility of merging our own trust – SALT – with another one. Quite apart from the economies of scale that a larger trust can generate, it was clear (as I acknowledged in the previous chapter) that a larger trust's ability to employ (for example) dedicated teams of subject specialists who can support individual schools where needed is a tremendous advantage. However, the number of trusts whom we would be allowed to join was limited, and my experiences of 2017 made me extremely wary. The old adage 'Marry in haste, repent at leisure' applies equally to the decision to join an academy trust, the main difference being that the latter arrangement is far harder to dissolve than the former. If that principle is true for single academies, then the decision to merge two whole trusts needs to be taken even more carefully.

In spite of my reservations however, I had confidence that our trusts had a similar ethos – the crucial starting point. First, we were both Church of England trusts – important for ensuring that our Christian ethos would be protected. Second, both our trusts expressed that ethos at a strategic level by investing our energies in pupils who would not necessarily make our respective trusts 'look good' in any of the performance tables. In our case, we had invested our spare capacity in Alternative Provision, and in HOPE's case, they had recently welcomed two highly challenging secondary schools into their trust.

As we have already seen, it is a sad statistical fact that, nationally, those children who start secondary school at the lowest level also make the least progress by age 16, especially if they are also 'white, working class'. Our respective trusts had however invested heavily in supporting young people in precisely this situation – the VYPs who are the subject of this book – and knowing this to be the case was of great mutual reassurance. Third, we had already begun to collaborate closely, with our main AP academy ASPIRE providing behaviour support to HOPE's two new challenging secondary schools. That had been working well and was further evidence that the merger would be a good 'fit'.

Maintaining confidentiality for this type of development is harder than you might imagine – as with any area of life, the world of education is rife with rumour – and with this in mind, Starbucks at Pocklington became our strategic and operational planning centre of choice. Before too long, we were in a position to put a concrete proposal to our respective Boards of Directors, and by the start of 2020, planning for the merger had begun in earnest. It was several months before we would be able to make any announcements, but when we were finally able to do so, we were both delighted that the news was well-received. Although I had retired before final approval to merge was given (Approval for the establishment of the Hope Sentamu Learning Trust was finally given by the DfE in a month later in September 2020) - I had no doubt that I would be leaving SALT as part of something much bigger, and ultimately, far more secure. ASA needed the support of a bigger trust to deliver the DfE's prescriptive curricular demands, and HOPE would need the ongoing support of our AP provision to deliver long-term improvements in its own challenging secondary schools.

That at least was the theory. However, 18 months after the two Trusts came together, in May 2022 ASA was once again judged to be 'Inadequate' and at the time of writing, is still judged to 'require improvement'. Clearly I cannot write with any authority on the reasons for this. However, two factors are clear. First, since my resignation as Principal of ASA in 2018 there have been no fewer than four successive principals – three of them within the past three years. This would appear to add weight to the view that it remains very difficult to attract leaders to the most challenging schools. Second, the 'Progress 8' score remains stubbornly low compared with the national average. This is certainly *not* meant to be a criticism of the school itself nor of its current leadership – not least because I of all people am in no position to do that - but rather of the accountability metric 'Progress 8' which, as we have seen earlier, is so unsuitable for pupils coming from highly deprived communities.

The unfairness of the measure is highlighted yet again in a recent set of tables produced by the Fisher Family Trust's (FFT) 'Education Datalab' (Natasha Plaister, 2024). The FFT is a highly respected organisation that specialises in analysing school performance data, and published its analysis of the 2023 exam results in February 2024. The report (amongst other things) analyses the Progress 8 scores of academy trusts with more than 10 secondary schools, and draws a number of conclusions, two of which are highly relevant to this topic. First, they note the strong correlation between levels of relative disadvantage (in this case, measured by the percentage of pupils in receipt of 'Free School Meals') and Progress 8. Broadly, the higher the level of disadvantage of its pupils, the lower the average Progress 8 score of the trust. Indeed, even the highly successful Outward Grange Academy Trust (which has a significantly high proportion of disadvantaged pupils) posted an average P8 score of below zero. Second, the report notes the correlation between pupils for whom English is an additional language (EAL) and P8 scores. In this case, those trust with averagely higher levels of EAL pupils posted higher P8 scores. This should be no surprise as, accordingly to the FFT, the average P8 score for an EAL pupil is +0.51 – a very high score indeed. With these two factors in mind, the FFT report concludes:

'So, what have we learned? Largely that, as ever, we need to keep context in mind when we look at league tables' (ibid P 98)

Indeed, in a reply to one of the comments on the article, an FFT staff member comments:

'Contextual factors like FSM and EAL are associated with P8. It's why we've always advocated creating contextualised value added (CVA) versions of P8'. (ibid, P 98)

And yet, the government resolutely refuses to acknowledge the value of taking such context into account when judging schools' performance, at least in so far is it is expressed in a statistical way as used to be the case with 'Contextual Value Added' (CVA) statistic which was used between 2008 and 2012. The government would of course point out that the current Ofsted framework doesn't necessarily require a direct link between the school's P8 score and its eventual judgement. However, judging a school to be 'Good' or better with a low P8 would require significant justification. At the very least, we can say that a school with a low P8 has the odds of achieving a successful inspection outcome stacked against them.

So, where do all these observations leave us? And what is their combined impact on our VYPs? It almost goes without saying that a climate of fear has built up around Ofsted – one that has been acknowledged by the governments' own education select committee as we shall see in a later chapter. Whilst it is true that an inspection with a negative outcome will always have been highly concerning to school leaders, I believe that the current levels of fear with respect to Ofsted began to ratchet up significantly in 2012 when on 16th January, HMCI Sir Michael Wilshaw began to clamp down on schools that were 'stubbornly satisfactory' (Ofsted, 2012) and abolished that particular outcome in favour of the term 'Requires Improvement'. This followed a government investigation into 'Schools that remain satisfactory', published the previous year (Ofsted, 2011).

The theory behind the policy made sense; obviously, I agree with the thinking that we should all aspire to be leaders of schools that are at least 'good'. However, the whole tone of the announcement was alienating, and seemed to imply that leaders of schools that were merely 'satisfactory' were lazy. There are two reasons I hold this view. First, Wilshaw used the phrase: *'**I make no apology** for making even greater demands of an education system...' (emboldened text my own)*. The aim of this phrase may well have been to 'demonstrate leadership', but I found the phrase pompous, and, sadly, typical of the 'grandstanding' which I saw over time as typical of his approach. The second reason was that he came up with the phrase 'coasting school', applying it in particular to *some 300 stubbornly satisfactory schools (which) currently serve the most affluent 20% of society.'(ibid, Ofsted 2012).* Again, whilst the desire to see all schools judged 'good' or better was laudable, the language used to make his point was highly insulting. I, for one, have never met a senior leader or headteacher who was satisfied with their schools being 'satisfactory', nor one who 'coasted'.

The psychology behind Wilshaw's announcements was interesting. Any teacher will tell you that those who exercise the most authority over their pupils (and who are therefore likely to see pupils' best efforts over the long term) are those whose love is most valued by their pupils, the withdrawal of which is, for the pupils, an awful prospect. This principle was driven home to me during one of my last years of headship, after a very difficult Year 11 boy whom I had been mentoring committed another heinous act in the academy. I was astonished to hear that when brought to book for his actions, his first words were: *'What will Mr. Chubb think of me? Will he stop mentoring me?'*, or words to that effect. I am not, of course, a special case; the way we ensured very high levels of discipline in an academy serving one of the most economically deprived areas of the country was through a whole network of relationships such as these, whereby (in the main) our pupils valued our love for them and didn't want to lose it. I would classify this as 'leadership through authority', and I would imagine that the same applied to the school that Wilshaw himself led. For whatever reason however, this principle was not applied through press releases from Wilshaw such as the one of 16th January 2012. Whilst the intention may well have been to 'rally the troops', the impact was to bring about a culture of fear which grew over the next decade to the point that the Education Select Committee itself recognised the issue as serious enough to comment on, as we saw above, in its own report of January 24th, 2024.

Back in 2012, our academy was judged to be solidly 'good', so in theory, I had nothing to fear from Wilshaw's comments. However, it was clear to me that should that ever change, the consequences could be very serious, so every single policy had to be viewed through the lens of Ofsted. At the time for example, Ofsted judged schools on the extent to which they promoted 'Community Cohesion', so we had to make sure that we could demonstrate that our practice here was exemplary. Fortunately for us, as we have already seen, there was still sufficient flexibility in the curriculum and examination system, so we were able to continue our development as an academy in the way we had planned, in the best interests of the pupils, and 'ticking the required boxes' to ensure success with Ofsted – to the extent that in our 2014 inspection, we were judged to be 'outstanding' in two of the four main areas of our practice. However, as we have also seen, when our practice on curriculum and exam entry did not align with 'what counted', Ofsted hammered us.

Critics would point out that in making these observations, I am dismissing out of hand any benefits of running a system based on a culture of fear. Those same critics would point to the long-term impact of Wilshaw's policies. At the time of the 'Satisfactory Report' in 2011, around 30% of schools were judged to be 'Satisfactory' (or worse). By 2024, the figure for schools judged 'Requiring Improvement' (the grade that replaced 'Satisfactory') or worse had fallen to 12%. Surely that demonstrates the effectiveness of Wilshaw's approach? To answer that question, I think we need to dig a little deeper than those headline figures. The advantage of fear is that it can be effective in bringing compliance, particularly in the short-term. At a human level, fear stimulates our 'fight or flight' responses, which are very useful in helping us stay alive when faced with a dangerous situation. It is now a truism however that exposure to extended periods of fear has a very negative long-term impact on our bodies. At societal level, fear of the potentially deadly consequences of catching the COVID virus achieved extremely high levels of compliance in terms of our being willing to give up freedoms that, hitherto, we had all taken for granted. As time went on however, the hypocritical behaviour of many of our own government ministers during that period demonstrated that 'rule by fear' simply cannot be sustained over any length of time.

Bringing this back to schools, I would argue that whilst Wilshaw's approach undoubtedly increased levels of compliance with government policy, it all but destroyed any sense of collegiality between leaders of the profession and the government. The question therefore has to be whether or not this trade-off has been worth it over the longer term. At this point, I'd like to return to another section of Wilshaw's speech of January 2012. A fuller version of the quote given earlier is this:

*'I make no apology for making even greater demands of an education system **which has to respond with greater urgency to increasingly difficult and competitive economic circumstances.'** (emboldened text my own).

Since 2016, at secondary level, compliance has meant ensuring that as many pupils as possible fill as many of the 'Progress 8' buckets as possible, based on a curriculum driven by the English Baccalaureate, or Ebac. I have argued however that the Ebac is as pitiful a concept as it is an outdated one. The impact of Wilshaw's approach has in my view therefore been to enforce compliance with Gove's fatally flawed vision of 'what pupils need to learn'. It may seem unfair to blame Wilshaw and Gove for their lack of ability to predict the rapidly approaching, era-changing impact of the AI revolution so soon (relatively speaking) after the introduction of their reforms. However, in destroying collegiality through establishing the fear culture now recognised by our own Education Select Committee, they effectively destroyed any possibility of addressing these issues effectively – at least until now. Put simply, Wilshaw and Gove should, in my view, have been more careful about 'what they wished for'.

Having looked in some detail at the workings of Ofsted, we are now able to begin to assess its impact on our VYPs. It is important to acknowledge from the outset that some academy trusts have specifically sought out schools with poor Ofsted judgements, brought them into their family of schools, and turned them around. Our current HMCI, Sir Martyn Oliver himself, led the highly successful 'Outward Grange' academy trust prior to taking up his current post, and there are several other examples including DELTA and the London-based Harris Foundation Trust (to name but two) which can point to similar successes. In these cases, the overall impact on our VYPs has to be seen as highly positive. It would be fair to say that the methods employed by some trusts to turn around such schools are often subject to criticism in the educational press, particularly around the numbers of pupils that have to be excluded in the process. There is not the space to discuss these criticisms here. Personally however, I think these criticisms can be unfair. Indeed, I had to use exactly this approach myself during my first headship to re-establish order in the school I was leading at the time.

As such, I think it would be churlish to be grudging about the achievements of these 'turn around' trusts, except to note that the model hasn't solved the problem of how to cater for our some of our 'top VYPs' - those excluded in the 'turn around' process.

Not every academy trust however is as outwardly successful (no pun intended) as the three mentioned above, and there will be many reasons for this. Church of England Trusts such as the one I led for example have little option other than to insist that every pupil studies at least a short-course GCSE in Religious Education, in order to fulfil the one of the requirements of an additional 'SIAMS' inspection to which they are subject. This effectively 'fills up' one of the optional 'Progress 8' buckets, thereby reducing the element of choice for all pupils, and making it more likely that they will either have to follow a more centrally directed curriculum, or turn in lower exam results for the school. This brings us to the first criticism I would have of Ofsted with respect to its impact on our VYPs. By acting as the main enforcers of government education policy through a culture of fear, they are making schools comply with a curriculum that is already outdated, and which by the arguments outlined in previous chapters, negatively impacts most seriously our VYPs. Put another way, if we accept that 'what matters gets measured' and 'what gets measured, gets done', then Ofsted are responsible for ensuring that, at least in part, 'the wrong things get done'.

The negative impact of Ofsted on our VYPs doesn't end there, however. In response to Wilshaw's comments on 'satisfactory schools', the review 'Headteacher Update' of March 2012 noted that in trying to improve to 'good' quickly, the temptation for schools to introduce 'quick fixes' can actually lead to more instability and problems with recruitment, which in turn exacerbate rather than improve the situation (Update, 2012). This report was of course referring to schools that were judged 'satisfactory', and facing pressure to improve. The pressures for schools to improve from an 'inadequate' judgement are all the greater, and with these comes the danger of even more 'short-term quick fixes' which, if they don't work, simply make matters even worse. With this in mind, it should perhaps be no surprise that even with the resources of a bigger trust

173

at its disposal, the journey back to 'Good' for ASA has proven so difficult under the current regime of educational policy. This being the case, the question has to be whether or not placing a school in 'Special Measures' as a consequence makes it easier, or harder, for a school to improve.

My own experience of leading two schools – one in a deprived area and one in a very highly deprived area – is that staff recruitment and retention are the biggest challenges. Having taught in both economically advantaged and disadvantaged communities myself, I can say without any doubt that teaching in the latter is far more tiring, even when behaviour in the school is good. It is therefore not surprising that attracting good quality teachers to schools facing challenging circumstances is, well, challenging. This problem can be alleviated in part by taking on newly qualified staff. As such, our own academy had several programmes to achieve this, including links with local universities. However, as we have already noted, when a school is put in to 'Special Measures', it is immediately barred from taking on newly qualified staff. This of course exacerbates one of the main reasons for which the school was in all probability struggling in the first place – namely its problems in recruiting staff. A second criticism of Ofsted with respect to our VYPs would therefore be that it reduces the pool of good teachers who would otherwise be able to teach them.

But we needn't stop there. As Headteacher Update pointed out *(ibid)* – it is schools in deprived areas, who are most likely to have the highest proportion of VYPs, that are most vulnerable of being placed in an Ofsted 'category'. Given the fear that surrounds this situation, many senior leaders will asking themselves whether or not it is worth the professional risk of 'taking on' such a school, especially when the prospect of improving the situation ,at least in the short to medium term, may be challenging for the reasons given above. I would argue therefore that a third criticism of Ofsted would be that it works at times, albeit unintentionally, to dissuade the very leaders who could effect improvements from applying for those jobs. In 2004 as a (relatively) young headteacher, I was full of optimism that, through building strong teams we would, over time, be able to turn around the fortunes of Campion. This proved to be the case. I had the same optimism in 2008 when taking on the challenge of leading Archbishop Sentamu Academy, believing, rightly, that governors would understand that it was a long-term project. Once again, this proved to be correct, and over the course of 7 years, we patiently and consistently built a flourishing school which served the interests of our VYPs very well. By 2018 however, it became clear to me that the heavy hand of Ofsted measuring the implementation and impact of a curriculum to which many of our pupils were inherently not suited was an unreasonably difficult task. Yet again, we see how government policy, this time with respect to the workings of Ofsted, had so often made things worse for our VYPs.

Part 4 – 'VIP Pass'

Abstract:

Having argued in detail in the first three parts of the book about how government policy since 2012 has impacted negatively on our VYPs, in this section I set out proposals for policy changes that would enable our VYPs to feel like VIPs, and how these policy changes might be achieved. Recent proposals for changes to Ofsted's practices in the light of the tragic suicide of Ruth Perry, including the launching of a major national consultation, are examined in detail. We see however that one of the key requests for change made by the profession - specifically the removal of one word summaries from inspection reports - was ruled out by the previous government before the consultation had ended.

Chapter 15: Re-setting the relationship between the education profession and ministers.

Abstract:

In this chapter, I outline the reasons why we need a 're-set' between the profession and ministers, who by their actions (not least in refusing to move away from the 'Progress 8' metric) would suggest they have little respect for the value of the opinions of current leaders of education. I demonstrate the precedent for this through an example of such a reset already being promoted by the government to improve relationships in another area of school life - specifically between PFI contractors and the leaders of those schools built under the scheme.

'Starting Over' (John Lennon, 1980)

I am very aware that the first three sections of this book make for pretty painful reading, as it seems that at every turn, no matter what their intentions, government policy in recent years has worked strongly against the interests of our VYPs. Specifically, we have seen how accountability system based on the performance metric of

'Progress 8' has led to schools being forced to drive students down curriculum pathways to which they are not suited, to try to find ways of removing them from their rolls, or simply to prevent them coming to their school in the first place. It would be easy to judge school leaders for displaying a lack of integrity if they choose to engage in these tactics. But that would be grossly unfair. Every single school leader I have ever met has genuinely wanted to 'do the best' for their students, but often finds themselves to varying degrees having to bend those principles simply to survive.

In my own case, my refusal to abandon the principle of 'early entry' for our own pupils was probably the key factor in Ofsted placing ASA into Special Measures in 2016. In order to be judged to be 'Good' again, I had no option but to preside over curriculum changes and entry policy with which I completely disagreed. In short, for the last four years of my career, I felt that I was leading a Trust with a gun held to my head. And of course, I am not alone. Schools who, quite justifiably and in the interest of their pupils, have placed their VYPs on the roll of Alternative Provision academies have had to do so with a constant eye on whether or not Ofsted will deem them to be 'cheating'. As I reflect on these issues, I have to admit to an anger that successive education ministers since 2010 have presided over what, in my view, has become a corrosive game of 'cat and mouse', where schools have been forced to find loopholes in the ever-tightening noose of accountability simply to survive, and in the process, damaging the interests of our VYPs.

Anger can, of course, be a highly destructive and negative reaction to given situation. During my time as Headteacher at Campion, I can remember complaining bitterly to one of my governors at the time about the behaviour of another governor. She had the grace to tell me: 'Andrew, when you get angry, you look weak'. I have always considered this one of the best and wisest pieces of professional correction I have ever received – and one by which I have always tried very hard to live. Nonetheless, a controlled anger that leads to positive action can be extremely beneficial. As such, I believe that it is time for the profession - the whole profession – to unite in their dismay at the general lack of trust from ministers in our collective expertise and judgement over many years – both explicitly and implicitly – and to call for a complete re-set in the relationship between government and school leadership. This may seem like a pipedream, but there is a very recent precedent whereby the government itself called for such a 're-set' between warring parties, one of which was, actually, schools themselves.

Earlier on in this book, I explained briefly how since retiring as CEO of our MAT, one of my activities has been to co-found a company which seeks to help schools obtain better value from their PFI contracts, following my own experience of leading an academy that was subject to this type of contract. For those who don't know anything about PFI, the following brief explanation will suffice. Under PFI, a private consortium is established to finance the construction of a public building such as a hospital, prison or school. The consortium then leases the building back to the 'end-user' (in our case, the school) to repay the capital costs, and also ties the school in to a series of contracts for maintaining and repairing the school during the life of the lease-back – typically 25 years.

The system was originally launched in the 1990s during John Major's government, but was hugely expanded by Gordon Brown in the early 2000s as a way of providing much-needed improvement of many public facilities, without the capital cost of these appearing on the government's books. Whilst this solved a problem in the short-term (many crumbling estates were renewed), it created a much longer-term problem as the maintenance contracts to which end-users had to sign up were in the vast majority of cases highly unfavourable to schools. For anyone interested in pursuing this further, I have included in the bibliography a number of papers I have written on the subject. (Chubb, 2019). Needless to say, as funding became progressively tighter, school leaders began to look more closely at these contracts, and upon this closer inspection, became very concerned about both their cost and lack of apparent value. This was certainly the case for me, where the maintenance contract costs of ASA were threatening to bankrupt the Trust.

As school leaders (and those in other areas such as hospitals and prisons) began to hold maintenance contractors to account more effectively however, relationships often deteriorated to the point where, in some cases, there was almost 'open warfare' between contractor and end-user. Personally, my sympathies lie entirely with the end-user – the reality is that many contractors have been 'getting away' unchallenged with poor service, dishonest practices and egregious profiteering for years. However, it is fair to say that this has led to, in many cases, a complete breakdown of relationships and trust on all sides, and it is within this overall context that the government has recently intervened.

In the White Fraiser report (Barry White, 2023), two consultants experienced in the PFI industry analysed the typical relationships between end-users and contractors. In many cases, they found them to be highly toxic, a state of affairs which was hindering the completion of remedial works and in some cases, leading to lawsuits. This analysis led the authors to call for a 're-set' - effectively a truce - at national level between contractors and end-users to give breathing space for unresolved problems to be tackled and solved. Without passing comment here on the specific terms of the truce the authors propose, it is my view that relationships between government and our own profession are characterised by similar levels of toxicity and gaping holes of trust. In saying this, I am afraid it is hard not to blame the government fairly and squarely for this state of affairs.

It is a tragedy that highly competent and committed teachers and leaders appear to have been held in such disdain by ministers, especially when the latter display such poor levels of professionalism themselves. Indeed, had any of ASA's pupils behaved like schools' minister Andrea Jenkyns outside Downing Street on 9th July 2022 (when she made an obscene gesture to reporters), or Education Secretary Gillian Keegan herself on 3rd Sept 2023 when she engaged in an expletive-ridden rant over her handling of the RAAC crisis, they would have been immediately excluded. Arrogant displays of behaviour like these clearly make it harder, although not impossible, for opposing parties to sit down for open and frank discussions. However, we now have a completely different government. This does indeed present the opportunity for a complete 're-set' in relationships between ministers and the profession, and it is my sincere hope that this could be achieved. But what would such a 're-set' look like?

When it comes to measuring school performance, it would appear that ministers responsible for standards in education take the view that unless the accountabilities for standards are increasingly rigorous, Headteachers and leaders will simply 'take the easy way out'. Their actions, as typified most recently by the introduction of the 'Progress 8' metric, would lead us to believe that the only way we are going 'to do the best' for our pupils is to ensure that their outcomes are measured against a set of extremely tight criteria. There are, to my mind, at least two problems with this view. First, it assumes that the objectives set by the government in the first place are correct. I hope to have shown throughout this book that I do not believe this to be the case. Former Headteacher and Education Consultant Tom Sherrington was initially not over-concerned by the introduction of this metric, as can be seen in his blog 'Teacherhead' of 30th September 2016 (Sherrington, 2016). Personally, I find his initial assessment of the metric over-generous, especially in relation to his views as to how it can help ensure a 'broad and balanced curriculum'. However, in under 12 months, his views had changed radically, and in an article for SchoolsWeek, he is positively scathing in his assessment of its impact. He states:

'I would argue that in Progress 8 (P8) we have created a measure that is so far removed from what learning is, from what an education is, from any sense of what the quality of schooling should be, that we should be embarrassed. We're descending into a vortex of delusional algorithmic data-worship…….Why not ditch this fetish for made-up aggregated numerical measurement and try to develop more intelligent, more nuanced qualitative and quantitative ways to determine the quality of the educational experiences and outcomes we actually value.' (Sherrington, 2017)

Well, indeed, and we will look at some ideas for how we might achieve this in the next section. But returning to our general critique of 'Progress 8', the underlying insult to leaders of our profession is the not-so-implicit implication that unless the government spells out in black and white how we are to educate the nation's pupils, we will simply take 'the easiest way out'. Underlying *that* implication, we then find two further implications: First, that it is government minister X who knows what is best for pupils, as opposed to the body of highly-trained professionals who have spent on average at least 15 – 25 years working extremely hard to reach the position where they are able to make these judgements, and second, that school leaders are somehow accountability-shy.

Naturally, I would totally refute this thinking. Readers more sympathetic to the government's views on the need for tight curriculum control would point of course to evidence such as that presented in the Wolf Report *(ibid)* which suggests that in some cases, pupils were being encouraged to take a large number of vocational 'equivalent' courses purely for the sake of the school performance tables. Whilst I don't doubt that there will always be people who will cynically manipulate a system for their own ends in any walk of life, I have personally never met a Headteacher who hasn't cared deeply for their pupils, and wanted the best for them. Put differently, the concerns of this nature expressed in the Wolf report with respect to 14-16 education would appear to have been used to justify an 'accountability noose' which has become ever tighter since 2015. The sad irony is that in putting this noose around the necks of school leaders in the name of 'tackling perverse incentives', it has actually put in place exactly that – a system of perverse incentives which unless complied with, make it very difficult for school leaders to demonstrate success. Most sadly of all, this enforced compliance works most strongly against the interests of our VYPs, who are forced down a programme to which they may well be ill-suited, and in which they may well have little interest.

Chapter 16 – Six proposals for policy change to improve outcomes for VYPs - Abstract:

In this chapter, I put forward the details behind my main six proposals for change if we are to improve outcomes for our VYPs. These are:

1. *Government policy should make it in schools' interests to have the most disadvantaged pupils on roll. Currently, the opposite is the case;*
2. *Linked to this, there need to be incentives for schools and academy trusts to collaborate at a local level to ensure the most vulnerable have quick access to school places. Currently, there are many disincentives for this;*
3. *The curriculum needs to promote equity, as well as equality. The dogma of the so-called 'English Baccalaureate' works against this, especially for our most vulnerable pupils who often achieve the lowest outcomes.*
4. *We need to allow pupils to be tested on a mix of exams and continuous assessment. At the moment, almost all assessment is exam-based.*
5. *In light of the above, the current measurement of a school's success known as 'Progress 8' needs a radical overhaul.*
6. *The inspection framework needs to evolve to take these changes into account.*

At the end of the chapter, I illustrate the points further by discussing how an E-Bac / Progress 8-driven curriculum would have prepared me for my two most recent careers – setting up a business consultancy and starting out as a DJ. Concluding that it would have led to some very specific gaps, I make the point that these gaps are all the more serious if experienced by our VYPs.

'Confident'

Demi Lovato, 2015

At university, I studied International Relations alongside Languages (French and Swedish). I was therefore very interested in a recent episode of the excellent 'Leading' series of podcasts, hosted by Alistair Campbell and Rory Stewart. In episode 67, 'A tale of two Spies', both the former head of MI5 (Eliza Manningham-Buller) and former head of MI6 (John Sawers) concurred that the most dangerous point the world had faced in terms of a potential nuclear war was not, as I had thought, the Cuban Missile crisis of 1962, but rather, a flashpoint in 1983 (Politics, 2024). At that time, it appeared that a pre-planned NATO exercise led the Russians to believe that NATO was about to launch a pre-emptive strike. In spite of all protests to the contrary, this in turn was leading the Russians to prepare for their own nuclear strike on NATO territory. Fortunately, this intelligence was taken seriously, and the NATO exercise was, in the event cancelled and the awful prospect of nuclear war was averted. This de-escalation was a good example of one 'player', in this case NATO, employing the principle of a 'confidence building measure' with respect to another 'player' – in this case Russia, to demonstrate that their words ('we're not about to launch a pre-emptive strike') were sincere.

Whilst it would of course be completely ridiculous to suggest that the current state of relations between government and the education profession could lead to such cataclysmic outcomes, I do think that it is time for the government to admit to themselves just how unfavourably – to put it as politely as possible – they have been viewed by educational professionals. Indeed, I would suggest that by maintaining the status quo with respect to curriculum, performance metrics and inspection policy, any words of trust or confidence in the profession are, quite simply, hypocritical. It is against this sorry backdrop that I think a series of 'confidence building measures' could be usefully deployed in an effort to restore trust and build an effective partnership between ourselves and future education ministers. In proposing this, I have three grounds for optimism: First, as of July 2024, we have a new government in place. This makes it far easier for the appropriate frameworks for discussions to be put in place, as ministers responsible for the corrosive policies of the previous 10 years have all gone. Second, embarking on a serious discussion with the profession about the issues raised in this book – specifically how we can improve the long-term life chances of our VYPs during their secondary education – would be viewed as a wholly positive initiative. Third, and crucially, the proposals set out below would not cost anything. Indeed, quite apart from marking a significant departure from the normal oppositional wranglings with the teaching unions around levels of pay, it could well mark an early 'easy win' for the new administration.

So, with these winds of optimism now blowing more strongly in our sails, let's return to the question posed earlier and investigate what a 'system re-set' could look like. At the end of chapter 2, I outlined six areas which such a 're-set' would need to address. These were as follows:

1. It is in schools' interests to have the most disadvantaged pupils on roll. Currently, the opposite is the case;
2. The curriculum needs to promote equity, as well as equality. The dogma of the so-called 'English Baccalaureate' works against this, especially for our most vulnerable pupils who often achieve the lowest outcomes;
3. We need to allow pupils to be tested on a mix of exams and continuous assessment. At the moment, almost all assessment is exam-based;
4. In light of the above, the current measurement of a school's success known as 'Progress 8' needs a radical overhaul;
5. There need to be incentives for schools and academy trusts to collaborate at a local level. Currently, there are many disincentives for this; and
6. The inspection framework needs to evolve to take these changes into account.

We will now look at specific proposals which would enable these changes. As we go through these, it will be clear that at times, any given proposal may contribute to more than one of the 6 priorities above. This perhaps underlines the point made earlier – namely that the effectiveness of policy initiatives should not be viewed in isolation, but rather as how they contribute to the effective working of the system as a whole. With this in mind, let's now look at how we can make it more in schools' interests to welcome our most disadvantaged pupils - our 'top VYPs' onto their rolls.

Earlier in this book, we saw how the principle of 'norm-referencing' GCSE exam grades (i.e., pre-determining the percentage of pupils who could achieve any given grade) based on how well those same pupils performed in their KS2 exams ('comparable outcomes') effectively made it impossible for all schools to demonstrate improvement in terms of GCSE outcomes. The analogy I used at that point was that of the film series 'The Hunger Games', in which young people were forced to fight to the death for a limited supply of food and resources. However, I believe there is a better analogy. In response to Tom Sherrington's excellent article mentioned above on the problems with the Progress 8 metric *(ibid),* an anonymous person (who would appear from their first sentence to be a headteacher too) makes the following comments, which I reproduce here in full (bold format is my own) as I believe they sum up perfectly the horrible position in which schools now find themselves as a result of the Progress 8 metric :

'Many headteachers would agree with Tom here, as do I...As Tom points out, the system is about sorting students on a bell curve and deciding which children and schools fail. Headteachers are focused on making sure their pupils are in the higher reaches of the bell curve. **It is a bit like a group of people trying to climb out of a swamp. You can only get out of the swamp by standing on other people and pushing them into the mud. You only get above the water line by drowning others. As a headteacher you cannot make a principled stand on this because other headteachers might then stand on you and drown you. So, it is a fight for survival of the fittest.**

The headteacher organisations could take a lead on this for the collective good. But they don't... The government's role seems to be to act as whip masters, extolling headteachers to climb on each other's backs even faster.

Ofqual's role is to make the slope out of the swamp even steeper, so that schools are now starting the slope climbing with younger and younger students.

So, what is the solution? No educationalist wants to be in this swamp! **We can only get out of this mess by some form of collective and consensual agreement on what education should be about, and how we achieve that for all our young people. Saying we don't like the swamp is a starting point, but it will not make it go away.'** *(ibid)*

The broad thrust of these comments is, I believe, fully justified, and identifies very well my own views on the root of what needs to change. Our starting point in this respect is to tackle the 'zero-sum game' of the 11-16 performance metric. But how might we do this?

We can begin with the research referred to earlier in this book by Hattie *(ibid)* who found in his meta-analysis of strategies used by schools to raise achievement that the single biggest factor to impact *negatively* on pupil performance is that of moving schools. This takes us right back to our second chapter where we saw that, certainly in the case of Hull, for many years local headteachers including myself were reluctant to take in pupils who had been expelled from other schools – pupil who were, of course, some of our most vulnerable young people – our VYPs. Was this because we were 'bad people'? In a later chapter, I will detail how we did eventually manage collectively to improve our practices in this respect. However, I think the real reason for many years that was driving our reluctance to admit this cohort of VYPs was simply this – we knew that each one we admitted would risk our sinking slightly deeper into the swamp so ably-described by the anonymous contributor referred to above. We all knew Hattie's research to be true - pupils who came into our schools from another school through the system of 'Fair Access' were highly likely to under-achieve. And yet, ironically, in another area of policy, the government itself recognises the unfairness of this situation, and it is their policy in set of circumstances which provides an answer to the first of our challenges, as we shall now see.

We saw previously how, as early as 2013, ASA decided to establish its own Alternative Provision Academy, the better to cater for both our own most vulnerable young people, and those in other schools in the city. In addition to having far greater flexibility of curriculum, the performance metrics for AP academies are very different to those of mainstream secondary schools.   Specifically, they are not judged on Progress 8 at all. The reason for this is that it is patently unfair to hold an academy to account for a Y11 cohort whose pupils may well have arrived at entirely different points (in the case of ASPIRE, at any point between Years 7 and 11), when they may have been out of school entirely for varying amounts of time – quite apart from the fact that, as Hattie has pointed out, a significant change in school has a highly negative impact on pupil achievement. (This is of course not to argue against the value of a move to an AP academy per se, but rather to point out the unfairness of judging the achievement of such pupils by the same criteria). Thus, whilst it is certainly true that exam results for pupils in AP are submitted to the DfE, in reality, pupil achievement (i.e. the progress made by each pupil during their time in the academy) is measured in a much more holistic way, to include (in the case of ASPIRE) a variety of measures based on social behaviours as well as purely academic performance. These issues lead us neatly to the first of the solutions I proposed in chapter 2 – namely that it must be in schools' interests to have the most disadvantaged pupils on roll.

How could this be achieved? A straightforward answer would be to give schools the option of not having to include in the main performance tables the achievements of any pupil joining their school through the system of Fair Access. As I suggest this, I can already hear the criticism that this would give schools a 'free pass' , leading to the 'lowering of standards' through a 'a lack of ambition'. However, this would be an excellent example of the 'confidence building measures' that I believe are necessary if the government and education profession are to work successfully in a partnership, so before it is dismissed out of hand, let's just consider the advantages that such a move would bring. First, it would play a significant role in ending any attempts to keep our must vulnerable young people out of education. Whilst it can be argued that accepting *any* pupil with a difficult history makes a school's life more difficult to a certain extent, removing the pressure of then having to force that pupil down curriculum and assessment pathways to which they will almost certainly not be suited would make a massive difference to schools' ability to welcome and integrate them successfully.

To be fair, it is true that in certain situations, schools may not be required to include a pupil's exam results in their performance tables. The two main examples of this are if within two years of sitting their GCSEs, either a pupil arrives from a country where English is not the official language in that country, or if a pupil is enrolled having been permanently excluded from another school. However, the former is relatively rare, and whilst it is true that pupils who are permanently excluded do indeed have to find another school Fair Access, we have seen earlier on in this book that in practice, many students opt to change schools before they have the stigma of a permanent exclusion attached to them. The 'accountability concession' also only applies to pupils excluded after the end of Year 9, and this does not therefore solve take away the very significant disadvantage of accepting a pupil permanently excluded from another school *before* this point in their education (i.e., during Years 7, 8 or 9).

I would, however, go further than this, and suggest that pupils with an 'Education and Healthcare Plan' (formerly known as a 'Statement of Special Educational Need' or even more simply, a 'Statement') are also removed from the main performance tables. In suggesting this, I can hear even more howls of protest; the government after all gives schools extra funding for these pupils, and surely has the right (as indeed they currently do) to measure the outcomes of these pupils strictly? I would argue that here again, it is a mistake to think that money can solve any problem. With respect to our VYPs it can certainly help, but it simply does not follow that money in and of itself can make up for a deficit in educational achievement.

In his book 'The boy who was raised as a dog' (Bruce Perry, 2006), Dr Bruce Perry uses a number of case studies to illustrate the impact of early childhood abuse, trauma and neglect on the lives of young people. One of the key points he makes is that these awful emotional experiences can have a direct physiological impact, in which the brains of children affected in this way are physically smaller than those in children who have had a more normal childhood. I look at the implications of this in more detail in my Masters' thesis on the design and setting up of the AP academy ASPIRE (Chubb, 2013) but for here, the point should be clear. To repeat - whilst money can indeed help improve provision for our VYPs, it does not necessarily follow that it can make up entirely for the challenges posed by emotional or physiological disadvantage. To hold schools accountable for their performance on exactly the same terms as their objectively less disadvantaged peers is, I would contest, extremely unfair.

My first proposal would therefore be to *give schools the option of removing from the 'standard' performance tables, any pupil who transfers through 'Fair Access', and any pupil who is given an Education and Healthcare Plan (EHCP).* Doing so would, I believe, vastly improve the chances of our VYPs, for the following reasons. First, the main reason for wanting to deter these pupils from joining a school in the first place would be removed. Whilst it is true (as we have noted earlier) that accepting any pupil with an 'above level of challenge' can indeed be difficult, the vast majority of heads and senior leaders with whom I have come into contact over the years are passionate about wanting to help the most disadvantaged pupils and would gladly welcome more into their schools if they were able to do so without fear of being driven down further into the 'performance table swamp' so well described by our anonymous writer above. At the same time, it would of course remove most of the incentives for 'off-rolling' pupils who present severe behavioural and attendance challenges. The following case will underline this point one more time.

In 2018, we had the opportunity to legitimately remove one of our Year 11 pupils with a highly dysfunctional family from our roll, as he confirmed that he had moved away. However, we knew that he would not enrol in another school and that in so doing, he would simply be giving himself more time to devote to what would be the start of a life of crime. This being the case, we kept him on our roll and devoted considerable resource to supporting him remotely, knowing full well that, through no fault of our own, we would be taking a significant 'hit' in the performance tables with this boy's exam results. Whilst this was an extreme case, the same principle applies to a greater or lesser extent with the majority of decisions both around in-year transfers through Fair Access, and the degree to which schools encourage the attendance of pupils with EHCPs – unless the pupil arrives after the 'cut-off' point for inclusion in the official performance tables, the school immediately disadvantages itself in those statistics. Third – it would cost precisely nothing to do this.

But why not go further, and actually reward schools who do take on the most challenging pupils? Whilst in some ways I am loathe to suggest yet more 'metrics' by which schools could be judged, it would nonetheless seem fair to me to measure the proportion of young people moving through Fair Access accepted by each school in any given area and for that level of inclusivity to be a part of any inspection, with the same being the case for pupils with EHCPs. At the very least, this would help contextualise the performance tables a little more effectively. If we coupled this acknowledgement with an acceptance that the academic performance of these VYPs would be measured through a different set of metrics, then the interests of these pupils would align with the interests of schools. This could be transformational for our VYPs – and again, would cost precisely nothing.

My second proposal would therefore be *for the Ofsted schedule to comment on the proportion of pupils taken on through Fair Access of any given school.* In addition to acknowledging and therefore rewarding the efforts of those who do so, it would draw attention to the lack of inclusivity of any school who simply refused to do so.

Elements 2,3, and 4 of our 'reset' (see above) all overlap, and my proposals for achieving them bring together changes in curriculum and performance metrics. In chapter 2, our definition of 'vulnerable' included those pupils who attract the 'Pupil Premium' – the initiative introduced under the coalition government at the insistence of the Liberal Democrats, which ensured that schools received additional funding for each pupil deemed to be in a qualifying category –

specifically those who are deemed to be disadvantaged, that is, those eligible for benefit-based free school meals (FSM) at any time in the last six years, those children who are either' Looked after' or formerly 'Looked after', and those from armed services families.

Here again, I would argue that additional funding, although welcome, is not the main challenge. Rather, the problem is the metric used to measure 'pupil performance'. Following the introduction of the pupil premium, a key requirement for schools was to show how much they had 'narrowed the gap of achievement' between those pupils who attracted the pupil premium, and those who didn't. In ASA's inspection of 2014, as we have already seen, inspectors noted that this 'achievement gap' had indeed been significantly narrowed. They said that (although)

'On average, they attain two thirds of a GCSE grade lower than their peers in English and mathematics by the end of Year 11', nonetheless:

'The achievement of students for whom the school receives the pupil premium funding is rising across all years. As a consequence, the margins between the progress that they make in English and mathematics, in relation to their peers, are closing fast.' (Swallow, 2014)

The detailed plans we had in place to 'narrow the gap' however relied much more on our opportunity at the time to 'early enter' pupils for English and Maths GCSEs, and also to provide a wider range of courses that were judged to be equivalent to GCSEs. Whilst it is true that the funding made these strategies more affordable, it was the curriculum adjustments rather than the funding itself, which were the key drivers in our success. Once these opportunities had been effectively withdrawn (or at the very least, significantly reduced) by the introduction of the 'Progress 8' metric, the encouraging trend became far harder to maintain. All of which brings me to my third proposal – *to decouple school performance metrics from the English Baccalaureate.*

It should be completely clear by now that I, and many others, see both the English Baccalaureate and Progress 8 as metrics which are fundamentally flawed. Without repeating the detail of my objections with respect to the former, I can find no good answers to the following questions:

1. Why are History and Geography seen as 'core EBac' subjects when Religious Education (RE) is not?

2. Why are Music, Art and Drama, Technology and a whole range of other vocational subjects not seen as important as either History, Geography or a modern language?

3. Why are languages a compulsory element? Personally, I love languages and studied them at university. However, when faced with the need to communicate in Slovakian with my upstairs neighbour whose toilet was leaking into the roof of my bathroom, I simply typed my letter into Google Translate, which communicated the problem effectively. I have been a huge advocate for the study of languages throughout my professional career, and would of course be the first to admit that studying languages brings a whole host of benefits additional to the ability to express yourself in a different tongue. But are these other benefits conferred through the study of languages of any higher intrinsic value than the benefits gained through the study of any subject?

4. Taking this argument one step further, how does the study of the EBac suite of subjects prepare our young people for the key challenges posed by the internet around disinformation? Indeed, at risk of being considered 'waspish', it's worth noting that, arguably, the success of the Brexit campaign was down to successful media manipulation which enabled large amounts of spurious information to be peddled as 'fact' (remember for example the '£350 million to the NHS every week ' emblazoned on the battle bus?). And yet media studies, a basic understanding of which would have underpinned the tactics employed by the 'Leave' campaign team (and, indeed, the tactics of any lobbying or political campaign) is clearly not seen as an important subject by proponents of the EBac.

5. In a similar vein, what are the implications of GPT 4 and future 'large language models' on the theory espoused by

E.D. Hirsch, whose research so influenced Gove's curriculum decisions, namely, that possession of a 'core body of knowledge' is a key element in ensuring social equality? If I want to find anything out now, my starting point is GPT4 – the crucial skill I need however is assessing the validity of the information I receive. It is outside the scope of this book to discuss fully the implications of AI on education. Suffice it to say that at the inception of the EBac, AI was a very niche topic of discussion. Over the past 15 years however, advances in AI have been so spectacular that hardly a day goes by without articles appearing in the press around its impact on jobs, the economy and indeed the existence of life on this planet. For readers who are interested in this area, Calum Chace's books 'Surviving AI' and 'The Economic Singularity' make an excellent starting point (Chace, 2015). But even without any further reading, it is clear that AI will have a massive impact on all our lives, and as educators, we need to prepare our young people for this revolution. When viewed in this light, the principles underpinning the EBac seem, at best, pitiful.

I could of course continue – but I find it difficult to conclude other than that the EBac was a bad idea in the first place, and that it is now an outdated and irrelevant concept. As such, I believe that it should be scrapped. If we accept this premise however, it follows that the 'Progress 8' metric should also be abandoned in its current form, as six of the eight 'pots' have to be filled with subjects that form a part of the 'English Baccalaureate' (English, Maths, Dual award Science, History or Geography and a Modern Foreign Language).

If we accept both these premises, then the question of course is how *should* we judge pupil performance at age 16? Readers who already have a deep knowledge of this issue would point out that we actually place far more importance on pupil outcomes at age 16 than is the case for many other countries. That is certainly the case, and knowing this, a further question would be whether or not formal assessment at age 16 needs to be as 'high stakes' as it is currently. I would certainly be sympathetic to this implied criticism of our exam system. However, to move away dramatically from a tradition of

'End of Key Stage 4' exams would indeed be a revolution of sorts, and as such, I consider it highly unlikely that any government would seriously consider such an option within any reasonable timeframe. The proposals that follow are therefore intended to be more a case of 'evolution' than 'revolution', in the belief that they would be politically easier to implement.

At this point, I would like to return to the point made earlier about the difference between providing 'equality of opportunity' and 'equity'. We said that the former involved curriculum decisions made in a 'top down' way about how schools should prepare their pupils for a particular set of opportunities determined as important by a government minister, whilst the latter involved a more 'bottom up' approach, in which highly experienced school leaders were able to evaluate barriers to opportunity at a local level, and put in place a curriculum which raised pupils' chances of success in life based on local circumstances and pupils' interests. The following broad example from my own experience will serve to illustrate this. The local community served by the ASA had many disadvantages, including the following 'top ten':

1. Extremely low levels of education historically;
2. Extremely high levels of unemployment;
3. Very poor levels of health, including significant numbers of pupils experiencing neglect, abuse and / or trauma;
4. Very little experience of travel outside of the city itself;
5. High levels of loan sharking;
6. High levels of drug abuse;
7. Incidents of right-wing extremism (sadly exemplified in the riots of August 2024);
8. Very little experience of pupils going to university;
9. Very few local opportunities to experience culture in any form; and
10. Low overall levels of pupil confidence.

Combined, these ten factors worked together to limit significantly the overall life-chances of our pupils. This being the case, I hope it is now even clearer why the supposed 'equality of opportunity' promised by the English Baccalaureate was so grossly inappropriate. What was needed instead was a curriculum which improved pupils' equity through removing as far as possible the barriers to a high quality of life imposed on them through no fault of their own. In practice, this meant that we had to consider the following as top priorities for our curriculum:

1. A significant emphasis on the skills of literacy and numeracy;

2. Significant 'agency' for pupils, whereby they were able to 'see the point of school' through their ability to determine their curriculum choices to a greater extent than was previously the case;

3. Explicit teaching around personal effectiveness and work-related skills, including a well-planned programme of work experience;

4. Significant time devoted to developing personal health and safety, including plenty of opportunity for sport;

5. A range of experiences outside the city itself;

6. Significant time devoted to the development of financial literacy; and

7. Significant time devoted to the Arts.

There is not the space in this book to go into details about what a more personalised approach to the curriculum based on individual need would look like. I believe that in general however, the philosophy behind our own 'Modern Baccalaureate' described in chapter eight is a good starting point, as it addressed all of the issues I have just raised. Before leaving this however, I would like to give the following case study as to why the EBac and 'Progress 8' are so woefully inapplicable to many of our pupils, and in particular, our VYPs.

The last class that I took before retiring was a group of Y11 pupils in the last term of their formal, compulsory education. All of the pupils concerned had just about 'given up' - they hated school, had no desire to attend, and had little ambition. The one person in the group who was able to articulate an ambition – he wanted to join the army – had no idea as to how to go about it. The aim of the class over the course of their last term was to help them identify a goal for the next stage of their lives, and how to achieve it. It was an intensely practical course, designed to build their resilience. Part of it involved me filming myself doing things at which I was pretty hopeless – painting / decorating / cutting down trees and so on, the point being to show how we have to persist in achieving our goals by breaking them down into a number of smaller, achievable steps. Needless to say, the group found my mishaps highly amusing.

I cannot claim that this relatively short course radically changed their lives, although the lad who wanted to join the army did persist and was eventually accepted, in spite of the fact that his application wasn't dealt with very efficiently. I was struck, however, by the problems experienced by one particular boy. Mikey (not his real name) wanted to join a local sixth form college for the next stage of his education, and to do so, all he had to do was telephone them to arrange an interview. Part of my course involved giving each pupil a small goal. Mikey's task was to make the phone call to the college, and each week, he produced some kind of excuse as to why he hadn't done this.

Eventually, I kicked myself for being so obtuse. In spite of possessing a mobile phone, this poor lad just didn't know how to make that sort of phone call – his confidence was so low that at 16, he was still utterly dependant on others to help him with even the most basic of tasks. He wasn't badly behaved or disruptive, just a quiet lad who 'kept his head down' and hoped nobody noticed him. For him, the supposed 'equality of opportunity' offered by the curriculum we were forced to follow because of the Progress 8 metric was, quite simply, pretty irrelevant, and did not give him the space to work on the skills that would maximise his opportunity for the next stage of his education or training and 'life in general.' Whilst this is perhaps an extreme example, it does I believe illustrate the thinking behind my second proposal – specifically, to move away from Progress 8 and the curriculum principles of the so-called 'English Baccalaureate' which underpin it. We now need therefore to look at what metrics we might reasonably put in place to assess the effectiveness of delivery of a much more personalised curriculum for our VYPs.

So far, I have made three proposals to underpin a 're-set':

1. That as a minimum, any pupil who comes to a school through the system of 'Fair Access' and / or who has an Education and Healthcare Plan (EHCP) should be considered 'highly vulnerable' and as such, schools should not be required to have their results included in the 'standard' performance tables, as it is highly likely that their individual needs will mean that they are not best suited to a curriculum based on the exigencies of 'Progress 8'. It is important to note however that it should be an *option,* which schools could exercise as appropriate, rather than a *requirement,* which could lead to charges of 'low expectations' or 'stereotyping'.

2. That schools report on the proportion of pupils they take onto their roll through 'Fair Access', so that their level of inclusivity in this respect can be measured and acknowledged as appropriate by Ofsted; and

3. That the key issue for the broader group of our VYPs (those we have defined as young people who attract the 'Pupil Premium') is to increase their level of equity with respect to their peers, and that to do so, they may need access to a more personalised type of curriculum such as the Modern Baccalaureate described in chapter eight. In light of this, school performance metrics should be formally decoupled from the English Baccalaureate, to ensure that there is no 'perverse incentive' to force the wider group of VYPs down an inappropriate curriculum path.

If the first two proposals were relatively easy to devise, the question as to how to hold schools to account for the outcomes of our VYPs is trickier. On the one hand, we are saying that their individual circumstances may well require a more personalised curriculum which doesn't 'fit' the current set of metrics. On the other hand, however, we don't want to highlight that difference to them in their daily school lives and through that possibility, further add to what can often be very negative perceptions of 'self-worth'. The solution to this dilemma, I believe, can be found in how we organised ASA's canteen.

Prior to the move into our new building, school dinners were provided by our local authority. These were, I'm afraid to say, woeful. The absolute low point for me was walking into the canteen one day to find that fish and chips were being served with no batter on the fish – it was just revolting. I vowed to change things as soon as possible, and the move to our new building coupled with our freedoms as an academy gave me the opportunity to do just that. In 2011, one of our excellent Food Technology teachers wanted to retire from teaching, indicating that she would very much like to run our new academy restaurant. Whilst this was a huge loss to our pupils in the classroom, it was very much a gain in terms of both our pupils' and our staff's stomachs.

Sandra was not only an excellent teacher – she was also an excellent cook and manager, with the added advantage that everyone was terrified of her. This winning combination of qualities meant she was ideally placed to cater for us all, and under her leadership, the quality of our food increased both rapidly and dramatically. I very much enjoy food, and some of the best I have eaten is that produced by Sandra and her team. The quality of her salads, lasagnes, sausage rolls and soups was amazing, and to this day, she has produced the only way I can enjoy eating broccoli – by chopping it up raw and adding it to bacon and some kind of sauce. The issue however was the payment system. There were essentially two options – cash, or a pre-paid card. In some ways, cash would have been convenient – at least as a back-up (certainly for staff), as pupils can be notoriously forgetful at bringing what they need to school – including a card to pay for their dinners. However, we decided (as would many schools, if not most,) to 'go fully cashless'.

Apart from the advantage of pupils not constantly having to carry cash around with them, it meant that those pupils on free school meals were not identified as 'poor' – the amount they needed having been credited to their accounts remotely. This was a major 'social equalizer', meaning that the 40% or so of our pupils benefitting from Free School Meals did not have to feel ashamed in any way of taking them. But we didn't stop there. By opting in to a programme called 'Fairshare', we were able for a relatively small annual payment to offer all our pupils a free breakfast. This was essential – we knew that many of our pupils were not properly fed at home, and that offering them a good breakfast was essential to their learning. But to avoid any form of implied discrimination, it was open to all pupils, whether they were entitled to free school meals or not.

What is significant about this is that in both cases, (deciding on cashless and offering free breakfasts to all pupils), we were actually basing our whole system around the needs of the most vulnerable – our VYPs. This principle, I believe, offers a solution to our school performance metric. Instead of expecting our VYPs to 'fit into' a system which ultimately benefits their already more advantaged peers, **why not design the metric around the needs of our VYPs instead?** This brings me to my fourth proposal – *to agree a revised set of metrics for pupil and school performance which has as its highest goal the promotion of equity for all pupils.*

At first sight, this would appear to contradict my first proposal – namely to drop the requirement for our 'most vulnerable' young people to be included in the standard performance tables, much as is the case (as we saw earlier) for those pupils who attend Alternative Provision (AP) academies. However, Proposal One is really only a short-term concession to remove the perverse incentives schools currently have either to avoid taking in the most vulnerable in the first place, to force them down curriculum pathways to which they are inherently unsuited, or simply to find a way of 'off-rolling' them. As such, Proposal One only removes a negative.

The aim of my fourth proposal therefore is to replace a negative with a positive, by developing metrics which are fair to *all* VYPs, and by extension, to all schools. In suggesting this, I am aware that some may question the wisdom in basing a whole system around a minority of pupils. However, I would counter this criticism with following points. First, I would argue that a system which bases its principles on the needs of the most vulnerable is morally superior to one which, even unthinkingly, does the opposite. Second, a system that can measure fairly the achievements of all pupils avoids the inherent problem of 'cliff edges' – a criticism which could easily be made of my first proposal, as it begs the question 'what about pupils who on a scale of 1-10 are quite at risk, but who don't fit into one of the definitions of being vulnerable?'. At this point, it is worth revisiting the success of ASPIRE, our Alternative Provision Academy. Readers will remember that pupils fortunate enough to gain a place there were able to follow a curriculum much more highly tailored to their individual needs, including a range of much more practical options than those offered in a mainstream school.

At any one time however, there was a queue of pupils who would have benefitted from this sort of flexibility, but for whom there wasn't space at ASPIRE. The main reason for not offering these qualifications in mainstream was not however down to a lack of facilities, but simply down to the fact that they didn't 'count' in performance tables, and therefore penalised schools for offering them. AP academies however are not judged by the same metrics as mainstream schools, for reasons there is not the space to go into here. This situation leads to the ludicrous position whereby a pupil who is not quite 'difficult enough' to justify a place at an AP academy is actually worse off, as they are forced to follow a programme of study that 'counts' in a mainstream school's metrics. Allowing greater flexibility in the 'courses that count' in mainstream schools would therefore go a very long way to solving this problem – and would cost the taxpayer precisely nothing.

Whilst the exam results for pupils aged 16 are important, they should not be viewed as an end in themselves, but rather as a means for young people to access further study, employment or training. Indeed, there is a formal measurement for those aged 16-24 who are *not* in Education, Employment or Training – the so-called 'NEET' metric. For the year ending 2023, the official figure nationally was 11.9% – almost one in eight of all young people (Publications, 2024). With the implications for young people who fall into this category in terms of their life-chances being quite obvious, it should be equally obvious that ensuring pupils progress to a 'positive destination' (i.e., further education, employment or training) is vital.

For those young people who want to continue studying in a sixth form or local college, a typical requirement is to gain at least 5 GCSEs at a basic pass (currently a 'level 4' grade), of which two would ideally be English and Maths. We have seen however throughout this book that the move to the 'Progress 8' metric radically narrowed both the choice of subjects available to young people, as well as the assessment method, which is now almost totally through a series of terminal exams. We have also seen how this can often disadvantage our VYPs. My starting point for revising the main performance tables would therefore be to re-introduce the concept of 'GCSE equivalence', through which a range of subjects assessed differently to GCSEs were given the same value or 'equivalence'. Examples of these, discussed earlier in the book, would include the former BTecs and ASDAN awards.

A key criticism of the period during which equivalencies were allowed in the school performance tables was that some pupils were encouraged to take increasing numbers of these equivalencies for the sake of the performance tables, rather than for their own benefit. Thus, for example, a pupil might have been encouraged to take English, Maths, two full BTecs (worth 4 GCSEs each) and an ASDAN award – giving them 11 GCSEs in total. Whilst achieving 11 GCSEs undoubtedly looked impressive on paper, it was arguably at the expense of the pupil experiencing a broad curriculum. In proposing that GCSE equivalencies are re-introduced into the performance tables, it would therefore be wise to legislate in such a way that a balance is achieved between giving pupils the best chance possible to gain at least the minimum 5 GCSEs needed for progression to further education, and the temptation for schools to 'rack up' the number of GCSE equivalencies taken for the sake of those performance tables. The exact formulation of this metric should be the subject of careful discussion between the profession and government, and I would not wish to make a definitive recommendation in this book. An example would be the 'Modern Baccalaureate' described earlier in the book, but there are other models to consider (see for example Wholeeducation.org).

However, I fully recognise that a reform such as this may be considered 'a step too far' and so would suggest as a starting point that the metric should be based on the following principles:

In terms of raw *attainment:*

1. *Either* English or Maths GCSE *or* Functional Skills in Literacy and Numeracy – the latter counting for a 'half-GCSE' in each case;

2. At least one science award, assessed either through GCSE or continual assessment as used to be the case with BTecs;

3. Four or five additional free choices (depending on whether a pupil took a single or dual science award), assessed either by GCSE or by continual assessment, but with no single subject worth more than 2 GCSEs or equivalent.

4. Pupils would be free to take more options, but the results of these would not count in the performance tables;

5. Additionally, the system of limiting the number of GCSE grades at any given level based on national results at KS2 (so called 'norm-referencing based on comparable outcomes') should be abolished;

6. The English Baccalaureate should be abolished, both as a concept which attributes greater value to a very limited set of subjects and as a performance table metric in itself; and

7. Schools should be allowed to count the 'best' exam result that a pupil achieves in any given subject.

This approach has the following advantages for our VYPs:

1. It gives them more ways of demonstrating competence in the key areas of literacy and numeracy;

2. It enables those who perform better through continuous assessment than terminal exams to demonstrate their abilities;

3. It gives pupils a far greater choice in the subjects they study from age 14 onwards, and thus increases significantly the 'agency' they have in their studies;

4. It gives pupils more than one chance to succeed in any given examination; and

5. It removes the perverse incentive for schools on the one hand to enter pupils for large numbers of equivalencies (as, arguably, used to be the case when these were allowed), or on the other hand to enter them for a set of subjects determined by the EBacc (as is currently the case with the 'Progress 8' metric).

The measurement of *progress* is trickier. We saw earlier that basing GCSE performance on KS2 SAT results was problematic, not least because nationally, pupils with lower initial attainment at KS2 also make less progress through secondary school. **All other things being equal, it follows therefore that secondary schools admitting pupils with lower attainment will be unfairly criticised when these pupils make less progress than their higher attaining peers.** Improving the relevance of the curriculum as outlined in the proposals above would arguably go some way to improve the chances of our VYPs to achieve better outcomes at 16; we are all far more likely to work harder at, and be more successful in, those subjects that we enjoy. That factor in itself would help resolve the issue of how to achieve a fairer measure of pupil progress. However, it is my view that we should look to re-introduce the concept of 'Contextual Value Added' (CVA) that was used between 2006 and 2010 to take into account the additional challenges faced by our VYPs. This is particularly important in light of my fifth proposal, which is to *highlight the importance of the NEET metric.*

Readers will remember that the term 'NEET' stands for 'Not in Education, Employment or Training'. Whilst the statistic is applied to young people aged 16-24, as far as secondary schools are concerned, it measures the proportion of young people who are NEET after leaving compulsory education (at the end of Year 11). It is true that schools are held to account for the proportion of pupils who are NEET, but it is not considered (at the moment) to be as important a metric as those that measure exam performance. I think this is a mistake; in many ways, the most important outcome of all for a person aged 16 is not the exam results themselves, but rather the fact that they are enabled to take the next steps to becoming a fully functioning member of society. Put bluntly, a person who achieves 9 GCSEs at a good level but who then subsequently 'drops out' is ultimately going to have a poorer set of life chances than a person who achieves fewer GCSEs at a lower grade, but who nonetheless goes on to 6th form study, an apprenticeship or indeed a full-time job. Viewing the percentage of NEETs as a key metric would therefore help redress the balance between the current position of seeing exams at 16 as an end in themselves ('How can we get each pupil the highest grades possible'?) rather than a means to an end ('How can we ensure that each pupil achieves a positive destination'?).

There is, of course, a significant overlap between these two concepts – in general, a pupil who achieves higher GCSE grades at 16 will stand a better chance of achieving a 'positive outcome' when they leave. However, this does not necessarily follow. Moreover, we have seen how an Ebac / Progress 8-driven curriculum may well not be the most appropriate for our VYPs; this being the case, having to follow this curriculum for the sake of the school performance tables could actually increase the risk of their becoming NEET. Increasing the relative significance attached to the percentage of a school's NEETs at age 16 would therefore give a very positive incentive for schools to find the most appropriate curriculum for their pupils, rather than one which simply resulted in their demonstrating their highest GCSE scores. If we accept the premise that the percentage of NEETs becomes a more important metric however, we immediately run up against the problem that schools with a higher percentage of VYPs will almost certainly, even with the changes put forward in my other proposals, be susceptible to further criticism. This is because it is, in the main, precisely our VYPs who become NEET. At this point, we have to return to my fifth proposal - the importance of re-establishing some form of 'Contextual Value Added' measure, which would take account of this fact.

In arguing that we should base our performance tables on our VYPs, it is of course only fair to assess what the impact would be on those who are *not* considered vulnerable. I would argue that *none* of the above measures would bring any disadvantage to this cohort of young people. Those pupils who still wished to study for eight (or more) traditional GCSEs, including the full EBacc, would still be completely free to do so. Those who only wished to take their exams once would be free to do so. Indeed, I would suggest that the proposals could actually benefit pupils traditionally considered not to be vulnerable, in a number of ways. First, and perhaps most obviously, they help any pupil who *becomes* vulnerable during their time at secondary school. There can be any number of reasons for this to occur, such as a change in family circumstances or a pupil's health. Second, removing both the limit on the number of times a pupil can sit a GCSE and also their 'comparable outcomes' link to KS2 outcomes benefits *all* pupils, not just those who are vulnerable. Returning to the image of the swamp, implementing the simple proposals outlined above would enable more pupils to get out of the swamp of low exam results without stepping on the heads of others in doing so. In short, prioritising the needs of our VYPs when devising school performance metrics would benefit all pupils. To emphasise this further, I would now like to turn to a specific example as to how basing everything around VYPs also helps those not considered to be vulnerable – myself.

I really did not enjoy school at all. Having passed the 11+ exam, in 1974 I started at Northampton Grammar School, where I experienced a diet of what would now be considered 'highly academic' subjects. I thoroughly disliked English, Maths, History, Geography, Science and Art. I was far too weedy and asthmatic to enjoy PE. I did however enjoy languages, music, woodwork and metalwork. Pursuing this 'broad and balanced curriculum' meant that I was broadly bored, in a balanced way, most of the time. On the face of it, this curriculum would not have served me well. However, I had two great advantages. Firstly, I had two loving and supportive parents who valued and stressed the importance of 'getting a good education'. And secondly, for some reason, I was good at passing exams. Having passed 9 'O' levels, the predecessors to GCSEs, I was finally able to spend my time studying subjects in which I was actually interested, and at 18, I passed my French, German and RE 'A' levels and even an 'S' level in French. Even there however, I found the requirement to study French and German literature utterly tedious, having little or no interest in the chosen books, their main characters, or endless analyses of stylistic devices and the requirement to learn line after line of quotes from the texts to demonstrate my skills in this area. I would have been far happier being able to study a course of business languages – but those options didn't exist at the time. My Head of Sixth Form was totally horrified when I informed him I had no desire to sit the Oxbridge exam, but rather wanted to apply for Middlesex Polytechnic, which would have enabled me to study for a degree in applied business French, two years of which would have been in Paris. In the end, I decided to attend Surrey University, where I spent four very happy years gaining a BSc in Languages, International Relations and Linguistics.

My first career was in teaching and for this, almost any of the various assessment regimes we have discussed would have worked for me. Whilst up until 2006 schools were not judged specifically on the percentage passing English and Maths, I was pretty good at both subjects, so succeeded without any extra support in those subjects. With the limited amount of choice available to me at the time, my 'O' level choices were French, German, Physics, Geography, and RE. This range of subjects would have been open to me through all the various changes in school performance measures. However, under the current system, I would have had to take 'balanced science' – a double award – probably at the expense of RE - which I would have found demotivating. Fortunately for me, this choice of options was no barrier to my first career – teaching. It is of course however increasingly common, if not the norm, for people to have more than one career in their lifetime. With this in mind, I now want to apply the same 'relevance test' of my schooling to my subsequent careers.

Post-retirement from teaching, my first venture, established in 2020, was 'ProjectPFI', a consultancy which set out to help schools with PFI contracts manage them better, and, if needed, renegotiate them. Let's start by seeing how well the English Baccalaureate and Progress 8 would have prepared me for this challenge:

English (written): Absolutely essential, as I have had to write a number of articles on the subject to explain in straightforward terms the pitfalls of these complicated contracts, and how best to overcome them.

English (spoken): Absolutely essential in order to simplify and clarify complex concepts for clients.

Maths: Only basic Maths needed – mainly to work out invoicing.

Science: Not at all

History: Not all

Geography: Not at all

Modern Languages: Not at all

Conversely, these are the skills I needed which were missing from that curriculum:

Setting up a company: Understanding the difference between establishing a limited company and a sole-tradership, understanding company tax, choosing an accountant, taking out Personal Indemnity Insurance

Website design: I needed to set up a website for my consultancy. In the end, my daughter did this for me.

Social Media: I have had to work out how to use Twitter, Linked-In and other platforms to promote what I do. Again, my daughter helped me with this – a good job as Linked-in gave me my biggest contract, completely unexpectedly.

Extensive Research skills: How best to use technology such as Chat GPT to research clients' needs.

Negotiation skills: How to identify win-win solutions with both clients and my work colleagues.

This might seem un unfair list of skills to expect schools to deliver. It could also be argued that these skills are better learned through experience. But in other ways, this is perhaps precisely the point - if I have struggled to set up the business with the benefit of all my experience, how much harder is it for fresh-faced and potentially highly vulnerable 18-year-old to make their own mark? Not everyone wants to be an entrepreneur – but what about those who do have this as an ambition? And anyway, we are repeatedly encouraging our young people to be bold, to innovate, to be entrepreneurial – but to what extent does the school curriculum give them the necessary tools? And has it ever done so?

Prior to 2015, the answer could well be 'more than you might expect'. For example, we saw that the Institute of Financial Studies (IFS) has a half-GCSE equivalent which addresses the need for basic financial literacy. We also saw that there used to be a full BTec (4 GCSE equivalent) in Business Studies, examined though continuous assessment, which went some way to preparing young people to run their own businesses. There was also a full BTec in ICT which developed the skills I have found I lack so woefully. More generally, ASDAN ran a suite of qualifications (which, we will remember, also had GCSE equivalence in terms of the school performance tables) which aimed to equip young people with the skills of problem-solving in a variety of ways. It was also generally accepted by schools that at the end of Year 10, every pupil would have around two weeks of work-experience, to at least give them some insight into the rigours of employment.

Since 2015 however, schools have had little incentive to offer these alternative qualifications; as we have seen, they are measured on how effectively they deliver the GCSEs that count towards the 'Progress 8' measure. Realistically, this takes up all the curriculum time available – time spent on any other courses is time taken away from ensuring that pupils achieve the highest grades possible in the exams in each of the Progress 8 'pots'. Moreover, the BTecs that still do exist are now mainly assessed through exams rather than continual assessment, which does not suit all pupils. Even the traditional work experience slot at the end of Y10 is considered by many schools to be too high a price to pay in terms of 'lost curriculum time' for the all-consuming goal of achieving as high a Progress 8 score as possible.

For this particular part of my life, the demands on schools (in terms of performance tables) for the period between 2006 and 2014 would have worked well for me. At Archbishop Sentamu Academy, I would have been able to study science through a BTec route, would have been able to follow another BTec in Business Studies, follow the IFS course in 'Financial Awareness', and an ASDAN course in 'Personal Effectiveness'. I would also have been encouraged to carry out a two-week work placement. However, from 2016 onwards, government assessment policy gave schools a perverse incentive to push the square peg of my actual needs for my second chosen career into the round hole of statistical expediency. At risk of labouring the point however, I want to look at my third chosen career which I currently pursue alongside my consultancy.

Having spent the last four years of my main teaching career dancing extremely reluctantly to the tune of government policy, in 2022, I decided to get others to dance to my own tunes, literally, by fulfilling a life-long ambition to become a DJ. Repeating the exercise carried out above, this how well a curriculum driven by the English Baccalaureate and Progress 8 would have prepared me for this particular venture:

English (written): Some.

English (spoken): Absolutely essential for good communication with clients.

Maths: Only basic Maths needed – mainly to work out invoicing.

Science: Not at all

History: Not all

Geography: Not at all

Modern Languages: Not at all

Conversely, these are the skills which would have been missing from that curriculum:

Music: This could have been taken as an option, but as it has been almost squeezed out at KS3 (from ages 11-14), I might not have had sufficient exposure to consider taking it

Use of social media: Absolutely crucial. For the second time in 2 years, I was struggling here, this time particularly with Facebook and Instagram (one of the main ways in which DJs promote themselves). I still find the latter extremely confusing, struggling with the difference between 'Your story' and 'Reels', let alone how best to film myself 'doing my thing' in any credible way.

ICT skills: Having the confidence to work with two fairly complex programmes (in my case, Serato DJ Pro and Ableton Live for Music Production) and crucially, fix them when something goes wrong.

Research and evaluation skills: Working out the most suitable on-line courses for DJ-training, and which 'record pools' gave me the best value for downloading music legally and professionally.

Marketing skills: Working out how best to research the local market for DJs, and how best to formulate a strategic plan that would ensure I was 'go-to' person for a variety of functions requiring a DJ.

Coping with failure: Whilst I found it relatively easy to get gigs in the UK, this was harder in Spain, where I now spend several months a year. Last Summer I gave out my business card to every beach bar in my area and was rewarded with a big fat 'Zero'. In the end, I found one bar prepared to take me on, thanks to spotting a request on Facebook – but I had many setbacks in the process.

Once again, and for the same reasons, it is fairly safe to say that the requirement on schools to demonstrate achievement in Progress 8 would probably not have served this particular career choice well either. Whilst it's true that I might have been able to follow a course in Media Studies in one of the 'Open Pots' of Progress 8 if the school offered it, the ICT courses examined through GCSE are far more theoretical in nature compared to the highly practical GCSE equivalency examined by 'TLM' that used to 'count' in performance tables.

If these are general problems for pupils whose interests and life goals don't really fit in with the education that schools are currently incentivised to offer, how much more of a problem is it for pupils who have either little *intrinsic* motivation to work hard in school (for example those who fail to see the advantages offered through the 'deferred gratification' of obtaining 'a good education') or the *extrinsic* motivation to do so (for example those who live in dysfunctional families and whose parents or carers are unable to push them).

As we come to the end of this section, it is important to note that none of these proposals to date actually involve spending any money – and so it is my contention that the curriculum and school performance measures can be made to work much better for our VYPs at no cost to schools or the taxpayer. With this in mind, we will now turn to how changes could be made to the third area of government policy which impacts schools – the inspectorate, Ofsted.

Chapter 17 – Proposals for changing the workings of Ofsted.

Abstract:

This chapter has no musical reference, out of respect for Ruth Perry and her family. Before making suggestions about how Ofsted could or should change, I felt it important to acknowledge the work done in this respect since the tragic suicide in 2023 of Ruth, following a judgement of 'Special Measures' on her school. I propose that when discussing Ofsted, it is important to bear in mind four separate factors:

1. *The principles underpinning Ofsted;*
2. *The processes by which Ofsted carry out their remit;*
3. *The suitability of the inspectors themselves; and;*
4. *The impact of inspections on schools (and of course in our case, VYPs in particular)*

Concluding that the proposals for change in recent months really only impact on factors two and three above, I put forward further suggestions. In particular, I draw attention to the opportunities for the profession to press for further changes, particularly with respect to the curriculum and performance metrics, during the consultation phase for how Ofsted will implement its response to its 'Big Listen'. The chapter ends by evaluating the specific problems that putting a school into a category of concern can cause our VYPs, and propose some alternatives for how schools could be helped to improve when faced with this challenge.

Chapter 17

My own experiences of the inspectorate between 2016 and 2018 were bad enough, but on January 9th, 2023, we heard the tragic news that headteacher Ruth Perry had taken her own life following an 'inadequate' judgement on her school by Ofsted. The senior coroner, Heidi Connor, subsequently found that the inspection had contributed to her death, and this in turn prompted an outcry from the profession about the practices of the inspectorate. In this part of the book, we are looking at how key elements of educational policy might change for the benefit in particular of our VYPs – and it is impossible to do this without looking in detail at the response to the tragedy of Ruth Perry's death. As we will see in the following pages, over the past 18 months a great deal of thought and energy has indeed gone into how Ofsted might improve its practices. We need therefore to consider these proposals for change in detail, ask ourselves whether or not they will help improve outcomes for our VYPs, and only then consider putting forward further proposals in light of this.

The immediate reaction to the tragedy provoked an outcry, with comments from a number of professional organisations summarised in 'The Independent' on 21st March 2023 (Kingsley, 2023). A petition calling for an inquiry into the inspection of Caversham Primary School gained more than 120,000 signatures, and Flora Cooper, executive headteacher of the John Rankin Schools in Berkshire, announced a plan to boycott their own forthcoming Ofsted inspection on Twitter posting: *'We have to do this! I'm taking the stand!'.*

On the 19th. December 2023, the coroner issued a report entitled the 'Prevention of Future Deaths', in which it examined the circumstances surrounding the death of Ruth Perry and concluded that the Ofsted inspection was indeed a contributing factor (Connor, 2023). On the 19th. January 2024, Ofsted published its own response to the report issued by the coroner, accepting all of her findings. In the response, it set out what action was taken before and immediately after the inquest as well as what it proposed to do next, including improvements in training for inspectors and a new appeals process (Ofsted, 2024). The report was prefaced by comments from the new Chief Inspector, himself a former headteacher, in which he openly expressed his shock and sadness at the death of Ruth Perry. He went on to announce the launch of a national 'Big Listen' to inform the development of Ofsted, stating clearly that *'nothing is off the table'* – a comment to which we will return shortly.

This is a book about the impact of government education policy on vulnerable young people. As such, I am not going to comment in detail on the inspection of Cavendish Primary School or the tragedy that followed. It is however impossible to discuss the impact of

Ofsted without reference to this inspection, as it crystalised for many people the problems with the way the inspectorate holds schools to account. Over the years, there have been many calls for Ofsted to reform itself, to abandon certain of its practices, or even for it to be abolished. There are, in my view, certainly good grounds for reform in so far as its practices impact on the life-chances of our VYPs. But before we get to these, it's important that we understand a little of Ofsted's history, and how we arrived at the current situation.

Prior to the introduction of Ofsted, schools were inspected by a combination of 'Her (now, of course, His) Majesty's Inspectors (HMIs) and local authority advisors. I can well remember my first experience of an HMI, who came to observe how I was getting on as a 'Newly Qualified Teacher' (NQT). At the time, the focus was not just on inspection, but also on continuing professional support. As such, the aim of the visit was to identify areas in which I needed to improve, and for these to be followed up in a subsequent visit. Supplementing this sort of visit were teams of local authority advisors, who would carry out similar work with individual teachers and indeed carry out whole-school inspections. At the time, almost all schools in the state sector were run by the local authority (the exception being the new City Technology Colleges, or CTCs), so it made sense for the local authority to be the inspectors of this service. However, under John Major, there was a concern that the system was not rigorous enough, and in 1992, the national inspectorate Ofsted was born.

Unlike the system of local authority inspections which it replaced, Ofsted's role was simply to inspect and report on their findings, rather than to offer ongoing support to schools in areas identified as in need of improvement, that latter role remaining the responsibility of local authority inspectors, HMIs and other 'advisory teachers'. In the thirty or more years since its inception, the framework or 'rules of engagement' under which Ofsted has operated have changed several times. Initially for example, schools were given months of notice of a forthcoming inspection. Whilst this gave schools plenty of time to prepare (too much, some people thought), it led to a situation whereby a school could have almost 'a year of Ofsted', in terms of the energy needed to prepare for, and then recover from, the very detailed inspections.

Over time, the period of notice was cut down; currently (in most situations) it is just one day, although no-notice inspections can also take place, as I discovered in 2016. Unsurprisingly perhaps, Ofsted has proved to be highly unpopular within the profession, and subject to much criticism over the years. This has included, for example, the validity of grading the quality of individual lessons and the extent to which overall outcomes are 'data-driven' (i.e., determined by pupils' exam outcomes). The former was abandoned in 2014, but the latter persisted until around 2019 when the latest framework at the time allowed, in theory, a school to be judged as 'Good' overall even it its exam performance data was 'below average', as long as it could show (in essence) that it was improving rapidly and the 'intent, implementation and impact' of its curriculum was solid. One feature of the inspection process has remained constant throughout Ofsted's history however, and it is this which is perhaps the most hotly contested – the 'one word' summary.

Originally, Ofsted had no fewer than seven possible overall outcomes for an inspection – 'Outstanding', 'Very Good', 'Good', 'Satisfactory', 'Unsatisfactory', 'Poor' and 'Very Poor'. Over time, these reduced to 4 categories – 'Outstanding', Good', 'Satisfactory' and 'Inadequate'. However, under the leadership of Sir Michael Wilshaw, the term 'Satisfactory' was replaced by 'Requires Improvement' – the argument being that a school was either good (or better) or not, and that if it wasn't good, then the term 'Satisfactory' could imply a settling for lower standards. Whilst the logic of this approach in and of itself is reasonable, the *application* of that logic was not. The criterion for being judged to be 'good' was to be 'Above average'. However, at the same time, the expectation was that all schools (quite reasonably) should aim to be good. The problem of course was mathematical – it is impossible for all schools to be 'above average' and therefore by this definition, impossible for all schools to be good. As we saw in a previous chapter, Michael Gove (the Secretary of State for Education at the time) failed himself to grasp this most basic of mathematical concepts when questioned on it by the Education Select Committee. We will return to the impact of this later on, but for now, I'd like to continue with what has perhaps persisted as the main criticism of OFSTED – namely the single word summary.

As I outlined earlier, during my career I experienced seven full Ofsted inspections, (five of them as a Headteacher and one as a Deputy Headteacher), in four different schools. I also trained to become an inspector myself, although as I explained, I never carried out an inspection as the rules for becoming an inspector changed during my training. Whilst I would never claim that this makes me an 'expert' on the inspectorate, I certainly had (I believe) at least my fair share of Ofsted 'at the sharp end'. Personally, I don't have any objection to the inspection of schools or indeed to OFSTED per se. Indeed, it is vitally important that all our public services are held to account, and that includes education. The inspectorate does however face huge challenges, which I will now do my best to unpick, after which we will consider the impact that Ofsted in its current form has on our VYPs.

When discussing the functioning of Ofsted, I think it is important to start by distinguishing between four factors. First, the principles that drive Ofsted, second, the process of the inspection itself, third, the people who actually run the inspections and fourth, the impact of inspection outcomes on the schools themselves. As I pointed out earlier on, the main stated aim of Ofsted is to provide parents with an accurate view of how well a school is doing, although over the years, these outcomes have become, as we will see, an increasingly important way of holding schools to account by the government.

Originally, full inspections lasted about a week – now, they last two days. Inspectors prepare for the inspection by analysing exam data, a self-evaluation form produced by the school, and other information that schools are now required to post on their websites. During the inspection itself, inspectors will observe lessons, speak to pupils, staff and governors, and make judgements in a number of areas. The exact format of these has changed a number of time, but currently, schools are rated on a 4 point scale ('outstanding', 'good', 'requires improvement' or 'inadequate') on the following areas: 'Quality of Education', 'Behaviour and Attitudes', 'Personal

Development' and 'Leadership and Management'. There is then an 'overall effectiveness' grade which, in one word, sums up the findings of the report. As for the individual areas, the options are 'outstanding', 'good', 'requires improvement' and 'inadequate'.

This way of reporting has been much criticised over the years, including, most significantly, the 'single-word summary'. This is viewed by many as problematic for a number of reasons. First, it is argued that to reduce the description of a school's operation to one word is overly reductive. The counterargument is that parents want a simple way of judging 'how well a school is doing'. Personally, I find this a rather patronising view – the parents with whom I dealt during my own 30-year career were well able to appreciate how 'some things worked better than others' within any of the schools of which I have been a part. A second criticism of the 'single word summary' however is that in practice, the individual judgements themselves are linked. A cursory glance at a random selection of reports would reveal that in many cases, all of the 4 individual judgements are the same, that in most cases, there is only a difference of one 'grade' (e.g., 'good' / 'requires improvement') between any of the individual areas, and that where there are differences, the 'overall effectiveness' grade is likely to default to the lower (or lowest) grade, especially when at least two of these are lower than the other two.

In addition to these general criticisms of Ofsted reporting, the following specific criticism was referred to by the coroner who led the inquest into the death of Ruth Perry. In the 'Prevention of Future Deaths Report referred to earlier on), she says:

'The current system allows a school that is inadequate in all areas to receive the same overall label as a school that is good in all areas, but with some safeguarding issues that can be repaired by the time the report is published.' (ibid)

An example of this would be a school being judged 'inadequate' owing to some clerical errors on the list which confirms the 'vetting' status of all its staff, even though in all other areas, the school was judged to be good. This is perhaps the most egregious example of one negative judgement affecting the overall judgement on a school, but it makes the point that the single word summary can effectively 'condemn a school twice over' for any of its practices that fall short of 'good'.

The format that inspectors are required to follow determines, quite naturally, the parameters in which they are required to work. My own observation over 30 years of inspection is that as in any field of human operation, the quality of behaviour varies enormously. My own performance has been both highly praised and highly criticised, as outlined in the opening chapter of this book. This in and of itself is of course perfectly reasonable, but the manner in which a number of inspectors have actually worked has, in my experience, been extremely variable. I can therefore well understand the criticisms levelled at Ofsted with respect to the conduct of some its inspectors. Here again, I am not alone in this view. Referring once again to the 'Prevention of Future Deaths Report (ibid), the coroner criticised Ofsted reports for their failure to balance the need for transparency to parents with teacher welfare. Specifically, she drew to attention an almost total lack of training for inspectors to deal with teachers' and leaders' distress during an inspection, the lack of a clear appeals process, and other issues around the confidentiality and timescales for production of reports.

As a Headteacher who has experienced a highly critical inspection himself, I find the coroner's conclusions utterly damning. For me personally, the biggest issue was the lack a clear appeals procedure. I knew that the lead inspector of our 2016 inspection had not followed process correctly, as I describe in Appendix 2, but I was not able to appeal this properly during the inspection. I would add to the above list that the appeal process following our inspection was also highly flawed – there was no independent assessment of inspectors' findings and the only other path open to us was, in effect, an extremely costly judicial review (which we ultimately decided against). It is tragic beyond words however that Ofsted's systemic failings with respect to the coroner's criticisms of Ofsted were found to have contributed to the death of Ruth Perry.

It would seem that MPs agree with this view. In its 68-page report released just 10 days after Ofsted's response to the coroner's report, on 29th January 2024, the Education Select Committee stated that that Ofsted's 'single-word summary' had led to a culture of fear developing in schools, and that both it and the Government must rebuild trust and make major changes to school inspections. The summary is, to my mind, is quite damning of the current approach to inspection, as it criticises the formulaic nature of Ofsted reports, and questions their usefulness to parents (which, readers will remember, is the main aim of Ofsted). The committee is particularly critical of the use of the single-word summary (outstanding, good, requires improvement or inadequate), echoing long-standing calls from the profession to changes in this policy. In particular they concur that the interventions linked to these summaries put undue and at times disproportionate stress on school leaders, who have 'an overwhelming fear' of losing their jobs. Helpfully, the report also noted that the appointment of the new HMCI gives a crucial opportunity to reset and restore relations between Ofsted and school leaders, and that doing so should be a key priority for Sir Martyn Oliver in his first year in post (Committee, 2024) .

As we have already noted, Sir Martyn Oliver, the new HMCI, subsequently launched Ofsted's 'Big Listen' on 8th. March 2024 (Ofsted, 2024). The introduction to the survey laid out four stated aims for the consultation - how Ofsted reports inspection findings, how it carries out inspections, how it can have a positive impact on the sectors inspected, and what it needs to do to be a world-class inspectorate and regulator, trusted by parents, children and the sectors with which they work. When I initially wrote this chapter, the consultation was ongoing. A key concern from the teaching profession and indeed the Education Select Committee (ibid) was the use of the single-word overall effectiveness judgement (outstanding, good, requires improvement or inadequate). Sir Martyn stated in Ofsted's response to the Prevention of Future deaths report (ibid) that 'nothing was off the table' (ibid), which by definition therefore includes the scrapping of single-word judgements. It was therefore extremely disturbing to learn on the 23rd. April 2024 that, in spite of this assurance, the DfE stated that single-word summaries would remain (Executive, 2024). Had this position indeed persisted, it would to my mind have completely undermined the legitimacy of the Big Listen. Fortunately, however, the government changed in July 2024 and this position has subsequently been reversed. Later on in this chapter, we will examine the extent to which Ofsted's response to its 'Big Listen' addresses these criticisms, and, of course, assess the likely impact of these changes on our VYPs.

Having looked at some key criticisms of the principles driving Ofsted and the behaviour of inspectors themselves, we can now look at our third area – the impact of Ofsted. There can be little doubt that the stakes of an Ofsted inspection are incredibly high. With around 88% of schools currently judged to be 'Good' or better, the ignominy for the remaining 12% that 'require improvement' or, worse, are deemed 'inadequate' is considerable. Quite apart from the general sense of shame and failure, there has been a growing fear over the past 10 years that a negative outcome to an inspection can easily lead to a headteacher losing his or her job, and / or (if the school is still a 'local authority' school) forced academisation. Once again, it appears that our MPs would agree with this view. As we saw above, the Education Select Committee in its report of 29th January 2024 *(ibid)* noted that there is an overwhelming fear among headteachers of losing their job following a negative inspection outcome, exacerbated by the extension of academy orders to schools with two consecutive judgements of 'requires improvement', and that, as such, it is vital that leaders are supported both through and after a difficult inspection.

Whilst these conclusions are of course welcome, the question we need to keep asking ourselves is whether or not these changes will help our VYPs. It is of course easy to assume that, if a school is judged to be 'Good' or better, then the VYPs in that school are being well-served. The arguments put forward in this book would question that this was necessarily the case, given that achieving the performance data necessary for a positive judgement could well entail requiring our VYPs to put up with options to which they are not inherently suited. However, we will leave that argument to one side for the moment, and at this point, focus on the impact of a negative inspection outcome on our VYPs. In our own case, as I described in chapter 16, the judgment had a devastating impact on the academy – one from which, eight years later, it still has not recovered. Worse, the cruel irony is that under the current system, the most secure way to improve the data upon which judgements are based is to ensure every pupil fills as many of the 'Progress 8 pots' as possible which, as we have said repeatedly, may not be in their best interests. In short, that inspection made matters far worse for our VYPs. With this in mind, let's look at how the proposals for changes in Ofsted's practice since the tragedy of Ruth Perry's death might improve outcomes for VYPs.

We outlined above four factors to take into consideration when discussing Ofsted – the principles underpinning it, the process driving it, the people involved in carrying out the inspection, and the impact on the school. With this in mind, let us now assess the extent to which the proposals laid out in Ofsted's response to its 'Big Listen' might improve its practice, especially with respect to our VYPs. The response pulled no punches in describing the extent to which the profession had lost confidence in the inspectorate, publishing a long list of criticisms of its practice given by teachers and senior leaders (Research, 2024). It is both appropriate and encouraging to read therefore that the Chief Inspector has pledged 'real change' to rebuild trust between the inspectorate and the profession (Ofsted, 2024), citing the following key points:

- A commitment to putting vulnerable children, such as those from disadvantaged backgrounds and those with special educational needs and/or disabilities (SEND), at the heart of its reforms;
- An increased focus on attendance, off-rolling and safeguarding;
- A new inspection framework with a greater focus on pupil outcomes 'to drive higher standards, alongside a range of measures to reduce teacher stress';
- The phasing out of the overall 'single word judgement' from Ofsted inspection reports, with these to be replaced with a report card;

- The pausing of the publication of inspection reports when safeguarding concerns are identified in an otherwise high-performing school, giving schools 3 months to remedy issues without intervention from the DfE;
- The announcement of all routine inspections on a Monday, with inspections taking place over the following 2 days, 'to reduce the stress of waiting';
- The launch of an Ofsted Academy, aimed at 'supporting a positive learning culture and embedding Ofsted's values of professionalism, courtesy, empathy and respect across the organisation', and which will 'share best practice from the sectors Ofsted inspects and make its own training materials and processes more visible';
- Specific training in mental health for inspectors, with the aim of reducing the stress of inspections; and
- A commitment to improving the investigation of complaints (ibid)

In terms of the biggest criticism of Ofsted – the use of single word summaries – it is extremely encouraging to note that Ofsted will indeed now be moving towards the use us of a 'balanced scorecard'. Equally, it is pleasing to see that safeguarding concerns in an otherwise high-performing school will be treated in a more measured way, thereby avoiding apocryphal situations of the past in which a school is put into a category of concern because of a mistake on the 'Single Central Register' of staffing or problems with the perimeter fencing. Finally, the decision to announce inspections on a Monday and improvements in the training of inspectors and the complaints process should also, in theory all contribute to a reduction in stress for teachers and leaders, and, as such, are all welcome. Based on our four factors for analysing the workings of Ofsted (its principles, processes, people and impact on schools), Ofsted's response certainly would appear to be clearly driving improvements in its processes and people, which, in turn, could lead to inspections having a more positive impact on schools. But is this enough? Crucially, to what extent have the principles of Ofsted changed?

At first sight, it is also very encouraging to see that a commitment to vulnerable children – our VYPs - is front and centre of the proposed reforms. Indeed, basing educational policy around the needs of VYPs is a key recommendation of this book. However, at the start of this book, I argued that successive secretaries of state have made changes to either curriculum or performance data policy without considering properly (or even, dare I suggest, fully understanding) how a given change will interact with existing policies in place. A key example of this is how the introduction of the 'Progress 8' metric, designed to reduce what were perceived by government as 'perverse incentives' for schools to offer pupils vocational qualifications, merely served to bring in a new set of 'perverse incentives', whereby schools need to ensure that, as far as possible, their pupils follow only those qualifications that count in one of the eight 'buckets' that make up the new metric. Whilst Ofsted's response to their Big Listen does indeed renew their commitment to ensuring schools serve the needs of the most vulnerable, little has been released so far as to how this will be achieved, particularly in terms of any changes to the curriculum or performance metrics.

There is however one notable exception. On November 2nd. 2024, it was reported that Professor Lee Elliot Major of Exeter University, an advisor to Ofsted, put forward proposals which would involve schools being judged on the extent to which they admit pupils from disadvantaged backgrounds and/ or with Special Needs as part of a range of new metrics being considered to measure a school's level of inclusivity (Turner, 2024). The stated aim was to incentivise schools with a traditionally more privileged intake to admit a greater proportion of more challenging pupils who, as we have seen in earlier chapters, statistically at national level make less progress than their more privileged peers, and who therefore risk depressing a school's overall Progress 8 score. An article appearing in the Daily Mail on the same day appeared to refute this, with the journalists claiming that a spokesman for Ofsted has already refuted the claim (Matt Drake, 2024). Measures to increase inclusivity are part of a wider consultation with the profession over how Ofsted's response to its Big Listen are to be implemented. Whether or not this particular policy is adopted is obviously not clear at time of writing.

It does however give an indication as to the approach that will be taken – an approach that does nothing to 'Fix the Foundations', to quote our current Prime Minister's slogan (Starmer, 2024).

It is the opinion of the author that in order to be effective, educational policy has to consider carefully the relationship between curriculum, performance data and inspection if pupils, especially our VYPs – are to be best served by our schools. Sadly (if perhaps understandably at this stage), the latest announcement from Ofsted deals mainly with the issue of inspection. It is true that their response to the Big Listen does also include a commitment to consultation on (yet another) review of the curriculum and on (yet another) inspection framework. But to date, no mention has been made of any flexibility around the current Progress 8 metric being changed. This is a very serious omission – as I have argued in previous chapters, it is the inflexibility of the Progress 8 metric which acts as such a disincentive for schools to admit, and retain, our VYPs, as it obliges schools to push all pupils down a curriculum route to which many, especially our VYPs, are not ideally suited. These policy areas are the 'foundations' that need 'fixing' before schools can be judged fairly on their level of inclusivity by the inspectorate. Indeed, if these issues are not addressed successfully, then it is hard to see how outcomes will improve simply by 'telling schools they have to do better with vulnerable pupils' through some new inclusivity metrics, as schools are already trying their hardest to do so anyway – not least because of current metrics around the progress of pupils who attract the 'pupil premium'.

Regardless of the final outcomes of the 'Big Listen', there is still the issue (for this book) of the impact of Ofsted on our VYPs. In Chapter 14, I noted that if a school deemed to be totally failing is taken into a strong trust, this course of action may, of course, improve the experience and outcomes for all pupils, including our VYPs. However, it is not always the case. My conclusion here is that in their current format, issuing a negative inspection outcome on a school is akin to throwing some dice. On the one hand it could improve matters if, as in the example above, it is able to join a strong trust. On the other hand, it could make matters far worse. For starters, there are at least two reasons for which a school deemed to be failing may not be able to find such a trust. First, if the school has a religious designation, the number of trusts allowed to accept such a school is limited. Second, if the school is subject to an expensive PFI contract, trusts may be unwilling to admit them on the grounds that they would drain their central funds too much. In this way, a negative Ofsted outcomes can lead to a school becoming a 'SNoW' school – a 'School Nobody Wants'. If as a consequence parents decide to send their children elsewhere (assuming they are able to), then 'falling rolls' and concomitant reductions in funding only makes matters worse. However, if the school doesn't join a trust, or doesn't do so quickly, it may well find it far harder to attract staff (and in the case of a judgement of 'Special Measures', prohibited entirely from taking on newly qualified staff), at the very time it is having to redouble its efforts. This in turn risks setting in motion a vicious cycle of staff-burnout, higher turnover and increasing problems in attracting new staff (see chapter 13 above for a detailed example of this). Overall, therefore, I cannot see how the changes to Ofsted's practice outlined in their response to the 'Big Listen' will make that much difference to any of this and consequently, to improving the lot of our VYPs. That said, there is every opportunity for the profession to redouble its efforts for change in the curriculum and performance metrics during the consultation period for the implementation of the new framework – a matter to which we will return in the final chapter of this book.

Part Five – Be the change you want to see.

Abstract:

This part of the book is a 'call for the profession to respond' to the challenge of how to rectify the situation whereby schools are currently having to work under the exigencies of a mishmash of educational policies which cohere badly, and which make it far harder than necessary to provide appropriately for the needs of our VYPs. Noting previous governments' unwillingness to act on concerns raised by the profession (as exemplified by the response in early 2024 to Ofsted's own consultation, outlined in the previous chapter), I suggest that achieving change could involve a struggle. Acknowledging this, extensive reference is made to a campaign I co-led to bring in significant changes to the ways in which the Local Authority in Hull made decisions that impacted on its schools (completely against the will of the Local Authority) , and from this, argue that pressure needs to be brought to bear from the profession at national level to achieve the policy changes that are needed to remove the disincentives that currently stand in the way of schools serving VYPs as best they can.

Chapter 18 – Causes of tension between the profession and ministers Abstract:

Citing the introduction of the E-Bac and some other examples, this relatively short chapter sets out the reasons for which I believe the profession is so critical of successive ministers' refusal to listen to and act upon, their concerns, in spite of the reasons ministers might give for this intransigeance – either explicitly or implicitly. It revisits my five key criticisms of current educational policy, and also my six general proposals to rectify these criticisms. Noting that successive ministers over the past 14 years have shown little willingness to act upon the concerns of educational professional raised by these issues, the chapter ends by posing the question: 'So what can we do?'

'A Little Respect'

Erasure, 1988

Few would argue against the vital role that education plays in the lives of all our young people, but particularly in the lives of those who are born into disadvantage – the VYPs whose educational experiences are the subject of this book. I cannot think of a single teacher or leader nor, to be fair, any politician, who would not want to make special efforts to ensure they succeed.   And yet the concatenation of educational reforms since 2012 has left school leaders frustrated by the demands of a succession of ministers, who for their part have trotted out pompous platitudes around how 'their' reforms will build a 'world class' education system. Where has it all gone wrong? And what can we do about it? In attempting to work out a way forward, I am acutely aware of the dangers of engaging in a 'blame game' or worse, yet another 'slanging match' – such approaches serve only to polarise opinion and as such, are perhaps doomed to fail from the outset. At the same time, I believe it is important for all sides to acknowledge mistakes, own them, and do their utmost to find solutions that will provide long-term improvements for our VYPs through a 'system re-set'. This being my belief, I will start with my own failures.

My biggest mistake as a leader, by far, was believing that I could convince an Ofsted team that our decision to 'carry on regardless' with our curriculum and exam-entry policy was in the best interests of pupils, in spite of changes to the performance table metrics. This was probably born of a combination of over-confidence, over-optimism, hubris and naivety. It is of course impossible to say what would have happened if I had taken different decisions on these issues. In all probability, ASA would still have been judged to 'require improvement' – a judgement I would have accepted (albeit grudgingly) as a snapshot of the academy's situation in 2016. However, bad as that would have been, it would not have prevented us from taking on newly qualified staff, and the overall stigma would have been nowhere near as great. We would not have wasted so much time fighting the 'takeover' bid, and arguably, it would have been a far easier pit from which to extricate ourselves. In spite of the great successes of our first eight years as an academy, I don't believe it has ever recovered from the shock of the 2016 inspection and that, for me, is a continual source of sadness and shame. Worse, the strategy to join forces with a bigger Trust (in line with government recommendations) appears to have made little difference even four years after that decision having been implemented. The 'take-away' from this for me is that any school taking a solitary stand against an aspect of government policy, however justified, is, in all probability, doomed to fail in its attempt. This was further illustrated by the stance taken by one brave headteacher shortly after Ruth Perry's suicide. On Monday, March 20, Flora Cooper, the executive headteacher of the John Rankin Schools in nearby Newbury, Berkshire, tweeted:

'I've just had the call. I've refused entry.' (News, 2023)

In spite of her bravery, she was subsequently forced to admit inspectors having been told that such non-compliance with national policy was simply not an option. Ofsted inspections were finally 'paused', but only after significant pressure from the teaching unions and the verdict from the coroner that the Ofsted inspection had indeed contributed to the death of Ruth Perry.

The main theme of this book is how government education policy has often (although not always) worked against the interests of our VYPs, so it should be no surprise that I revisit this theme here. Looking at the period between 2010 and 2024 in the round, an overarching criticism I would make is that overall, I find it impossible **not** to conclude that the government simply doesn't trust the professionals who are paid to develop effective strategies for delivering school improvement – i.e., teachers, senior leaders and headteachers themselves. I find this quite staggering, and often wonder why the situation has been allowed to continue for so long.

One example will serve to illustrate the point – Gove's obsession with the English Baccalaureate. Pronouncing on 'what he thinks is best for the nation's children' is rather like a health minister telling doctors how long patients with any particular condition should be allowed to stay in hospital, or what combination of drugs they should be given. Doctors would rightly be outraged by meddling micromanagement of this type, and the teaching profession should be equally displeased when they are told 'they have got it all wrong'. Ministers would, of course, deny that this was the case, and would talk of 'wanting to work with the profession' to 'raise standards for all'. But actions speak louder than words. Not one of the professional associations for teachers or leaders thinks that the E-Bac is a good idea, but still it persists.

It is not hard however to identify other areas of ministerial intransigeance in the educational domain. Many of the aspects of the 'Progress 8' metric have been similarly criticised, and yet it persists. The lack of a contextual value-added measure has been criticised by one of the most respected bodies analysing school performance data (the Fisher Family Trust), and yet no new measure is being considered. The call for the removal of 'one-word' summaries has been quashed, even though all the professional associations are saying it is a bad idea. Worse, it has been quashed in the middle of a consultation which purports to let everyone 'have their say' on this (and other) issues. Overall, any claims of 'working with the profession' have, to put it politely, an extremely hollow ring to them.

But what of the profession itself? One criticism the government would make is that without 'rigorous and robust regulation', schools will 'play the system', pointing to practices such as 'off-rolling' or, in the past, schools allowing pupils to take larger numbers of qualifications than were necessary in order to 'boost their position in the performance tables'. But let's just look at these criticisms for a moment. First, 'the system' is one which has been created by government and imposed on the profession – it is certainly not one that the profession has requested. Second, 'the system' is built on the principle of a zero - sum game; as we saw in previous chapters, it is actually impossible for all schools to demonstrate improvements in GCSE performance owing to the system of norm-referencing linked to comparable outcomes. Third, in order to score the necessary points to remain 'good', schools have to ensure that as many pupils as possible fill as many of the Progress 8 'buckets' as possible – so 'the system' has actually created a whole new set of 'perverse incentives' for schools to base their curriculum and exam-entry policy on what will work best for the school. Fourth, the consequences for school leaders who cannot deliver the government's demands are extremely severe – even if the reasons for failure are not fully their own. In noting this, I am not trying to justify or make excuses for any bad practice. Simply dropping a pupil off-roll is, as we saw, illegal. I would however make the point that in setting up such an inherently brutal accountability regime, the government is responsible for having instigated a culture of fear, the reality of which, as we saw earlier, has been acknowledged by its own education select committee. People living in a culture of fear generally have no love for their leaders. The new government should therefore not be surprised to learn that much of the profession has had a very low view of educational ministers from Gove to Keegan and, at best, tried to find ways to work around legislation that simply hasn't make sense.

In sum, it would appear that up until now, we have been at an impasse. And yet, if we are to achieve the changes in policy I believe are necessary to ensure our VYPs receive a better deal, the new team of government ministers will need to be prepared to make some significant changes. To remind readers, in Part One of this book, I outlined five key contentions:

1. That curriculum policy over the past decade has been influenced more by misguided notions of equality than by principles of equity, and that this has negatively impacted our most vulnerable young people, or 'VYP's;

2. That government metrics around pupil performance continue to force schools to act in the interests of the performance tables themselves rather than pupils, in spite of having tried to abolish these so-called 'perverse incentives';

3. That curriculum, examination and accountability systems have been neither viewed nor developed as a whole, and that this piecemeal approach to educational reform that has impacted with disproportional negativity on our most vulnerable pupils. Put another way, a succession of education ministers, starting with Michael Gove, have acted like insouciant doctors, dishing out an ever-increasing

number of pills to be taken without considering how they interact with previous prescriptions;

4. That we have a long-term moral duty to ensure our 'VYPs' become 'VIPs', and that the solutions proposed in this book will not only help achieve this, but also raise aspirations for all pupils; and
5. That many (though not all) of these problems can be solved through a 'system reset' without either the state or individual schools incurring any further costs.

These contentions led to six general proposals outlined in Part Two:

1. Government policy should make it in schools' interests to have the most disadvantaged pupils on roll. Currently, the opposite is the case;
2. Linked to this, there need to be incentives for schools and academy trusts to collaborate at a local level to ensure the most vulnerable have quick access to school places. Currently, there are many disincentives for this;
3. The curriculum needs to promote equity, as well as equality. The dogma of the so-called 'English Baccalaureate' works against this, especially for our most vulnerable pupils who often achieve the lowest outcomes;
4. We need to allow pupils to be tested on a mix of exams and continuous assessment. At the moment, almost all assessment is exam-based;
5. In light of the above, the current measurement of a school's success known as 'Progress 8' needs a radical overhaul; and
6. The inspection framework needs to evolve to take these changes into account.

These proposals, even when elaborated in Part Four, have been deliberately 'broad brush', for two very good reasons. First, there may well be issues that others would consider even more pressing, and second, I believe it is down to current practising professionals to determine the details of change. Whilst it is true that the whole of this book has been written with my own specific concerns in mind, I certainly am *not* claiming to have a 'monopoly of wisdom' on this subject. Indeed, I hope that the topics covered will provoke debate in the profession about these issues, and that these ideas will be robustly analysed and challenged. That said, I very much hope that a 'case for change' has been made through this book. However, given the highly depressing picture I have just given with respect to relationships between government and the profession, the obvious question remains - how then can any real progress be made when it would appear that there is a huge imbalance of power in favour of government ministers? An attempt to answer this question is the subject of our final chapter.

Chapter 19: Campaigning for Change

Abstract:

Our last chapter looks at how change might be achieved. Acknowledging that the recently elected government presents a genuine opportunity, it also proposes that the profession prepares itself for a tough campaign to ensure its voice is heard loud and clear, should the new team of ministers be reluctant to make the decisive changes which would give our VYPs the best possible chances of long-term success. The chapter begins with an example of 'direct action', in this case taken by Spanish farmers earlier this year to draw to attention their disaffection with EU policies on agricultural subsidies.

From this introduction, I give an account of how a small group of us led some direct action of our own with a view to changing practices within our Local Authority for the benefit of our own VYPs. The example chronicles our efforts to make the 'Fair Access' panel (responsible for the efficient admission of pupils to schools in-year) work more effectively. In the second example, I give a detailed account of how we established Hull's 'Learning Partnership', in order to rewrite completely the way in which Hull's Local Authority worked with schools. Both cases involved significant struggle with vested interests at Local Authority level – the latter particularly so. However, the campaigns were carried out professionally and the end-result was that the needs of our VYPs stood a far greater chance of being met effectively in both the immediate and longer term. On the back of these examples, I end the book with a vision of how relationships between government and the profession could be so much better. I challenge the leaders of the main teaching and headteacher unions to agree on a series of proposals to improve education policy for our VYPs, and to agree on strategies for how the government might be 'brought to the table' to discuss them if they will not do so willingly.

'Things… can only get better…'

D:Ream, 1993

Our drive back from Spain in February 2024 was put at risk by some *'accion directa'* on the part of Spanish farmers. Inspired by their French counterparts who had successfully blockaded most of the central routes into Paris, a group of tractor drivers decided to drive their huge machines calmly, peacefully and completely legally around the main roundabout in San Pedro. Their action, in protest at the perceived immense increase in their production costs perpetrated on them by Brussels, essentially stopped all traffic on the A7, the main (and pretty dangerous) arterial route along the Costa del Sol. This in turn threatened our long journey back to the Eurotunnel – if the A7 was blocked, we would be stuck in the South of Spain. Now, you may think that there are worse problems for a semi-retired couple and their golden doodle to endure – but to avoid falling foul of post-Brexit regulations, we absolutely needed to be out of Europe by the time of our planned departure. Fortunately, the farmers did eventually disperse, and we were able to drive the 1500 miles to the Eurotunnel without any hitch.

How does any of this relate to driving change in educational policy? In the previous chapters, we have looked at ways in which future administrations could develop policy on a more coherent, rational and less ideologically driven basis. We have noted that the current body of legislation has built up over a number of years without any minister having properly considered how new policies could, or indeed would, interact with existing legislation. We have seen how on occasions this lack of foresight on the part of ministers led to school leaders taking action which in turn led to accusations of us 'gaming the system'. This in turn led to more legislation, and so this cycle of 'cat and mouse' has continued. In light of all this, we have suggested that a policy 're-set ' is needed – a period during which the government listens genuinely and humbly to the concerns of school leaders and professional associations and works with them, to ensure that at 'system level', the interplay between curriculum, assessment and inspection is sensible, logical and effective.

History suggests however that it might be pretty difficult to achieve this. I remember a conversation I once had with my local MP on the train, during which I was bemoaning the fact that governments never appeared to listen to the concerns of our profession.

'Well,' he replied, *'Governments govern'.* The simple truth expressed in those three words has always stuck with me. Certainly, as far as education is concerned, that has been my observation. It should be clear from this book that there is little evidence over the past 15 years that government wishes genuinely to work with the profession and bring in policies which experts working on the ground – i.e. headteachers and their staff – know will work in terms of improving outcomes for all. Rather, ministers have simply pronounced changed and effectively told the profession to 'get on with it'. The introduction and perpetuation of the 'English Baccalaureate' (or E-Bac), coupled with changes in 'what counts' in school performance tables are perhaps two of the most egregious examples of this, but it is not hard to find other examples. The seriousness of this is compounded in my mind when we consider the quality of leadership shown by our government over recent years. I have endeavoured to avoid party political criticism throughout this book and to keep it as objective as possible. But objectively, it is hard not to conclude that the standards of leadership shown by the administration in office between the general election of 2019 election and June 2024 have been somewhere between dismal and woeful. This matters. Why should the highly trained, highly intelligent and highly practical leaders in our profession be subjected to the whims of ministers who often appear to lack at least one or more of these qualities at any given time?

In the previous chapter, we looked at a few ways in which government ministers could find fault with aspects of professional practice of some leaders in education – perhaps the main one being that of illegal 'off-rolling'. Whilst not in any way justifying that practice where it exists, my own main criticism of the leadership of our profession is that we are simply too polite, and not skilled enough in working together collectively to effect change in government policy. Thankfully, we live in a democracy, and can use our vote to change governments, as has just been the case. Indeed, a new team of ministers gives perhaps the best chance in over a decade for a genuine dialogue with the profession and a re-set of policy. In this respect, we can 'hope for the best'.

At the same time, I believe that we should also 'prepare for the worst'. Just as we can vote for a change of government, our democratic processes also allow us to organise ourselves collectively to push for policy changes during the life of a government. This may seem a huge challenge, given our inability in recent years to achieve this. But I believe it is perfectly possible to do so calmly, peacefully and legally, fully respecting our democratic processes. To illustrate this, we will now look at Hull's own recent version of Spanish *'accion directa'*.

As leaders in Hull, our first experience of taking collective action to improve matters was in the context of the Fair Access Panel (FAP). Readers will remember from the first chapter that this particular panel was the forum through which our highest level VYPs had to pass in order to move into a new school. We noted that the process was fraught with conflict, and was characterised by schools doing all they could to avoid taking the most challenging pupils, the result being that many VYPs were in effect excluded from full-time education for far longer than was necessary. One of the reasons for this was that headteachers, myself included, would typically send our Vice-Principals to the panel with strict instructions as to whom we would, and indeed would not, accept. A secondary reason however was that the FAP was chaired by a representative from the Local Authority (LA). This led to the perception that our academy leaders were being 'told what to do' by someone else - in this case the LA.

It turned out that the LA itself was under huge pressure for the panel to work effectively as, in 2017, it had been severely criticised by Ofsted in a report on its provision for pupils with Special Educational Needs (SEND). The consequence of this report was that the LA had to produce a 'Written Statement of Action' for how it would improve its provision in this area. Reading this particular Ofsted report of

2017 now, it is clear that the work of schools has a significant bearing on the provision for pupils with SEND on which the LA was being judged. An example of this overlap of responsibilities is indeed the FAP, which was tasked with placing VYPs into schools, many of whom had SEND; the longer these pupils were out of school, the harder it would be for them to access the support they needed, and the harder it would be for the LA to demonstrate that this cohort of pupils' needs were being well-met.

Ironically, to the best of my knowledge, this report had not been formally shared with school leaders – by this time, I was CEO of our Trust and I had certainly not been called into any meeting to discuss how we could help the LA with its challenges in this area. Had we been aware of this, there might have been more sympathy towards the LA person tasked with chairing the panel. However, in the period leading up to around 2018, relationships between the LA and schools surrounding Fair Access had become increasingly fraught, to the extent that good will towards the LA had almost completely disappeared. That situation notwithstanding, by 2018 I for one had become extremely uncomfortable with the workings of the FAP, and thought that as headteachers, we could do better for our VYPs. I therefore approached a colleague CEO and proposed that we changed the way it worked. Basically, I suggested that the FAP would be attended by headteachers and CEOs rather than their deputies, that the monthly meetings would be chaired by an academy head or CEO rather than the Local Authority's, and that we would all agree to draw a line under 'who was perceived to have stitched up whom' in the past and give ourselves a new start.

Happily, my colleague agreed to this plan, and when we presented it jointly to the other headteachers, the plan was backed by everyone. That is, everyone except the LA, who wanted to retain the chairing of the FAP. We patiently explained our reasoning, and eventually, the LA accepted the proposal as well. It will perhaps come as no surprise that none of the Headteachers wanted to chair it, me included, seeing it somewhat as a 'poisoned chalice'. As I had proposed the idea however, I agreed to do so for the first year of operation in its new format.

Working in this way, the FAP almost immediately became much more effective in its task of placing VYPs into schools as quickly as possible. I think that there were two reasons for this. Firstly, the psychology of the meeting was turned on its head. With the LA chairing the meetings, it became a battle between a group of people (headteachers) being told to do something they didn't want to do to solve someone else's problem. With headteachers controlling the meeting however, it became 'our' problem to solve. Secondly, we were able to hold each other to account far more effectively. A 'tally' was kept of the number of pupils that each school had both on the one hand excluded, and on the other accepted through the panel. Whilst this system wasn't *perfectly* 'fair', it at least enabled us to ensure that we all took our share of challenging pupils. Over the course of the two years that I experienced of the panel working in this way, such was its success that only one academy in the city was perceived to have acted unfairly – by which I mean to have acted in the narrow interests of their academy as opposed to the city as a whole.

This experience led me to believe that these principles – enabling headteachers to own and then share problems and hold each other to account for solving them – were crucial if we were to find solutions to some of the most intractable problems we faced – many of them being around how to cater effectively for our VYPs. These reflections were key to the next example of how we saw that taking collective action could be really effective.

In the autumn of 2018, our Local Authority was still grappling with the challenges of delivering the goals of its 'Written Statement of Action' following the critical report of 2017 into its provision of children with SEND (Special Educational Needs and Disabilities) (Kirby, 2017). Part of its work in this respect was to establish a number of 'workstreams', which were duly produced. However, these were simply presented to schools without any real consultation to heads in the city. This was bad enough, but when a number of fellow headteachers and I reached out to offer our own perspectives, we were met with intransigeance and, frankly, arrogance - the expectation was simply that we would comply. There were two problems with this approach. Firstly, even though the statutory duty for provision lay with the LA, in practice, it was of course delivered through schools. This led to the second problem. By 2018, almost every single school in Hull had 'academised'. This meant that in practice, authority over their running lay with individual academy trusts, not the LA. Their failure to recognise this sowed the seeds of a quiet revolution which was to change Hull schools' relationships with the LA permanently.

The imposition of the five 'workstreams' mentioned above became the touchstone for this mini revolution. As headteachers, we could see immediately some serious flaws in the LA's strategy for improving SEND provision, but believed that we could offer improvements. Infuriated by their lack of interest in our suggestions, I approached my colleague CEO for the second time, as well as the local district secretary of the NEU (the biggest teachers' union) to propose that we worked together to form a new city-wide Learning Partnership. Buoyed with optimism following the successful relaunching of the city's Fair Access Panel earlier on that year, the three of us quickly pulled in another small group of CEOs and headteachers, and this 'City Strategy Group' began work on drafting both terms of reference and a strategy to launch it. We realised from the outset that leaders in the LA would not give up their assumed position of authority without a battle, so we planned our campaign carefully. First, we came up with the following terms of reference, published below in full:

Hull Learning Partnership Purpose and Remit:

- The main purpose of the Hull Learning Partnership (HLP) will be to support the Local Authority in the discharging of its statutory duties.

- The HLP will do this by providing the Local Authority with regular, reliable and high quality advice on all matters pertaining to the delivery of high quality educational services across the city. These issues will include, but are not limited to:

- SEND strategy;
- The strategy for Teaching Schools and other CPD / intervention support across the city;
- Improving attainment;
- Improving attendance; and
- Reducing the level of exclusions

- The HLP will bring together MAT CEOs, Teaching School Heads and other representatives from academies and colleges, along with elected members and officers from the local authority, to enable open partnership working to take place;

- It will consider the constituency and organisation of SEND and other work-streams as needed, including the Schools' Forum, and will make recommendations to the LA as to how these could link together and run in the most effective and efficient manner.

- The Learning Partnership recognises the Local Authority's statutory role in decision making, but expects that these decisions should only be made after discussion with, and wherever possible full agreement from, all parties involved in the Learning Partnership.

Membership and Organisation:

- The Learning Partnership will comprise the following:
  - All MAT CEOs and Teaching School Heads who wish to participate;
  - At least one senior LA officer, preferably the DCS and / or the Assistant City Manager for education;

- o The LA finance officer

- o At least one elected member;

- o Representation from the teachers' professional associations; and

- o Other members, who may be co-opted as needed.

- The Learning Partnership will elect a chair and vice-chair on an annual basis.

- The Learning Partnership will meet monthly.

- All meetings shall be formally recorded, with minutes distributed to all partners and head teachers in the city.

Reporting:

- The workings of the HLP will be scheduled to link in effectively with the following:

  - o The current series of Heads' meetings (such as Fair Access Panel) to promote good communication with City Heads;

  - o Any work-streams established in the city;

  - o The Schools' Forum; and

  - o The SAF and CIB series of meetings

- Feedback and updates from the meeting will be given to head teachers at Head teacher briefings to avoid generating further meetings;

- It is proposed that these briefings replace the current round of meetings held by the Assistant City Manager for Education;

- The Learning Partnership will provide termly reports to the RSC, to ensure that he is aware of developments and kept in the best position to support us;

- Termly reports will be shared with all elected members, who will be able to call on representatives from the Learning Partnership to answer any questions they may have;

- The Christmas term report will be issued in advance of MAT CEO's annual meetings with the RSC, to make the preparation for, and running of these meetings more efficient.

I have reproduced this in full to illustrate four key principles we wanted to enshrine. First, we identified key goals that we shared with the Local Authority. Whilst this started with the immediate challenge – achieving the goals outlined in the LA's five workstreams to deliver improvements for pupils with Special Educational Needs – they also included other key goals, such as reducing exclusions and raising achievement across the board. In other words, we worked hard to ensure that all the challenges were 'our' challenges, the resolving of which would require collective planning and collective responsibility. The aim was to remover the 'us and them' atmosphere which had existed up to that point.

Second, we recognised that the development of policy would genuinely require the views and skills of all relevant parties. In this respect it is important to note that we recognised the LA's role and accountabilities and wanted to help them discharge these effectively. We just didn't want them to dictate to us, which was our perception of how they had worked in the past. By the same token, we recognised the importance of involving the professional associations so that they in turn didn't feel 'done unto'.

The last two principles aimed to ensure we could work together effectively, so third, we 'kept it simple'. We wanted to achieve absolute clarity of purpose, and in the end, a completely new way of working was described in under 500 words. Finally, we wanted to ensure that regular communication between all relevant stakeholders was 'hardwired' into the system, to avoid for example the situation we looked at above, whereby schools were not routinely made aware of issues faced by the LA as a result of Ofsted or any other inspections.

Having decided fairly quickly what we wanted to achieve, the challenge remained as to how to arrive at the point where the LA agreed to fulfil its role as part of a learning partnership, rather than by simply dictating policy. In the end, we decided to invite the LA to a meeting with all the Headteachers and CEOs, at which we had decided we would hold a vote of 'No confidence' in the LA. Once again, I have reproduced this communication in full, with a view to illustrating some more key principles of our strategy:

Meeting to discuss the development of SEND strategy in Hull:

City Strategy Group

'During the last academic year, the City Strategy Group was established, to examine ways in which we might attract more funding to an area which all agreed was badly underfunded. The group comprised a range of MAT CEOs and Teaching School heads, representing Primary, Secondary and Special Schools, as well as the Local Authority. At our first meeting, the group unanimously identified SEND as the biggest priority to tackle, and commissioned a report to investigate this. Having received the report, which looked into the percentage of pupils with EHCPs in Hull relative to its statistical neighbours, the group has reached the following conclusions:

1. Data suggests that errors in the way in which the LA calculated the need for statements / EHCPs since 2010 has significantly underestimated the level of SEN need across Hull;
2. These errors mean that there are currently between 150 and 250 pupils across Hull without an Education and Health Care Plan (EHCP) who should have one;
3. Based on national averages, around half of these should be in a Special School;
4. Because SEN funding historically has been based on LA assessment of need, it is estimated that Hull has lost around £4.5m per year for each of the last 8 years;
5. The LA has not worked with schools effectively, as required by the DfE's 2017 High Needs Strategic Review policy;

6. In addition to failing pupils, the current strategy is putting increased pressure on mainstream schools to meet the needs of pupils who should be in a special school or on SEN support. This is having an inevitable impact on exclusions, and puts schools at greater risk of criticism from Ofsted for failing to meet individual need adequately.

Based on these findings, the strategy group wishes to register with Hull's executive officers and elected members that it has no confidence in the ability of the LA to analyse SEND sufficiency accurately, no confidence in its ability to formulate a coherent strategy for children with SEND, and no confidence in the Executive's ability to oversee SEN sufficiency planning and strategy effectively.

In order to ensure that appropriate arrangements and actions are put in place to produce a collaboratively agreed, coherent strategic plan (SEND Sufficiency Strategy) for Hull that will enable SEND needs to be effectively identified, planned for and met, the City Strategy Group proposes the following steps are taken:

1. Drawing a line under past mistakes, we all need to work together urgently to lever in the funding that Hull needs to support the true number of children with SEN;
2. To this end, Hull establishes a new Learning Partnership, comprising MAT CEOs, Teaching School Heads, and representation from the professional associations, LA officers and elected members;
3. The remit of the partnership, in the first instance, is to develop a comprehensive SEND 'strategy for change' for the city, including sufficiency planning, spending on 'out-of-county' placements, spending from the High Needs Block (HNB) and future needs for the city, taking into account the findings of the independent SEND review;
4. The current city SEND strategy is put on hold, pending a full review of the above. School Representatives will not be attending any associated meetings (including SAF and High Needs Strategy Group, for example) until we have agreed a new way of working in line with these proposals. *The City Strategy Group does however fully support the Special*

244

School Bid and has received reassurances from the Regional Schools' Commissioner (RSC) that this bid is not affected in any way by these proposals.

5. The proposed new role of City Manager for Education is put on hold for 12 months, and that some of the money is allocated to the Learning Partnership to commission further independent research as needed;
6. The new Partnership agrees a schedule for reporting to the Executive, elected members and the Schools' Forum with their findings and proposals for a new strategy; and
7. The Partnership agrees to present its findings and case for additional funding to the Regional Schools' Commissioner (RSC), demonstrating a genuine partnership approach that includes all major stakeholders.'

Perhaps unsurprisingly, this meeting managed to attract almost every one of Hull's 100 or so headteachers and CEOs. After the proposal had been presented we immediately held a secret ballot electronically on whether or not to accept its principles. Around 85% of those present did so, which we believed was a very positive endorsement, and the following day, the Hull Learning Partnership was formed.

That, however, was not the end of the matter. In spite of having demonstrably lost the confidence of Hull's headteachers and CEOs, the LA still demanded to chair the partnership. When we refused this request, our actions were reported to the Regional Schools' Commissioner. As we have seen in previous chapters, RSCs hold an extremely powerful position in the regional administration of schools and academies. To use a school-based analogy, The LA's reporting of our actions to the RSC was the equivalent of a pupil 'dobbing someone in' to a teacher. Fortunately for us, the RSC clearly had the good sense to realise that this particular battle was one whose outcome it was going to be very hard to influence, given the level of support for it across Hull. I believe that collectively, Hull heads were in some way 'put on the naughty step' for a while, but in reality, faced with such a united response, there was little to be done but to accept the new status quo, especially given the fact that, objectively, the new partnership stood a much better chance of tackling and solving the problems around SEND provision than was previously the case. If any more justification had been needed, In January 2019 Ofsted issued another highly critical report of the LA in its Inspection of Children's Social Care Services, highlighting again the need for support from it schools to effect certain improvements. Thus finally, Hull's new way of working was accepted by all parties.

The new Learning Partnership elected its own chair and vice-chair, and ensured that representative headteachers and CEOs from the Partnership sat on all of the workstreams established by the LA to improve SEND provision. In spite of some opposition, our (in the main) quiet revolution had succeeded, and from that point onwards, the planning of educational strategy in Hull had a much more cohesive approach. It is perhaps too soon to judge the long-term effectiveness of the strategy, but there were certainly some 'quick wins'. First, we had a forum in which primary, secondary and special school headteachers could all meet up regularly. Prior to this, meetings for each of these categories of schools had been held separately – bringing us all together at the very least gave us the opportunity to understand each other's issues and support each other better. Second, we were able to obtain some private sponsorship from a local law firm, who attended our conferences and gave us all useful legal advice on a range of issues of common interest. Whilst these successes might on the surface appear a little trivial, I believe they contributed to an enhanced sense of our value and professionalism, which in turn have a positive impact on morale. Perhaps the biggest 'quick win' however was how we were able to navigate the Pandemic.

In March 2020, a large number of key leaders in the Learning Partnership gathered in a relatively small room at the Local Authority's Headquarters to receive updates on the LA's progress towards meeting the goals laid out in its 'Written Statement of Action' following the critical 2017 report of its SEND provision. A week later, we were put into lockdown. That same day, I looked into video-conferencing solutions, and following the briefest of google searches, hit upon 'Zoom'. We bought it that day, and set up our own academy accounts as we faced this new challenge. By that time, we had a new (and excellent) Local Authority Director of Education. I suggested to her that to help manage communications, we added all the Learning Partnership leaders to a Zoom group.

It seems remarkable now that only 4 years ago, this was a relatively new way of working. Needless to say, the suggestion was accepted, and we were able right from the outset to plan how to navigate the crisis. Whilst Zoom was indispensable, it was the work we had done through establishing the Learning Partnership 15 months beforehand that proved so useful in those early days. By March 2020, trust between Hull's academies and the LA had been much improved, and in a series of weekly (or in some cases more frequent) meetings, we were able to navigate the challenges of the Pandemic extremely effectively. Our decision to include representation from the teaching unions also proved invaluable as we did our best to resolve tensions around dates for 'locking down'. Although our discussions in this respect were not easy, I believe that we did manage, ultimately, to reconcile conflicting views from the government and the unions. Indeed, from being on 'the naughty step' just over a year previously, the Regional Schools' Commissioner congratulated Hull on its response to the crisis as a model of best practice.

But what of the SEND provision which had been the trigger for the establishment of the Learning Partnership in the first place? We made the point earlier (without going into great detail) that whilst there is indeed an overlap between how well schools provide for pupils with SEND and how Local Authorities specifically are judged on their overall provision for these pupils, it would perhaps be over-stretching the point to draw direct causal links impacting the outcome of inspections on this issue, either for schools or LAs. That notwithstanding, the outcome of the November 2023 Ofsted area inspection of SEND was much more positive than the one of January 2017. In 2017, inspectors had judged that, overall,

'There was a lack of an effective strategy for jointly commissioning services across education, health and social care.' (ibid)

By November 2023 however, inspectors noted the following significant improvement:

'Leaders have strengthened the quality assurance of the administration of EHC (Education and Health Care) plans…Newer EHC plans more fully reflect the individual needs of children and young people and the support they should receive.' (David Mills, 2023) And furthermore:

'The local area partnership closely monitors school suspensions and permanent exclusions… This ensures children and young people receive appropriate support, such as through local authority-commissioned AP places, to help avoid permanent exclusion.'(ibid)

Whilst it would be neither possible nor fair to attribute these successes solely to the establishment and working of the Learning Partnership, it certainly would be fair to acknowledge the contribution it made to the improvement in EHC plan delivery, as would it be to acknowledge the contribution of the renewed Fair Access Panel to improvements in efforts to avoid permanent exclusions. So, with this in mind, what lessons can we draw from this episode?

A key contention of this book is that the 'higgledy-piggledy' approach to education policy has had a disproportionally negative impact on our VYPs. It should perhaps be no surprise therefore that the trigger for the establishment of Hull's Learning Partnership was linked closely to this exact issue – a collective failure to provide adequately for our VYPs, owing, in the main, to poor leadership from the Local Authority. How we provide for our VYPs is very close to the hearts of almost every educational professional I have ever met. Indeed, we are in the main quite passionate on this issue. The first conclusion I would draw therefore is that if we are to unite successfully as a profession to lobby ministers on education policy, its impact on our VYPs would be a good issue with which to start.

The second conclusion to draw is the value of a detailed analysis of the problem. In our case, we had very specific examples of how Hull had got its calculations wrong, and how these mistakes had impacted on the funds it was able to draw down from central government. This book, for its part, has attempted to show in some detail how at the national level, it is the lack of coherence between curriculum, assessment and inspection policy which has in many cases impacted disadvantageously on our vulnerable young people. I would suggest that when tackling government on these issues, our profession needs continuously to explain how these issues are linked, and how altering one part of the workings of this 'Swiss watch' risks causing the watch itself to malfunction, or even to stop altogether. A good example of this would to the impact of Archbishop Sentamu Academy's 2016 inspection on its long-term success, eight years after the event.

Returning to the Learning Partnership, it's worth noting that our complaints were not specifically linked to lack of funds. It is true that we were critical of the poor leadership that had led to our not receiving all the funds to which were entitled, but it was this poor leadership in general rather than a lack of funds per se that was our real focus. Generally, all public services want more money. However, it is clear that this is unlikely to be forthcoming any time soon. Rather (not unreasonably in many ways), we will be exhorted to 'do better with what we've already got'. A third conclusion, possibly more controversial, is therefore that lobbying on government educational policy would perhaps stand a better chance of success if it was restricted to changes that didn't increase costs. The changes advocated in previous chapters all fall into this category, and therefore avoid the otherwise easy dismissal of 'we can't afford this'. This leads us onto a fourth conclusion – in taking a stand against the LA's leadership, we were not disagreeing with their aims. Indeed, our own aims were fully aligned with theirs – in this case, better provision for pupils with Special Educational Needs. Our differences were around how to achieve those goals, not the goals themselves. Extrapolating this to the national level, we need to articulate clearly and concisely how the wishes of ministers – broadly to achieve better outcomes for all - align fully with our own as educational professionals. The only difference is in how we can best achieve these ends. The following example might serve to illustrate this.

A justifiable concern held by our current administration is a relative lack of economic growth nationally. As school leaders, this is something about which we should be concerned, and as such, we would want to see how we could put in place some long-term solutions which could contribute to solving the problem. Now arguably, one of our stronger areas nationally is in the creative arts – this being so, it would make sense for educational policy to foster this existing strength. And yet at national policy level, the insistence on the Ebac curriculum and the 'Progress 8' points system for assessment against which schools are judged does exactly the opposite, as we have seen in previous chapters.

The actor Simon Pegg draws attention to this issue in broad terms, through an expletive-ridden 'to camera' critique of Rishi Sunak's announcement in 2023, in which he proposes the compulsory study of Maths up until age 18 as a solution to our lack of competitiveness. Whilst Simon Pegg's piece is both rude and insulting to the Conservative Party in general and former Prime Minister Rishi Sunak in particular, the point is strongly conveyed (Pegg, 2023). I am neither condoning this approach nor suggesting for one minute that, as educational professionals, we should adopt it, but we most definitely *should* be seeking ways to convey convincingly how our proposals can help governments of all persuasions to meet nationally identified objectives. A fresh approach from our profession to lobbying government could therefore perhaps include a detailed analysis of both our short and longer-term national priorities, with a full analysis of how changes in policy could enable both the current and future administrations to meet those aims.

This all takes time however, and ministers new in post are generally keen to make a name for themselves. It would be wonderful if future ministers were prepared to do so by taking a long-term view, for example by being remembered as the person who led lasting and effective change, drawing on the immense pool of professional educational talent and building with recognised leaders in education systems that tackle the issues raised here, and indeed many others which this book has not covered. If, however, this proves not to be the case with our next administration, then a fifth conclusion from our experience in Hull is that collective action can effect powerful change for the better.

When we were setting up our Learning Partnership, we were keen that our actions would not prejudice in any way the Local Authority's bid for a funding for a new Special School, which we saw as crucial for our area. In order to convey our determination to effect change however, we did withdraw all support for the delivery of the five workstreams the LA had put in place to resolve other challenges around the provision of support for pupils with SEND. We therefore instructed all our staff not to take part in them. Without this support, we knew that the workstreams would founder, quite apart from the fact that if the situation had continued over any significant period of time, the LA would face the prospect of having to explain to authorities such as Ofsted why they had failed to deliver their objectives. Overall, we felt that this was a reasonable balance between forcing the issue on which we felt most strongly, namely wanting to redefine the working relationship between ourselves and the LA, without prejudicing a key plan which we all wanted to see succeed – namely the building of a new Special School in our area. Extrapolating this principle to the national level - finding the balance between being professionally assertive whilst avoiding the charge of holding people to ransom or worse, as has arguably been the case with the disputes around nurses' and doctors' pay, of prejudicing people's life chances – is not at all easy. However, I would put forward humbly and respectfully the following ideas as a 'starter for 10'.

First, and most importantly, the profession needs to address the issue of unity. When we confronted our Local Authority with our concerns, our proposed plan of action had the support of approximately 85% of all the Headteachers and CEOs in the city. With this level of determined cohesion, it was always going to be very hard for either the LA or the RSC to 'divide and conquer'. At national level, there are seven main unions representing the profession:

- ASCL (broadly representing secondary heads and senior leaders)
- NAHT (broadly representing primary heads and senior leaders)
- NEU and NASUWT (both broadly representing teachers)
- Unison, Unite and the GMB (all broadly representing teaching assistants and other support staff)

As a headteacher, I was always grateful for the support I received from my own union – ASCL – and for the representation that the other associations offered to the rest of our staff. The two main unions representing teachers – the NEU and the NAS – may at times get a 'bad press' nationally. However, it was, in my experience, healthy to hear uncomfortable messages within a structured framework, and as time went on, I worked increasingly closely - both formally and informally - with the representatives of the two main teaching unions in particular, to resolve both individual concerns and issues affecting all our staff. The best example of this was perhaps during the early days of COVID. Whilst we did not by any means agree on everything, we had learned over many years how to 'disagree agreeably'; these strong relationships of trust and mutual respect that had been built up enabled us to navigate a very difficult set of circumstances often characterised by conflicting priorities.

However, it is my observation (somewhat ironically) that the unions appear to find it hard to agree amongst themselves on issues that affect the profession as a whole, such as those raised in this book. It is true that during the Covid crisis, collaboration was improved as they worked closely to support schools, staff, and pupils. Here are some examples of their joint efforts:

- ASCL, NAHT, and NEU provided joint advice on managing the crisis, emphasizing the importance of keeping schools running for key workers' children and vulnerable children, while ensuring staff safety (NAHT, 2020);
- Workload caused by the 'Test and Trace' programme: A joint statement from NAHT, NGA, and ASCL addressed the workload challenges school leaders faced due to the test and

trace system, advocating for the well-being and welfare of school leaders (NAHT, 2020);

- Management of Long COVID: The NEU, ASCL, NAHT, NASUWT, Unite, Unison, GMB, agreed on a protocol for the workplace management of those diagnosed with Long Covid, ensuring fair and supportive treatment (Union, 2022); and
- Quarantine and Self-Isolation Guidance: ASCL, LGA, and NAHT issued joint guidance on quarantine and self-isolation for staff (ASCL, 2020).

More generally, we can find some other examples of joint working on issues relating to both funding, and teachers' pay and conditions:

- In 2016, ASCL, NAHT, NASUWT, and NEU all lobbied the Education Secretary to express concerns about the revision of the National Funding Formula, which they argued reduced the value of the NFF by £370 million (ASCL, 2023);

- In 2018, they issued a united call to the Secretary of State for urgent measures to improve teacher pay and conditions with a view to tackling the recruitment and retention crisis (Union, 2023);

- In 2022, in response to the School Teachers Review Body (England) report, ASCL, NAHT, NEU and NASUWT collectively called for the removal of the obligation on schools to operate Performance Related Pay (PRP), in efforts to reduce bureaucracy (Trinder, 2023), (NAS/UWT, 2023).

However, these examples only serve to underline the fact that joint action on educational policy appears to be rare. Indeed, even during the national crisis of COVID, only one of the joint agreements (that which related to the management of Long COVID) obtained the support of all the major unions. Nonetheless, joint working can indeed produce change. In response to the call to remove the obligation for schools to operate Performance Related Pay (outlined above), the requirement was indeed dropped by the Education Secretary in March 2023, with the change set to take place from September 2024 (for example, see (SchoolsWeek, 2024)). Given this success, it would be wonderful in my view if the major unions could all agree to lobbying ministers jointly on the themes of this book – namely the constant tinkering of curriculum, assessment and inspection policies which make it so hard for schools to serve our VYPs, and which are arguably some of the main root causes of many of the issues about which the unions separately, (if not yet jointly), do already complain – namely worsening pupil behaviour, teacher burn-out and teacher recruitment to name but three.

As we have seen earlier on in this book, individual teaching unions have produced policy statements on these issues – ASCL's excellent 'Blueprint for a self-improving system' (ASCL publications, 2015) and 'Blueprint for a fairer education system' (ASCL publications 2021) being two such examples. If we are to convince future governments that we are serious about this sort of 'policy re-set' however, we need agreement on the proposals from all the unions in order to bring the power of collective action to bear on ministers. As a first step to achieving this, I would urge the general secretaries of all the unions to reach agreement on key changes they would press the government to implement. As a starting point, this should include the acceptance of a broader curriculum (aspects of which could be based on the local economic context) which is more flexibly measured, and which takes into account pupils' social context.

With respect to improving accountability systems, perhaps our greatest hope is that the introduction of the 'balanced scorecard' could be linked to new ways of schools improving those areas in which they were found to be weak without the automatic assumption that they will have to join a trust, or be re-brokered into a new one. For example, a school with significant weaknesses in a core subject would, under the current inspection framework, normally result in a judgement of 'inadequate', leading to the application of 'special measures' and with it, a requirement to join a (new) trust. However, an alternative could be to work in close partnership with, for example, local or regional teaching schools with specific expertise and surplus capacity in those areas. An approach such as this would be far less disruptive to the workings of the rest of the school, and could help avert setting in train the vicious cycle of staff-burnout, higher turnover and increasing problems in attracting new staff, to which we alluded above. Of course, none of this should preclude the occasion where a school has completely imploded and really does need either to join a trust or be re-brokered into a new one. I do suggest however that such a move should be a last resort, rather than an automatic assumption.

Whilst I clearly believe in the merit of the arguments put forward in this book, I would expect current leaders in the profession to find other issues; I certainly am *not* claiming to have all the answers. If agreeing on a joint set of challenges and proposals is the first step however, the next step is identifying 'which levers to pull' to require government ministers to come to the table. To this end, I would like to highlight three possible options.

Option One involves invoking the 'common sense' and 'good will' of ministers. In 'hoping for the best', I would certainly not rule out the possibility that our new government would agree to a substantial review of curriculum, performance metrics and Ofsted practice if presented with a clear and united case for doing so by *all* the teaching unions. Indeed, a review of the curriculum has already been announced at the time of writing. I would note however that a curriculum review by itself is not enough – performance metrics and the workings of Ofsted also need a similarly comprehensive review for the reasons outlined in this book. However, such good grace cannot, in my experience, be counted upon, for which eventuality other plans need to be prepared. This being so, another option could involve industrial action. I would personally not support that at all, on the grounds that it would harm pupils, especially and disproportionately the very VYPs whose opportunities we are trying to improve. There is, however, a third option. In chapter 20, we saw how one brave headteacher, Flora Cooper, decided to boycott Ofsted and refuse them entry into her school in response to the tragic death of Ruth Perry. Whilst her own protest was quickly overruled, it would have been very difficult to overrule a national stance on this issue. In 'preparing for the worst', another option therefore could be for all the teaching unions to unite in instructing their members not to admit Ofsted to their schools at all, until there was at least an agreed process in place to resolve the sorts of concerns around educational policy covered in this book.

If this were to be the case, I would however advocate two exceptions to this general withdrawal of co-operation. First, inspections should be allowed to continue where a genuine safeguarding concern had been formally identified. This would, in practice, lead to a tiny number of inspections taking place. The second exception would be for a school to be able to request an inspection itself if it was working hard to come out of either the 'inadequate' or 'requires improvement' category – it would be tragic if a blanket ban on admitting Ofsted inspectors made it harder for those schools being told to improve to demonstrate that they had indeed done so (as was indeed the case for our own academy, as we saw in chapter 12.

Those exceptions notwithstanding however, an almost total ban on Ofsted inspections being carried out for a certain period of time would be highly embarrassing to the government, would cost nothing, and would have a minimal impact on pupils. If this option were considered to be too risky from a legal perspective, then other strategies involving the withdrawal of cooperation could be considered. Ultimately it will be down to the profession to decide how best to press its case. I would simply re-iterate that unless it does 'prepare for the worst', there is the risk that educational policy will continue to be dominated by ministers who, frankly, have little or no experience of 'what really works' – to the continuing detriment in particular of our VYPs.

Concluding thoughts:

Walking into a Post Office the day before writing this chapter, I witnessed the utterly miserable scene of a woman's desperate and unsuccessful attempt to have some credit put onto her electricity account. She was highly distressed, and it was clear to me that at school, she would have been one of our high-level VYPs, subsequently joining society at adulthood without the skills needed to live a normal, fulfilling life. We know that this individual tragedy is being repeated daily across the land – VYPs leaving school unprepared for life's challenges and condemned to a soul-destroying existence where they constantly feel 'at the bottom of the heap'. Whilst it would be unrealistic to expect schools to be able to solve all of life's problems for everyone, I believe that the situation could be vastly improved for many who risk falling into this situation, with some simple changes. And so, to end this book, I would like to indulge us with a vision for how our VYPs could indeed be enabled to feel more like VIPs, at least when at school, experiencing equity rather than just equality of opportunity, and an education tailored fully to their needs.

The key, I believe, is for the relationship between the profession and ministers to be renewed, where all parties agree to 'down weapons', genuinely 'take nothing off the table', and work hard to build a lasting partnership. A partnership where the profession accepts the need for accountability (as I am convinced it already does), but where it also is allowed to play a key role in developing the principles underpinning that accountability. A partnership in which the views of highly skilled leaders in education are genuinely valued and fully taken into account when policies on curriculum and performance metrics are developed. A partnership which removes all perverse incentives to off-roll or block entry for 'difficult pupils', and which instead actively rewards those schools who can demonstrate the most inclusive practices. A partnership focussed on delivering equity for our VYPs, based on the needs analyses of local educational leaders rather than the personal whims of a government minister. A partnership which enables our VYPs (and indeed, all pupils) to feel that they have 'agency' in their education and a partnership where the inspection process takes all of these principles fully into account.

Given that improving outcomes for our VYPs is such a high priority, and given the fact that none of the changes proposed in this book would cost any real money to implement, achieving such a reset should in theory be quite straightforward. I would accept, of course, that whatever government ministers may think of the ideas put forward here, current leaders in our profession may take exception to some or indeed all of what I have written, and may well have better ideas as to how matters can be improved for our VYPs. That is a cause for celebration; to repeat, I certainly do not claim to have a 'monopoly of wisdom' on system redesign. However, I do believe there is an urgency to impress upon ministers the need for some radical change to our curriculum, performance metrics and inspection processes if we are to improve chances for our VYPs. So, what stands in the way of such a reset? And how hard would it be to get started?

When planning our own 'system re-set' in Hull, we secured the agreement of 85% of the 100 or so headteachers in the city within a matter of weeks. Here however, we are talking about a far smaller number of union leaders agreeing on a key set of issues to be resolved with the government. These issues are not new, having been the subject of concern for many years, and I cannot believe it would be so hard for the unions to agree on priorities. There are already encouraging signs here, with both leaders of the two main Headteacher unions (ASCL and the NAHT) for example issuing statements over Ofsted's 'Big Listen'. These would however be far more powerful if issued jointly, and more powerful still if they were issued jointly by the leaders of all the unions. Over to you....

Bibliography

Abrams, F., 2012. *Cultural Literacy: Maichael Gove's school of hard facts.* [Online]
Available at: https://www.bbc.co.uk/news/education-20041597

ASCL, 2015. *Blueprint for a self-improving system,* s.l.: ASCL.

ASCL, 2020. *ASCL, LGA and NAHT Joint School Workforce Guidance COVID-19: Quarantine on entering or returning to the UK and self-isolation prior to admission to hospital.* [Online]
Available at:
https://www.local.gov.uk/sites/default/files/documents/Joint%20schools%20guidance%20current%20rules%20on%20quarantine%20and%20self%20isolation%20with%20regards%20hospital%20admission%2019%20June.pdf

ASCL, 2021. *Blueprint for a fairer system,* s.l.: ASCL.

ASCL, 2023. *Education unions call on Government to restore £370m NFF funding.* [Online]
Available at: https://www.ascl.org.uk/News/Our-news-and-press-releases/Education-unions-call-on-Government-to-restore-%C2%A337

Barry White, A. F., 2023. *White Frasier Report.* [Online]
Available at: https://www.gov.uk/government/publications/white-fraiser-report-private-finance-initiative-sector/white-fraiser-report

Benton, T., 2016. *Comparable Outcomes - Scourge or Scapegoat?.* [Online]
Available at:
https://www.cambridgeassessment.org.uk/Images/346267-comparable-outcomes-scourge-or-scapegoat-.pdf

Bruce Perry, M. S., 2006. *The boy who was raised as a dog.* 1st edition ed. New York: Basic Books.

Campbell, 2024. *'But What Can I do?'*. Penguin books

Chace, C., 2015. *Surviving AI: The promise and peril of artificial intelligence*:Three Cs.

Chubb, A., 2013. *Planning the opening of an Alternative Provision Academy under the DfE 'Free School' programme,* Newcastle: Northumbria University.

Chubb, A., 2019. *I'm a PFI, get me out of here!'*. [Online]
Available   at:
https://headteachersroundtable.wordpress.com/2019/10/19/gues t-blog-im-a-pfi-get-me-out-of-here-from-andrew-chubb-salt_ceo/

Committee, E. S., 2024. *UK Parliament: Ofsted's work with schools.* [Online]
Available   at:
https://publications.parliament.uk/pa/cm5804/cmselect/cmeduc/1 17/report.html

Connor, H., 2023. *Ruth Perry: Prevention of future deaths report.* [Online]
Available at: https://www.judiciary.uk/prevention-of-future-death-reports/ruth-perry-prevention-of-future-deaths-report/

Cowley, S., 2002. *Getting the Buggers to Behave, 2.* 2 ed. London: Continuum International Publishing Group.

David Mills, C. M., 2023. *Ofsted inspection report.* [Online]
Available at: https://files.ofsted.gov.uk/v1/file/50238910

Executive, E., 2024. *NEWS: Government defends single-word Ofsted judgments.*   [Online]
Available   at: https://edexec.co.uk/news-government-defends-single-word-ofsted-judgments/

Fazackerley,   S.,   2023.   *The   Guardian.*   [Online]
Available   at:
https://www.theguardian.com/education/2023/dec/16/strictest-academy-schools-in-england-suspend-30-times-more-pupils-than-the-national-average#:

George Leckie, H. G., 2017. The evolution of school league tables in England 1992-2016:

Contextual Value-Added, Expected Progress and Progress 8. *British Education Journal.*

Gicheva, P., 2018. *Vocation, vocation, vocation,* London: The Social Market Foundation.

Gove, M., 2012. *Education Select Committee* [Interview] (31 January 2012).

Gove, M., 2013. *Statement to Parliament* [Interview] (11th June 2013).

Green, D., 2013. Michael Gove's planned national curriculum is designed to renew teaching as a vocation. *The Spectator,* 1(2nd April 2013).

Hattie, J., 2012. *Visible Learning for Teachers: Maximising Impact on Learning.* 1 ed. London: Routledge.

Independent, T., 1997. *So what is a GNVQ worth?.* [Online] Available at: https://en.wikipedia.org/wiki/General_National_Vocational_Qualification

Jadhav, C., 2017. *The Ofqual blog.* [Online] Available at: https://ofqual.blog.gov.uk/2017/03/17/mythbusting-3-common-misconceptions/

Jonathan Simons, N. P., 2015. *A collection of essays to accompany E.D. Hirsch's lecture at Poliucy Exchange.* [Online] Available at: https://policyexchange.org.uk/wp-content/uploads/2016/09/knowledge-and-the-curriculum.pdf

Kingsley, T., 2023. *Everything we know about Ofsted protests following Ruth Perry death.* [Online] Available at: https://www.independent.co.uk/news/education/ofsted-ruth-perry-boycott-b2304920.html

Kirby, C., 2017. *Ofsted insepction report.* [Online]
Available at: https://files.ofsted.gov.uk/v1/file/2743093

Learning, S., 1999. *GNVQ Science.* [Online]
Available   at:
https://www.stem.org.uk/resources/elibrary/resource/28373/gnvq
-science-your-questions-answered

Learning, S., n.d. *GNVQ Science - your questions answered.* [Online]
Available   at:
https://www.stem.org.uk/resources/elibrary/resource/28373/gnvq
-science-your-questions-answered

Matt Drake, R. F., 2024. *Ofsted hits back and insists it WON'T mark down schools for taking in too many children from middle-class backgrounds amid furious row over controversial rating revamp plan.* [Online]
Available   at: https://www.dailymail.co.uk/news/article-14033707/ofsted-mark-schools-middle-class-children-labour.html

NAHT, 2020. *Coronavirus - information and resources for school leaders Coronavirus: joint union advice.* [Online]
Available   at: https://www.naht.org.uk/Advice-Support/Topics/Coronavirus-information-and-resources-for-school-leaders/ArtMID/764/ArticleID/327/Coronavirus-joint-union-advice

NAHT, 2020. *NAHT Members' Area.* [Online]
Available   at: https://www.naht.org.uk/Membership/Members-home/ArtMID/675/ArticleID/1021/NAHT-NGA-and-ASCL-joint-statement-on-school-leader-workload-from-test-and-trace-system-support

NAS/UWT,   2023.   [Online]
Available at: https://www.nasuwt.org.uk/article-listing/education-unions-coordinate-industrial-action.html

Natasha Plaister, K. B., 2024. *Secondary school and MAT performance tables 2023: What have we learned?.* [Online]
Available   at:
https://ffteducationdatalab.org.uk/2024/02/secondary-school-and-mat-performance-tables-2023-what-have-we-learned/

Nelson, F., 2008. Ed Balls gets it wrong, wrong, wrong.. *The Spectator,* Issue 12th June.

News, I., 2023. *Ruth Perry: Unions urge Ofsted to pause school inspections after teacher's death.* [Online]
Available at: https://www.itv.com/news/meridian/2023-03-20/headteacher-plans-to-refuse-ofsted-entry-to-school-after-ruth-perry-death

Ofsted, 2011. *Schools that stay satisfactory.* [Online]
Available at:
https://assets.publishing.service.gov.uk/media/5a7cbe97ed915d63 cc65c981/110080.pdf

Ofsted, 2012. *Ofsted scraps 'satisfactory' judgement to help improve education.* [Online]
Available at: : https://www.gov.uk/government/news/ofsted-scraps-satisfactory-judgement-to-help-improve-education

Ofsted, 2024. *Building a better Ofsted: the response to the Big Listen.* [Online]
Available at: Chief Inspector pledges 'real change' as Ofsted unveils plans to rebuild trust with all those it inspects and regulates following the 'Big Listen'. Ofsted commits to putting vulnerable children, such as those from disadvantaged backgrounds and those with special educational needs

Ofsted, 2024. *Ofsted responds to Prevention of Future Deaths report.* [Online]
Available at: https://www.gov.uk/government/news/ofsted-responds-to-prevention-of-future-deaths-report

Ofsted, 2024. *Ofsted's Big Listen.* [Online]
Available at: https://www.smartsurvey.co.uk/s/ofstedbiglisten/

Owen, D., 2019. 'What is off-rolling, and how does Ofsted look at it on inspection?'. *Ofsted blog: schools, early years, further education and skills,* Issue 23rd December.

Pegg, S., 2023. *Simon Pegg sends Rishi Sunak furious message over plan to make pupils study Maths until age 18.* [Online] Available at: https://www.independent.co.uk/arts-entertainment/films/news/simon-pegg-rishi-sunak-maths-instagram-b2257693.html

Politics, T. R. i., 2024. *Leading, episode 67, 'A tale of two spies'.* s.l.:Goalhanger productions.

Publications, G., 2024. *NEET age 16-24.* [Online] Available at: https://explore-education-statistics.service.gov.uk/find-statistics/neet-statistics-annual-brief#releaseHeadlines-summary

Research, I., 2024. *Ofsted Big Listen research report: findings from professionals.* [Online] Available at: https://assets.publishing.service.gov.uk/media/66d06d137c42acbece502c8b/ofsted-big-listen-research-report-findings-from-professionals-IFF-Research.pdf

Roberts, J., 2019. Ofsted asked to investigate 'off-rolling' row MAT. *Times Educational Supplement,* Issue 21st. October.

SchoolsWeek, 2024. *Performance-related pay in schools to be scrapped from September.* [Online] Available at: https://schoolsweek.co.uk/performance-related-pay-in-schools-to-be-scrapped-from-september/

Sherrington, T., 2016. *Dissecting Progress 8: The good, the bad and the ugly..* [Online] Available at: https://teacherhead.com/2016/09/30/dissecting-progress-8-the-good-the-bad-and-the-ugly/

Sherrington, T., 2017. *Schoolsweek: We need to ditch Progress 8.* [Online] Available at: https://schoolsweek.co.uk/we-need-to-ditch-progress-8/

Starmer, K., 2024. *Keir Starmer's speech on fixing the foundations of our country: 27 August 2024.* [Online]

Available at: https://www.gov.uk/government/speeches/keir-starmers-speech-on-fixing-the-foundations-of-our-country-27-august-2024

Susan Bowles, H., 2011. *Archbishop Sentamu Academy Inspection Report.* [Online]
Available at: https://files.ofsted.gov.uk/v1/file/1978933

Swallow, A., 2014. *Archbishop Sentamu Academy inspection report.* [Online]

Trinder, M., 2023. *Tory ministers forced to agree to 'intensive talks' with education unions on pay and workloads.* [Online]
Available at: https://morningstaronline.co.uk/article/b/tory-ministers-forced-to-agree-to-intensive-talks-with-education-unions-on-pay-and-workloads

Turner, C., 2024. *Schools face being marked down for taking in too many middle-class children.* [Online]
Available at: https://www.telegraph.co.uk/news/2024/11/02/schools-face-being-marked-down-too-many-middlle-class-kids/

Union, N. E., 2022. *National Education Union: Management of long COVID-19.* [Online]
Available at: https://neu.org.uk/latest/library/management-long-covid-19-model-policy

Union, N. E., 2023. *Education unions in united call to Secretary of State for urgent measures to improve teacher pay and conditions.* [Online]
Available at: https://neu.org.uk/latest/press-releases/education-unions-united-call-secretary-state

Update, H., 2012. [Online]
Available at: https://www.headteacher-update.com/content/best-practice/ofsted-a-satisfactory-performance/

Walker, A., 2023. *Are schools in poorer areas now getting better Ofsted grades?.* [Online]

Available at: https://schoolsweek.co.uk/are-schools-in-poorer-areas-now-getting-better-ofsted-grades

Wiseman, E., 2023. *The Guardian.* [Online] Available at: https://www.theguardian.com/education/2023/dec/10/eva-wiseman-the-real-reason-why-schools-are-failing

Wolf, D. A., 2002. *Does Education Matter?: Myths about Education and Economic Growth.* 1 ed. London: Penguin.

Wolf, D. A., 2011. Review of Vocational Education: the Wolf Report. *Government Publications.*

Appendix One – The Modern Baccalaureate Framework:

Modern Baccalaureate Intermediate **GCSE A*-C** QCF/NQF Level 2   :   EQF   L3

To be awarded.. *A learner will have to gain the following grades...*

	Best five...	...*in a best eight minimum of*
DISTINCTION*	Grade A* in English and Maths and 3 others (GCSE or equivalent)	*Grade A GCSEs or equivalent, or with Level 3 qualifications (AS-Level, CoPE L3, Vocational etc.)*
DISTINCTION	Grade A or above in English and Maths plus 3 others (GCSE or equivalent)	*Grade B GCSE or equivalent*
MERIT	Grade C or above in English and Maths and 3 others (GCSE or equivalent)	*Grade C GCSE or equivalent*
PASS	Grade C or above in five subjects (GCSE or equivalent) Level 2 threshold	

Modern Baccalaureate Foundation GCSE D-G QCF/NQF Level 1 :
EQF   L2

To be awarded..   A learner will have to gain the
following grades...

	Best five...	...in a best eight of
DISTINCTION*	Grade D or above in English and Maths and 3 others (GCSE or equivalent)	*Level 1 qualifications*
DISTINCTION	Grade E or above in English and Maths plus 3 others (GCSE or equivalent)	*Level 1 qualifications*
MERIT	Grade G or above in English and Maths and 3 others (GCSE or equivalent)	*Level 1 qualifications*
PASS	Grade G or above in five subjects (GCSE or equivalent) Level 1 threshold	

Modern Baccalaureate Entry QCF/NQF Entry Level EQF L1

To be awarded..   *A learner will have to gain the following...*

	Criteria
DISTINCTION*	4 or more Entry Qualifications at Entry 3 (or above) **to include an Entry 3 qualification in English and Maths** (Functional Skills or Basic Skills)
DISTINCTION	3 or more Entry Qualifications at Entry 2 (or above) **to include English and Maths** (Functional Skills or Basic Skills)
MERIT	2 Entry or more Qualifications at Entry 1 **(to include English and/or Maths at Entry 1 (Application) or above (Functional Skills or Basic Skills)**
PASS	1 Entry Qualification at Entry 1 (inclusive of E1, P1-8) or above

- Internal accreditation through a curriculum experience
- External accreditation through a Modern Baccalaureate 'accredited provider'
- External accreditation through an award

The final level awarded to students for the honours section depends on the number of components completed, and how many of these are externally accredited. This very flexible approach makes it much easier to identify a completely individual pathway for each student, just as for the 'Core' award, whilst still ensuring they have coherence within an overall framework.

The Honours Programme – detail:

ICT / Computing

The Modern Baccalaureate recognises that the 21st Century learner has to be fluent in the creation and application of digital resources. This can be supported through a wide range of learning contexts, from stand-alone qualifications to challenges within programmes such as COYO's 'Design, Engineer, Construct!'

Internationalism

The 21st Century learner needs to appreciate their place in a global community. Through this part of the programme, students will be introduced to cultures, and experience a developed sense of internationalism through the themed humanities programme.

Enterprise / Financial Capability

The focus is on 'real enterprise', taking on real challenges rather and simulated, and improving financial capability through applied numeracy. All ASA students will complete the IFS' Financial Capability exam, in order to be prepared for managing their finances.

Work Experience / Careers Education

All ASA students will follow a programme that gives them knowledge of the world of work, exploring future possibilities and career planning , to prepare them for the flux and change anticipated in future employment patterns. This will include a high quality work placement.

A Community / Citizenship Experience

In line with our Christian ethos, we will develop opportunities for ASA students to serve others, and/or show awareness of community issues, needs, problems and solutions.

A Personal Challenge

All ASA students will have opportunities to build character and confidence, to 'step outside their comfort zone', in a variety of possible contexts – for example through participation in a range of activities at our residential centre.

An Extended Project

We want all ASA students to develop their independent learning skills, and will provide them with opportunities to do this by their showing sustained commitment through investigating something that interests them, and then going on to produce a single piece of work that represents their findings.

Accrediting the honours section:

The Modern Baccalaureate award opens up the option for the honours section to be accredited through a range of means – either internal, external, or a mixture of both. The final level of this part of the award will depend on the balance of assessment – the greater the number of elements accredited externally, the higher the level of this part of the award. Giving this breadth of assessment choice however once again underpins ASA's commitment to inclusion – all students can undertake a wide variety of tasks in this area of the curriculum, but can have them accredited in different ways. This strengthens our ability to personalise the curriculum for all learners, whilst ensuring everyone receives breadth and balance.

The tables below gives examples of how this part of the award may be accredited.

External accreditation of Honours Programme - some examples

HONOURS ELEMENT	External accreditation in core qualifications	External accreditation through ASDAN Bronze/Silver/ Gold Personal Development Programme	External accreditation through Other Quals/Awards / Approved Provider Programmes
ICT / COMPUTING	IT GCSE TLM INGOTS	Module 1 Communication Module 9 Science and Technology	ASDAN IT Short Course ECDL QCF IT Unit Quals Sector-specific IT Quals NAICE Awards Digital Media Quals
Enterprise / Financial Capability	Free standing Maths Qualifications that 'count' ASDAN CoPE*	Module 6 Number Handling Module 8 World of Work	Young Enterprise Programmes HTI Go4IT Award Scheme IFS Qualifications NCFE award ASDAN

			Enterprise/Personal Finance Short Course
WORK EXPERIENCE AND CAREERS EDUCATION	Edexcel Work Skills * NCFE Developing Skills in the Workplace * ASDAN Employability* ASDAN CoPE*	Module 8 World of Work	ASDAN Experience of Work Short Course
LANGUAGES / INTERNATIONALISM	GCSE Modern Languages ASSET Languages Applied GCSE, NVQ Business Languages * ASDAN CoPE*	Module 10 The Wider World	FCSE ASDAN International Short Course

EXTENDED PROJECT	½ GCSE Extended Projects* ASDAN CoPE*	Module 13 Combined Studies	COYO 'Design, Engineer, Construct!' project, STEM Activities and Extended Project Award
COMMUNITY / ACTIVE CITIZENSHIP	ASDAN Community Volunteering Qualifications* ASDAN CoPE*	Module 2 The Community	The Young Arts' Leader Award The Young Health Leaders' Award (developed by ASA academy) The Junior Sports Leaders' Award The Archbishop of York's Young Person's Award The Duke of Edinburgh Award ASDAN Citizenship Short Course ASDAN Volunteering Short Course

PERSONAL CHALLENGE	ASDAN CoPE*	Module 1 Communication Module 3 Sport and Leisure Module 4 Home Management Module 5 The Environment Module 7 Health and Survival Module 9 Science and Technology Module 10 The Wider World Module 11 Expressive Arts Module 12 Beliefs and Values	Outward Bounds or other Residential / Expeditions ABA Boxing Awards World Challenge Operation Wallace Operation Raleigh NCS (these are just illustrative examples)

Listed below are some examples of how the honours section can be accredited *internally:*

ICT / Computing

- designing, building and managing a website for school, club or community group
- using CAM/CAD to design and build a model drag racer for a national competition, or Christmas decorations for an OAP party.
- DTP the school magazine, a Year Book, and advertising campaign for a chosen local charity
- using a spread sheet to track income and out-goings for a school or community play, a sports' club.
- a blend of the above or similar

Enterprise / Financial Capability

- tracking expenditure of the family shopping bills for a month, and working out how to make a 10% saving.
- planning the family holiday within a set budget
- raising money for a charity, but anticipating income and expenditure to maximise profit.
- involvement in a Young Enterprise project or related enterprise activity

Work experience / Careers Education

- *work experience (many schools are choosing to continue with their 14+ programmes because they see the importance and relevance to young people)*
- *workplace visits, and meeting local employers and employees.*
- *mock-interviews (preparation, participation, de-briefings)*
- *a blend of the above or similar*

Languages / International Studies

- *self-study key words and phrases, as well as customs and practice, prior to visiting a country or going on holiday.*
- *foreign exchange trips*
- *host visitors from another country*
- *prepare a guide to your locality highlighting places of interest.*
- *communicate with students from a foreign school, or an e-pal.*
- *a blend of the above or similar*

Personal Challenge

- *Residential and outward bounds experiences*
- *A performing arts or creative challenge,*
- *Participation in school and community sports teams, dance clubs and related*
- *A technological, scientific or environmental challenge*
- *Activities through Youth Clubs*

- Health and Well Being challenge (sports and fitness, healthy eating, drugs awareness, etc.)
- Public Speaking and Debate

An Extended Project

- written report, diary or record
- digital media presentation
- participating in a school performance, a concert, a community event, a sports or activity event (with a write up and evidence)
- producing an artefact (sculpture, textiles/fashion, mechanical model, etc.)

Community / Citizenship

- a period of voluntary service within the community
- peer mentoring
- St Johns Ambulance volunteering
- serving on School Council or Youth Parliament
- Guides/Brownies/Scouts activities
- Reporting to local politicians on facilities for young people, , or comparing local issues with a twinned community in another country.

Combining internally and externally assessed components:

GRADE	Number of Elements	External Accreditati
DISTINCTION*	6 or 7 Honours elements	externally accredited
DISTINCTION	5 elements minimum...	externally accredited
MERIT	4 elements minimum...	externally accredited
PASS	3 elements evidenced in learner transcript	no requirements for

Appendix Two: Inspection of Archbishop Sentamu Academy May 4th/5th 2016 - Complaint to Ofsted

Dear Sir / Madam,

Having now received a draft version of the written report on the inspection of Archbishop Sentamu Academy on May 4th and 5th 2016, I now wish to add to the complaint already submitted. This new complaint takes into account a number of factual inaccuracies in the report, which have already been submitted through the required channel. It also refers to other areas of the report, and indeed omissions from it, which add to the concerns expressed in our original complaint. Taken together, I now believe that there is a compelling case that too many conclusions were drawn on either factual inaccuracies and / or a collective failure by the team to look at a sufficiently broad evidence base, which makes the inspection incomplete under Ofsted's own definition. There are also contradictory pieces of evidence in the report itself that undermine the PDWB judgement. For these reasons, we now formally request a re-inspection by a new team, in which all the evidence presented by the academy can be taken correctly into consideration. This request will be made in a separate letter to the Regional Director, as laid out in the Ofsted document: *'Gathering additional evidence to secure an incomplete inspection' (January 2016).*

There are now five main areas of complaint:

1. In reaching her conclusions, the Lead Inspector did not consider all the evidence presented to her, particularly the evidence linked to the academy's self-evaluation processes which are significant both in quantity and evaluation, and also evidence of the academy's context. As such, we consider the inspection to be incomplete;
2. The written report contains a number of serious factual inaccuracies, upon which some key judgements have been made, as well as some serious omissions of key areas of academy leadership and management;
3. The key judgement of PDWB is based on two pieces of contradictory evidence in the report itself;
4. The link between comments made in the verbal debrief and the draft written report is evidence of an imbalanced

judgement having been made; and

5. The unprofessional conduct of the Lead Inspector during the final meeting at which the Executive Principal and Associate Principal were present;

Taking these in turn:

Complaint One: Basing judgments on an incomplete evidence base:

As per our original complaint, we would like OFSTED to understand that we are not calling into question all of the issues which inspectors raised with us as needing to improve; on the contrary, with very few exceptions we have been, and are working on, these significant challenges already and have plans in place to effect further improvement - we have evidence of the positive impact of these actions in documents not scrutinised by inspectors although they were made aware of them on several occasions. We also fully acknowledge that the exam results for 2015 based on first entry were poor. However, it is our strong contention that the team did not take into account significant amounts of evidence that provided an alternative view to the one that the 2015 Raise online (based on first entry) clearly gave, including an amended Raise online given to the team that was based on final entry results, and which was evidence of the significant improvements made between first and final entries. Extracts from the Ofsted inspection handbook say the following should take place at an inspection:

Student outcomes:

'Ofsted will take a range of evidence into account when making judgements, including published performance data, the school's in-year performance information and work in pupils' books and folders, including that held in electronic form'; and

'During inspection, inspectors should consider performance information presented by the school for current pupils across year groups and previous cohorts, including that provided by external organisations. They should also consider the published data available to them before the inspection.'

Performance data provided on KS3 was not looked at, nor discussed, during the inspection, even though it was provided. There appears to have been some confusion in the team as to who received that particular set of data. There was a very brief discussion around Y9/10 performance data, but no discussion of the detailed tracker of Y11 performance submitted, that contained key evidence for our contention that current progress was good. The Lead Inspector makes no reference in the report to the significant amount of in-year performance data that was given to her.

'In judging achievement, inspectors will give most weight to pupils' progress. They will take account of pupils' starting points in terms of their prior attainment and age when evaluating progress. Within this, they will give most weight to the progress of pupils currently in the school, taking account of how this compares with the progress of recent cohorts, where relevant'.

During the inspection, more time was spent discussing the data of the previous year's Y11 cohort. Furthermore, the discussion around outcomes in 2015 failed to acknowledge the impact of government policy on the decline in outcomes at 16, which was the most significant determining factor in this decline. There was also no discussion of the Raise online we submitted, which had been amended to take account of final entry results, nor was there any discussion of outcomes from previous years, which would have painted a very different and much more positive picture.

'Inspectors will take account of current standards and progress, including the school's own performance information, and make a relevant judgement on academic and other learning outcomes for pupils by evaluating the extent to which all pupils':

- *progress well from their different starting points and achieve or exceed standards expected for their age nationally (at the end of a key stage), or within the school's own curriculum;*
- *attain relevant qualifications so that they can and do progress to the next stage of their education into courses that lead to higher level qualifications or into jobs that meet local and national needs.'*

The discussion on outcomes did not cover these points adequately. For example, there was hardly any discussion around our predictions for GCSE results this year, which pointed to a much more favourable picture than the previous year's.

- *'Inspectors should consider a wide range of information. No single measure or indicator should determine judgements. Inspectors will consider the progress of pupils in all year groups, not just those who have taken or are about to take examinations or national tests. As part of pupils' progress, inspectors will consider the growth in pupils' security, breadth and depth of knowledge, understanding and skills.*

There was very little discussion about the performance of students in year groups other than Y11.

The Lead Inspector told us she did not receive any data for KS3 progress. However, this was given by one of our senior leaders to the inspector called Malcolm Kirtley. This issue has still not been resolved, and there is no clear discussion of standards in KS3 in the report at all, other than for students attending AP, which, is based on a **factual inaccuracy.**

- *When considering the school's records for the progress of current pupils, inspectors will recognise that schools are at different points in their move towards adopting a system of assessment without national curriculum levels.*

There was no discussion around how we are tackling this issue in Years 7 and 8. This was due to the team's confusion over who had the data.

The draft written report contains no reference to the academy's in-depth use of data, nor to its projections of student outcomes for this year or subsequent years. Whilst there are comments that refer to work seen in books, this view has not been triangulated with the academy's own evidence of monitoring of progress, which is considerable. The judgements made about progress, particularly, in mathematics and science, are based on incomplete evidence. No account of the amended Raise online to show the impact of final entry was taken until at least the start of the second day of the inspection, and there is also no mention of this in the draft report. The judgements made on progress across all subjects are also incomplete and therefore the inspection team were unable to come to a rounded and fair judgement on the progress made by students in all year groups and across all key stages.

We therefore contend that the judgements made around student outcomes were based on an incomplete evidence base.

Teaching and Learning:

'Ofsted will usually expect to see evidence of the monitoring of teaching and learning and its link to teachers' performance management and the teachers' standards, but this should be the information that the school uses routinely, and not additional evidence generated for inspection.'

During the inspection, 16 lessons were observed jointly on the second day with members of the leadership team. In every case, inspectors and senior leaders agreed on the quality of teaching and learning observed (there is no mention of this strength of leadership in the report). This being the case, it should have given the Lead Inspector confidence that lesson observations carried out in a similar way during the year would confirm the accuracy of our judgements, including our contention that **current** levels of progress were, over time, Good. A file containing evidence of over 600 lessons visited, including actions arising from these, was ignored by the team and is not mentioned in the report. Given that senior leaders agreed with inspectors' judgements on the quality of learning in every instance during the inspection, this body of evidence should have given inspectors confidence in the judgements of senior leaders that over time, learning in the academy was of a good standard.

Equally, significant and well-presented evidence of book scrutinies were not taken into consideration. Our internal monitoring documents were candid about identifying practice that needed to improve, and gave good evidence that leaders were taking action to improve practice where needed and that this is having the required impact. This evidence also demonstrates our dedication as a leadership team to continually improve the quality of our work. We fully believe that this evidence demonstrates that the leadership of the academy has improved further since our last inspection two years ago when leadership was judged to be outstanding. Without taking all of this evidence in to account the inspection was incomplete;

We therefore contend that judgements made around both teaching and learning (and indeed leadership and management) are also based on an incomplete evidence base.

Leadership and Management:

'Inspectors will request that the following information is available at the start of the inspection':

- *a summary of any school self-evaluation or equivalent.*

- *the current school improvement plan or equivalent, including any strategic planning that sets out the longer term vision for the school.*

At no point were we asked to provide a copy of either of these key documents. The academy's self-evaluation process is central to the effectiveness of leadership and management in the academy and is crucial in the academy's own evaluation of the impact of actions and academy's capacity to improve further. We contend that it demonstrates the rigorous nature of our self-evaluation process, the impact actions have had and the further actions that we have taken to accelerate the speed of improvement. Many of the outcomes of this process have led to very challenging actions being taken, including significant staff changes. There was no mention of the quality of the academy's self-evaluation in the report.

There were however several other omissions in the evidence base used to make this judgment:

As mentioned above, we presented extensive amounts of information linked to the monitoring of teaching and learning (approximately 600 learning walkabouts carried out this academic year, significant amounts of book scrutiny and the high level of moderation on the progress made by students all carried out by the Senior Leadership Team that year), the significant work we have done with teachers and leaders at all levels to improve this, including 5 specific case studies (more could easily have been provided), the CPD support put into place, and the positive impact this had on their practice. Whilst documentation relating to performance management was discussed, the very large body of evidence relating to improving teaching and learning was not.

Indeed, there is no reference in the draft report to this whole body of evidence presented to the Lead Inspector, nor of the actions taken and the impact that this has had on improving colleagues' practice and / or in persuading them to seek alternative employment if they judged that, in spite of considerable support (all documented) they were not able to reach the high standards expected of them. As explained above, the inspection team unanimously agreed that the judgements made by the SLT during joint inspection activities were 100% accurate. Therefore, to a large degree, this validated a significant amount of evidence which contributes to the evidence base needed to come to an overall judgement on the effectiveness of leadership and management.

This confirms our view that the judgements on leadership and management were based on an incomplete evidence base.

Judgements relating to AP:

With respect to the evaluation of *AP*, the handbook states that *'Inspectors will also scrutinise the school's records and documentation relating, for example, to pupils' academic and vocational achievement and the welfare and safety of pupils in alternative provision.'*

The team's view on students in AP was based on a series of factual inaccuracies (see above, and also the factual accuracy check). However, they did not look at evidence provided that we do monitor carefully the performance of students who actually are accessing AP. This evidence was offered, but was not examined. The conclusions arrived at on the progress of students attending AP were therefore based on both factual inaccuracies and an incomplete evidence base.

Judgements relating to Post-16 provision:

Post-16 provision was judged inadequate on the basis of one aspect of the provision (which had been resolved by the end of Day One), when other evidence, including significant improvements in student progress achieved this year, pointed to a very different 'best-fit' judgement.

Lack of evidence of the context of the academy

In addition to the incomplete nature of the evidence base mentioned above, the team also failed to take account of a number of contextual factors:

1. The decline in results is attributed in the draft report solely to poor teaching. However, no consideration is made of the facts that the academy was obliged to move away both from the successful strategy of early and multiple entry of students for English and Maths (the success of which was acknowledged by inspectors in our Ofsted report in 2014), in response to government policy that only final entries would count in performance tables, and also the previously highly successful BTEC course to GCSE Science – again a response to a change in government policy whereby only GCSE Science would 'count' in the new Progress 8 measure. Moreover, the report reads as if the academy chose to do this - in fact we had no choice.

2. No link was made between the fully inclusive nature of the academy, and the fact that this can have an impact on the attendance and behaviour of certain groups of pupils who can be extremely challenging, but who nonetheless show

good improvement thanks to the actions taken by the academy to ensure they are included in mainstream education.

3. No account was taken of the difficulties in recruiting high quality staff in mathematics and science to a highly deprived, white working class coastal area, nor of the amount of continuous professional development needed to bring these teachers up to the standards expected by the academy, which can in itself lead to teachers leaving when they are unable to meet the high standards expected of them.

Taken as a whole, we conclude that the evidence base on which judgements were made was both highly selective and limited, and that as a consequence, the inspection is incomplete.

Complaint Two: The level of factual inaccuracy in the draft report

There are a number of significant **factual inaccuracies** in the report, especially around the judgements relating to Alternative Provision, the monitoring of it, attendance of students and their outcomes. These have been addressed in the official 'Factual Accuracy Check' process, but also form part of the complaint. They are explained here:

The Definition of Alternative Provision and its application to students at ASA:

The Ofsted document 'Alternative Provision - The findings from Ofsted's three-year survey of schools' use of off-site alternative provision' (February 2016) defines AP thus (page 4 footnote),

'Alternative provision can be defined as something in which a pupil participates as part of their regular timetable, away from the site of the school or the pupil referral unit where they are enrolled, and **not** led by school staff.'

(*Alternative provision*, Ofsted, June 2011
www.gov.uk/government/publications/alternative-provision-education-outside-school)

1. During our inspection, inspectors looked at the progress of students at our 'Progress Centre', that supports Year 7 pupils with basic literacy and numeracy. In spite of our view to the contrary, inspectors took the view that it constituted AP, because it was off-site. However, it is staffed fully by our own staff, and therefore does not meet Ofsted's own criteria for AP. **This is a factual inaccuracy**, and we therefore assert that the following comments in the report should be removed:

'There is a lack of a strategic overview of pupils who attend alternative provision. Achievement of many of the pupils attending the off-site Year 7 and Year 8 literacy and numeracy lessons is poor and their attendance is considerably lower than the national average.';

'Ensure the progress of all pupils learning at alternative provision increases rapidly, by:

- *rigorously monitoring their absence and taking swift action to improve their attendance.*

- *ensuring pupils receive the right provision at the right provider.';*

'There is no strategic overview of alternative provision. Pupils' attendance is monitored day-to-day, as with all pupils. However, no one checks on the overall attendance levels of pupils at alternative provision. In some cases their attendance is less than 60%. Catch-up literacy and numeracy classes for pupils in Years 7 and 8 are taught on one day a week at an alternative provider.'; and

'The progress made by pupils who attend Year 7 and Year 8 alternative provision for literacy and numeracy lessons varies considerably. A significant proportion of these pupils made little or

noprogress between Christmas and Easter 2016. The progress made by pupils who attend other alternative provisions varies greatly, with many pupils making inadequate progress.'

By the same token, at the end of the report, it states the following: *'The school uses the following alternative providers: Aspire, Elvin, Taboo and BEST for part time and full time placements.'* **This is factually inaccurate**, because as for the Progress Centre, both BEST and the Elvin Centre are fully staffed by ASA staff, and therefore do not meet the criteria for Ofsted's own definition of AP. This further compromises the judgements made with respect to AP, as it demonstrates clearly that the team were making judgements based on a **factual inaccuracy** with respect to which students were actually accessing AP.

2. The statement *'no one checks on the overall attendance levels of pupils at alternative provision. In some cases their attendance is less than 60%'* is **factually inaccurate.**

At the time of the inspection, there were 3 students in AP whose attendance was less than 60% (none of whom were attending the Year 7 and 8 Progress Centre). The parents of one of these were being prosecuted for non-attendance. There were clerical errors with the two other students. One of these was being educated at home pending a permanent exclusion which governors subsequently upheld, and the other was attending an alternative provider. In actual fact therefore, only one student attending AP had an attendance rate of less than 60%, and this was being pursued through the courts. We therefore ask that the above statement: *'no one checks on the overall attendance levels of pupils at alternative provision. In some cases their attendance is less than 60%'* be removed.

3. The issue of a strategic overview of AP:

In the section 'What the school needs to do to improve further', we read:

'Ensure the progress of all pupils learning at alternative provision increases rapidly, by:

- *rigorously monitoring their absence and taking swift action to improve their attendance;*

- *ensuring pupils receive the right provision at the right provider.'*

Under the definition of AP as given by Ofsted (see point 1 above), there were in fact only 16 pupils at ASA attending AP at the time of inspection. Of these:

- Three are dual-registered with ASPIRE, an academy in its own right with an URN, where all three are making good progress;
- One is highly criminalized, but whom we have nonetheless managed to retain, who attends another AP provider 4 times a week; and
- Twelve attend the AP provider 'Taboo' two days a week, all of whose behaviour has improved significantly so that they are now at a significantly lower risk of exclusion, and whose progress has also improved significantly.

Moreover, full information on the progress of these students was provided as requested to the team. It was left with the Executive Principal's PA, but was not referred to by the team. The information contained evidence of progress both at ASA, and at their AP provision.

It is our strong contention that under Ofsted's own definition of AP, we can demonstrate that there is indeed a strong strategic overview of students accessing AP, and that in all cases, it has led to improvements for the students, all of whom were at significant risk of long-term exclusion from full-time education. Furthermore, it is our contention that the comments made about this to the contrary in the report are based on a **factually inaccurate** view on who actually qualified as accessing AP, as well as a failure by the team to examine all the evidence provided. We therefore ask the statement below to be removed from the report.

'The progress made by pupils who attend other alternative provisions varies greatly, with many pupils making inadequate progress.'

'Ensure the progress of all pupils learning at alternative provision increases rapidly, by:

- *rigorously monitoring their absence and taking swift action to improve their attendance.*

- *ensuring pupils receive the right provision at the right provider.'*

Other inaccuracies in the draft report:

Comments on governance:

The report states that: *'The governing body has aspirations for the pupils but has not acted with sufficient decisiveness to support and challenge leaders in addressing the declines in outcomes and the quality of teaching over the past two years.'* This is **factually inaccurate.**

It is a matter of record that governors have challenged the principal on the decline in exam results. The minutes of the relevant governing body meetings which state this were offered to the team but were not reviewed. Moreover, it is also a matter of record that concerns have been shared by the principal at several governors' meetings, where support and challenge from governors were clearly given. Again, these minutes were offered to the team, but they were not examined.

Furthermore, as mentioned in the first complaint above, we have significant evidence that the quality of teaching has in fact improved over the past two years. All of this evidence was offered to the team, but it was ignored. Significantly, members of the SLT and inspectors agreed on the quality of learning in all 16 lessons that were observed on Day Two of the inspection. This should have given inspectors the confidence that the significant amount of evidence provided to the team about ongoing judgements on the quality of teaching and learning were reliable. It is also a matter of record that governors have discussed the quality of teaching and learning with the principal at governors' meetings. We therefore request that the comments highlighted above be removed from the report.

Interviewing members of the governing body:

The report states that inspectors met with members of the governing body. Only the Chair of the Local Governing Committee was in fact interviewed and one other Governor contacted by telephone, even though the Chair of the Trust, John Downing (who is also vice-chair of the LGC) was available at the academy for three hours for this purpose, but was not interviewed. This is a **factual inaccuracy.**

Changes to the school curriculum:

The report states that *'Changes made to the curriculum had an adverse effect on the progress of pupils in Year 11 in 2015. The school replaced vocational qualifications with GCSEs.'* Whilst this is true in itself, it is also highly misleading. The changes were made, as the team is aware, in response to a change in government policy through which only Science GCSEs would count in the new Progress 8 measure, leaving the academy no choice but to make the change. As it stands, the report reads as if the academy wanted to do this, and in so doing, made a strategic mistake. This leads to a highly **inaccurate interpretation** of the academy's actions. We therefore request that this statement is either removed, or altered to give an accurate representation of the reasons for the change.

Complaint Three: The judgment on PDWB:

In addition to the above, we would also like to draw attention to a serious internal contradiction in the report that, as such, amounts to **a factual inaccuracy** in that a judgement has been made on the basis of two contradictory pieces of evidence, as explained here:

The draft report states at the start of the section on PDWB that: *'The school's work to promote pupils' personal development and welfare requires improvement. This is because, although safeguarding is effective, there were issues with the single central record, which might have compromised the safety of pupils.'* However, the draft report also states at the end that: *'At the beginning of the inspection the single central record had minor administrative issues: these were resolved by the end of the inspection.'*

The judgement of RI based on the SCR is contradicted by the statement at the end of the report, namely that these minor errors had been rectified by the end of the day. If the minor errors had been resolved by the end of the day, it is not reasonable to state these same errors might have compromised pupil safety. This in turn undermines the basis for the judgement of RI on this section.

Complaint Four: The link between the verbal debrief and the draft report:

In the final verbal debrief to the executive and associate principals, these strengths were mentioned:

- With almost no exception, all our students said how happy they were here. In particular, our vulnerable students said they felt very nurtured, and that the academy was a safe place for them;

- Inspectors were impressed with our commitment to equality, and the fact that the students said that there was zero tolerance towards bullying of any kind. They were also very impressed with our highly inclusive ethos and very low exclusion rate;

- The team were impressed with our students' appearance, their uniform, the tidiness of the site and the lack of graffiti, as well as the fact that the students confirmed that they liked being in such a nice environment;

- The team found SMSC to be a real strength across the academy, and praised our Christian ethos. They told us that the students smiled as they articulated our values of Trust, Love and Community. They really liked the House system and the links we have through that with other countries;

- In Teaching and Learning, they also found many positives. The team saw many examples of good or better learning in English, History, RE, PSHE, Drama, PE and Music, both in the main academy and Post-16. They were also impressed with the strides in improvement that had clearly been made with Post-16 achievement over the past 2 terms.

Whilst some of these points have come through in passing to the final report, the sense of praise for these outstanding features of the academy has been omitted from it, the exception being the reference to our highly inclusive ethos, and the strategies used to support this. Set against these strengths, plus the fact that our English GCSE outcomes for 2015 were outstanding, (based on final entry), the judgement that we require Special Measures is made not only against an incomplete evidence base and on a significant number of factual inaccuracies, but also in a biased report that does not give credit where it is due, thereby leading to an unfair representation of the academy to the general public.

Complaint Five – the conduct of the Lead inspector:

The final feedback from the Lead Inspector to the Executive and Associate Principals, prior to governors being invited, was unprofessional and did not meet the code of conduct expected from Ofsted. For example, at one point she appeared to be genuinely delighted when one of her team found a negative comment to make, and exclaimed excitedly that she would have to put it in bold in the report. This 'modus operandi' continued with the final feedback to governors, who received hardly any indication of the strengths found (SMSC was mentioned in passing). The feedback was therefore unbalanced and an unfair representation of the academy as a whole.

Conclusions:

We acknowledge the concerns raised in particular by the team around the Raiseonline 2015 data linked to Maths and Science, which we have recognized and are addressing with some good improvement evident within our current progress data. We also acknowledge that our monitoring systems can improve, and that we need to ensure greater consistency in stretching higher attaining pupils, particularly in Maths and Science. Where these issues exist however, they relate to weak teaching which has been extremely difficult to shift, despite the many actions of support and challenge that have been provided.

However, it is our view that owing to the highly selective and incomplete nature of the evidence that was analysed, the judgements in the report take no account of significant improvements already made this year in these areas. Neither does the report take full account of our outstanding English outcomes in 2015, nor of the considerable weight of evidence provided to the team that exam results at both GCSE and A level are set to improve significantly this year.

Moreover, the considerable number of judgements in the report relating to AP are based on **factual inaccuracies**, as evidenced by Ofsted's own criteria for determining what constitutes AP.

There is also a contradiction in the actual report itself as to the seriousness of the errors found on the SCR, which means that the judgement on PDWB cannot reasonably be maintained.

Taking all this together, it is our view therefore that the final judgements given in the report are seriously flawed, and as such, can give parents and other stakeholders little confidence in its validity. In light of this, we are therefore asking:

1. That the judgment of 'Inadequate' leading to Special Measures is overturned on the grounds that a highly selective and incomplete evidence base was used to reach the judgement, and that the report contains both a number of serious factual inaccuracies and an internal contradiction that seriously undermines the validity of the report;

2. That the Lead Inspector is held to account for her manner in the final debrief, which senior leaders and governors found to be clinically unprofessional, lacking in any empathy, and failing to acknowledge any of the strengths found during the inspection; and

3. That ASA is granted a re-inspection with a new team, who will analyse all of the evidence presented to them. The inspection of May 4th / 5th was carried out following an anonymous complaint. It is our view that the fairest way to resolve the situation would be for a normal Section 8 inspection for Good schools to be carried out in the normal inspection window – from the third year since the last inspection onwards – meaning one after the next set of results have been received in September 2016.

Andrew Chubb, Executive Principal,

June 2016.

Appendix 3 – Letter from Malcolm Greenhalgh to the Regional Schools' Commissioner

Dear Alison

I was considering writing directly to the RSC to offer our support for Andrew as things move forward but rather than this Andrew suggested that I write to you direct.

As you are probably aware, we have a long relationship with ASA having provided support when it was on the old site and not long after Andrew took up post there. The school initially was not in a good place and needed a strong improvement programme to be delivered. Caroline McKee took the role of school improvement partner in 2009 and working with Andrew, saw a significant improvement in the school over a period of time resulting in the school's Ofsted grading of Good/Outstanding in February 2014. Since then we have taken a minor role in ASA but provide significant support for the three primary schools in the MAT.

During this MAT period, Andrew has worked tirelessly to ensure the MAT is in a place to provide as high quality an education to the pupils as is possible under very challenging circumstances. The personal support and challenge he is provided for the primary schools during this time has been excellent. Also, during this period, ASA's leadership capacity has not been at full strength and was only resolved last September. Developing a MAT and the demands and challenges that a change of role from Headteacher to Executive Principal provides is in itself a significant task and Andrew has shown the capacity to rise to the extra demands of this new role.

Andrew has been fully aware of the challenges that ASA has been facing as a result of exam changes, especially in maths and science, and, as a result, he has been well aware of the need to develop high quality teams for in these subjects. Andrew has put a wide range of actions in place to ensure these changes have had minimum adverse impact. This has proved extremely challenging despite the actions. As a result, the impact of these major changes has been slower than was hoped for. However, this academic year, the significant efforts from the leadership team at ASA have begun to show through. In fact, it is difficult to suggest anything else that could have been done, therefore indicting effective leadership and management.

In the last year Jan Lomas (a very experienced inspector and consultant), has provided some guidance and support to Andrew, and then in September, the appointment of Gulshan Kayembe as the academy improvement partner strengthened the support that Incyte is providing. Not only is Gulshan one of the most experienced inspectors in the country, but she is also a science specialist. Her view of the academy from her first two visits was much the same as the academy's own view – a cusp Good/RI. Gulshan is very accurate in her own judgements and therefore there is little doubt, from the evidence collected thus far, that this is probably where the academy is at the moment – certainly not special measures.

Caroline McKee, Gulshan Kayembe, Jan and myself have more than seventy years' worth of Ofsted experience behind us. We have all quality assured inspections during this time as well as training new and experienced inspectors. There are few people that could match our experiences and expertise in inspection. Andrew is aware that we are honest and fair when making judgements on school performance and do not hold back from providing hard but honest messages. Jointly and independently, we all believe that the judgement made by the inspection team was based on a single track of thought and that the evidence therefore collected was engineered to meet a specific judgement. As a result of the inspection practice that took place (only accepting certain evidence and not accepting evidence that may not agree with the outcome expected) the outcome of the inspection was predictable.

As an Ofsted contractor for more than ten years I was responsible for dealing with complaints both for Bench Marque and Tribal. My view is that it is highly unlikely that the judgement will be overturned – simply because the evidence base collected will match the judgement. However, our advice to Andrew has been to make a complaint about the inspection to show that there is disagreement over the end judgement (rather than the evidence collected) and the way that the inspection was conducted. The reason for this is not to be in denial about the issues that were raised (they are well documented in the academy's documentation over a significant period of time) but to put a more 'realistic' view point forward that is much more in line with how effective the academy is.

The evidence base that the academy has and the knowledge that Incyte has is much more comprehensive than that which can be collected on an inspection and therefore likely to be much more accurate.

It is our view that Andrew is the right person to move ASA forward at this moment in time and the right person to develop the SALT MAT. We all have great faith in his abilities as he has consistently shown over a long period of time that he knows what makes a good school and what actions are needed to achieve this. We are therefore writing to give full and comprehensive support to Andrew retaining his current position as we believe that the fair judgement for the academy at the moment is around a grade 2/3. Taking in to account the significant challenges the academy has faced in raising standards in science and maths – not something unique to ASA as issues in recruiting and retaining high quality science and maths teachers have been well documented in the national press for many years now – we believe that leadership and management is good.

We are more than happy to discuss any of the points we have made.

Yours sincerely

Malcolm Greenhalgh, Caroline McKee, Gulshan Kayembe and Jan Lomas Directors Incyte International Ltd

Malcolm Greenhalgh

Director

Incyte International Ltd and MGA Education Ltd

Appendix 4 – Recommendation to Board to fight 'Insider Dealing' with respect to potential re-brokerage of SALT (Strategy was accepted by the Board)

The Future of SALT – updated following Directors' Meeting on 5/1/17.

Following recent developments, it has become clear that the RSC apparently wishes to re-broker SALT into another MAT. At the time of writing this paper, it is not known which Trust that may be, although it would either have to be an existing Diocesan MAT, or one whose membership had been reconstituted in line with the MoU between the National Society (NS) and the DfE.

Ultimately, it is the members of the company who would 'sign up' to a re-brokerage. It is my contention that not only is this unnecessary, but also that such a move has the potential to slow down the improvement journey of ASA. This is because I believe we can evidence good progress against the POAP (approved by Ofsted), and good capacity to improve further (evidenced by the Incyte review). Consequently, I believe that it would be more in the interests of ASA, its pupils and the other constituent academies and their pupils for SALT not to be re-brokered.

In addition to the practical issues that re-brokerage would cause, I believe that there are three further principles at stake.

First, in terms of 'natural justice', we have not been afforded the slightest opportunity to demonstrate that we are making substantial progress on all the four heads of improvement identified in May 2016 by Ofsted. We have also carried out the review of our use of pupil premium and a review of governance as we were instructed. We are acting on the advice received. Evidence around our improvements in exam results appears to have been ignored, as have all the improvements we are making against the POAP.

Second, it seems grossly unfair that the primary schools, who academised and joined SALT under one set of circumstances, now be forced into a MAT whose vision, ethos and working practices they may not share, and certainly have not had the opportunity to shape.

Third, re-brokerage puts at risk the jobs of employees in the support service of SALT (such as HR and finance), who have 'signed up' to the vision of the MAT. When it would appear that there is a good chance that we will no longer need Special Measures within a year, losing this strong skills base of educational support seems both short-sighted and morally wrong.

Following from this, I am proposing that the Board asks to meet with the members to put to them the case for their 'pushing back' more strongly against the RSC's decision for re-brokerage, and asking for a much more detailed debate around our original plan which involved closer working with the Pathfinder MAT. It is my view that this is urgent if we are to avoid being presented with a 'fait accompli'. This paper looks at the legal basis on which members could pursue this, and what the implications of such a course of action could be.

The legal issues surrounding re-brokerage:

There are 5 documents relevant to this discussion. In turn, these are:

- Our Master Funding Agreement (MFA);
- Our Supplemental Funding Agreement (SFA);
- The Church Supplemental Agreement (CSA);
- The MoU between the National Society and the DfE; and
- Our articles.

From these, our legal advice is that the RSC cannot actually force us to be re-brokered, so that is our first line of argument. The RSC's power rather lies in being able to terminate our funding agreement, subject to a number of fetters. Thus the real debate is around ability to terminate our FA and the risks involved therein, rather than re-brokerage per se. Termination of FA however would in practice involve us closing our doors completely, so the second line of argument is really will the RSC a: make that threat at all, and b: attempt to enforce that threat?

Issues around termination:

Clause 5f of ASA's SFA of 2014 states that the Secretary of State (SoS) can serve a termination warning notice in the event of the academy going into SM. The Education and Adoption Act of 2016 then added further clauses to that, (which in effect varied everyone's FA by legislation). However, because the latter did not remove clauses from the former, our legal advice is that the SoS would still have to issue a warning notice before actually terminating the FA, and indeed, the current model in use does include the same clauses as we have. To date, there have been 7 different types of warning notice issued across the country, even though in the FAs there are only really 2 - a warning and an actual notice of termination. This indicates the extent of flux with the application of this principle.

The worst case scenario to date has been typified in the Durham Free School, which went from a warning in January 2015 with 15 days to respond, to the actual termination of the academy's FA in March. Our legal advice is that this particular 'high water mark' was the end product of a much longer set of negotiations. Other cases, such as the Durand case (which involves related-parties allegedly benefitting unduly from the Trust) have taken much longer. Certainly, as a Church academy, the SoS (which in our case means the RSC) cannot jump to a notice to terminate without following a process with several steps.

If members refuse the re-brokerage, there are two options initially. The RSC could agree to our plan (perhaps unlikely!), or she could threaten to (and maybe follow through on the threat to) move to terminate our Funding Agreement. However, in summary terms before doing so, she would have to show that she is having due regard for the following, to avoid the risk of the decision being potentially subject to judicial review or a breach of contract claim.

First, she must take account of the Church Supplemental Agreement (the CSA). Under clause 20 of the CSA, the SoS agrees that before termination, and in particular before serving a 'termination warning notice', the SoS must notify the Diocese of its intention to do so, and must have due regard to the Diocese's representations before moving to issue the warning notice.

Second, under section 5G of the School Funding Agreement (SFA), the SoS has to take account of the overall performance of the Trust. In this respect, we could draw attention to the following:

- 6 years of success for ASA between 2008 and 2104, resulting in a very good Ofsted report in February 2014, and which gave the DfE confidence for ASA to open up an AP Free School in September 2014;
- Our good exam results Post-16 in 2016, at both AS and A2 level.
- Our P8 score of -0.17 in 2016, which put us above the 'coasting' threshold, and which represented an improvement of +0.77 over the previous year.
- The highly positive and documented reaction of parents to the announcement of SM;
- The continued popularity of the academy, as evidenced by the increase in both the number of first choices and the total number of choices for ASA in 2017 compared to the previous year;
- The quality of the POAP that was approved by Ofsted, and against which we are making good progress;
- The outcome of the Incyte review of ASA in November 2016, which acknowledged the progress made since May, and deemed that we had good capacity for further improvement;
- The outcome of the second monitoring visit of ASPIRE by the DfE, which judged that it will be outstanding on its Ofsted visit;
- Two primary academies that are good and improving (However, we have to note that Stockwell academy has contacted the DfE asking to leave the MAT and join a bigger local one. This is disappointing, not least because we have invested much time and effort in supporting Stockwell);
- One primary academy that is RI and improving strongly;
- The fact that there are two other local primary schools that would like to work closely with SALT;
- The financial strength of the Trust; and
- The strength of the support services (HR, finance, facilities management) of the trust

Third, under the MoU between the National Society (NS) and the DfE, there is an expectation that the DfE will work in partnership with the Diocese, and that where there is a failure to reach an agreement, that a mediation process can be invoked in conjunction with the NS. Thus, before the RSC even considered termination of FA, she should under the terms of the MoU engage with the NS to try to reach a mediated agreement.

Fourth, as part of the whole process, the RSC must show under clause 22 of the CSA that she has had 'due regard' for any plan submitted by the Diocese, and in good faith considered funding implications. To my mind, this simply has not happened. In the initial meeting between the Diocese and Pathfinder at the RSC's office, the officials were incorrectly briefed as to the history of ASA's many successes. Moreover, at no point (to my knowledge) have we had proper debate with the RSC as to why our plan is so unsuitable - to my mind, 'due regard' has not been given.

If the RSC proceeded with issuing a termination warning notice without doing all of the above, she would open herself (and therefore the SoS) up to criticism that due process had not been followed; any subsequent decision would therefore potentially capable of challenge under judicial review. In this respect, the RSC may need to be reminded that the DfE recently found itself on the wrong end of a judicial review application which, although it did not go all the way as the facts of the case changed, very much left the DfE in the position of needing to make sure it follows its own guidance (let alone contracts) in the future.

Conclusions:

First, until the RSC can persuade us otherwise, I think that the solution that we put forward is in the better interests of our children as I believe it gives us the best chance of improving quickly and coming out of SM. Once we are out of SM, the specific powers referred to above to serve notices fall away in any event.

Second, the MoU, SFA and CSA have all been negotiated to ensure that Church schools are not simply 'railroaded' by the RSC in this sort of event. They have been hard fought-over, and I would think it somewhat of a travesty if full use were not made of them. Otherwise we are basically saying the state runs the affairs of our schools.

Third, in the light of the two points above, I think that there are still a number of options open to the Diocese in terms of resisting the move to re-broker.

I would therefore like the Board to agree to ask to meet the members to discuss this strategy, with a view to opposing the RSC's preferred option more robustly. I think we should ask to meet with the Archbishop himself to discuss this with him, not least of course because he is a member.

I think this is urgent, as the members may already be on the point of agreeing a deal, whatever it may be.

Andrew Chubb

December 2016

<u>Update following Directors' meeting on 5th January.</u>

On 5th January, we were made aware that the Trust involved is the YHCLT. Following a wide-ranging discussion, it was the general view of the Board that this proposal, as it stands, gave no hope of speeding up ASA's improvement process – indeed, the reverse was judged to be the case. There are several reasons for this:

1. The Trust concerned is new, (constituted this academic year);

2. We are not clear of any track record it has in supporting schools, although we have based our revised QA procedures on a more rigorous version of processes introduced by Kelvin when they were RI;

3. The Trust is also taking on another local secondary school – Newland School for Girls. Currently judged to be RI, their Progress 8 data was worse than that of ASA (around – 0.3 – potentially in the 'coasting' category) and has been the destination for a number of our own science staff whom I have moved on. Consequently, they would be in the

position of having to support 2 schools deemed to need improvement;

4. At Christmas, they lost their overall Maths Director, the Deputy Director of Maths, and the 'Third in Charge' of Maths. Given that our most pressing need is to improve Maths, it is hard to see how they have any capacity to do so;

5. Kelvin's own concern about this situation can be illustrated thus: During the last week of the Christmas term, we interviewed their deputy Director of Maths. Although he did finally accept our job offer, he asked during the interview whether or not it was true that we were going to re-brokered the following week, adding that the Head and Deputy had spent the last two days trying to convince him to stay for this reason;

6. The actions taken by Kelvin in point 5 above indicate three things:

   a. They are prepared to used privileged and confidential information to further their own organisational ends ('insider dealing');

   b. They are prepared to act in this way against the very organisation that they are stating they are able to help, in the exact subject which is presents us with the most challenges; and

   c. They would not appear to be adhering to the values of the Cooperative Trust, that they purport to hold;

7. Upon hearing of the identity of the Trust, Chris Mulqueen, Principal of ASPIRE, stated that he would be seeking permission from the RSC to join another Trust, or indeed to stand alone. ASPIRE would be in a position to join any Trust that would want them, as they are not a designated Church Academy; the Diocese would be unable to invoke the MoU to steer the decision;

8. The loss of effective control of ASPIRE would be extremely serious for ASA. Forming ASPIRE was part of a long-term

plan to ensure that we were able to ensure that all those ASA students who needed ASPIRE's specialist type of provision were able to access it. Without it, exclusion, both fixed-term and permanent, would, without doubt, rise;

9. A further implication is that SALT's reserves and assets (including the hard-won Mouthlock Centre), totalling well over £1m, would transfer to the new trust. This would make future investment in our development much more difficult, as the new trust would almost inevitably take the view that these reserves would have to be used across the whole Trust, and not just SALT academies. This factor alone would put serious constraints on our ability to drive improvement further.

10. In the face of all of these disadvantages, it was not possible to identify a single advantage to ASA joining YHCLT. The plan, as presented, gives no indication as to any additional resources that would be offered to rise standards, nor any indication as to what costs (both initial and ongoing) that ASA and the other academies would incur, nor any indication as to what would happen to the several people in Finance and HR in particular whose jobs are currently dependant on the MAT rather than one particular academy;

11. It was further acknowledged by all that the process involved in joining YHCLT would deflect ASA almost inevitably to a greater or lesser extent from its core purpose of raising standards, at precisely the time when standards are demonstrably rising. This includes the very real possibility of an exodus of staff (whether teaching, support, or our highly experienced 'back-office' staff), who may feel very unsettled by the whole prospect of joining a new trust.

In short, the general view expressed by SALT directors was that the proposal is complete nonsense. All the advantages lie with Kelvin, and all the disadvantages lie with ASA. On the next page, I offer some suggestions as to how members could respond to this.

Responding to the RSC's decision:

I believe that before anything is formally agreed or 'signed off', that these concerns are lodged with the RSC. Specifically, I believe that the Headteachers' Board (HTB) should be made aware of these, as they are tasked with advising the RSC. This is urgent, as the HTB meets in the very near future. I do not believe that any Headteacher would see this as either a sensible or a just solution;

I believe that we should ask to be given the opportunity to speak directly with the HTB and present our concerns to them.

Should this opportunity not be afforded, then I believe we should formally voice our objections and ask for further mediation through the terms of the MoU, involving the National Society;

If this fails to resolve our concerns, at that point the Diocese will have to take a view as to the extent it wishes to tackle the RSC further (see the first part of this paper from 16th. December);

If, having tried everything, the RSC still forces the issue, then the diocesan members of YHCLT will need to consider how they can best use their influence as majority members to protect ASA's interests. These could include, but not be limited to:

- Lobbying the RSC to ensure that ASPIRE remains with ASA;
- Requiring YHCLT to ring-fence existing SALT funding at point of transfer, to be used for the benefit of ASA and other SALT academies;
- Requiring YHCLT to use existing and highly experienced SALT 'back-office' staff to support the development of YHCLT, before taking on any new staff to perform these functions;
- Obtaining assurances around being allowed to retain those processes and systems which are now driving improvement in ASA and the primaries.

Andrew Chubb

January 2017

Printed in Great Britain
by Amazon

58010316R00175